The
Essential
Guide to
XML Technologies

ISBN 0130655565-1

Prentice Hall PTR
Essential Guide Series

The Essential Guide to XML Technologies

RON TURNER

 Prentice Hall PTR, Upper Saddle River, NJ 07458
www.phptr.com

Library of Congress Cataloging-in-Publication Data

CIP date available.

Editorial/Production Supervision: *Mary Sudul*
Acquisitions Editor: *Mark Taub*
Editorial Assistant: *Sarah Hand*
Manufacturing manager: *Maura Zaldivar*
Art Director: *Gail Cocker-Bogusz*
Interior Series Design: *Meg Van Arsdale*
Cover Design: *Bruce Kenselaar*
Cover Design Direction: *Jerry Votta*

 © 2002 by Prentice Hall PTR
Prentice-Hall, Inc.
Upper Saddle River, NJ 07458

Prentice Hall books are widely used by corporations and government agencies for training, marketing, and resale.

The publisher offers discounts on this book when ordered in bulk quantities. For more information, contact Corporate Sales Department, phone: 800-382-3419; fax: 201-236-7141; email: corpsales@prenhall.com Or write Corporate Sales Department, Prentice Hall PTR, One Lake Street, Upper Saddle River, NJ 07458.

Product and company names mentioned herein are the trademarks or registered trademarks of their respective owners. The Electronic Commerce Game™ is a trademark of Object Innovations. Inc.

All rights reserved. No part of this book may be reproduced, in any form or by any means, without permission in writing from the publisher.

Printed in the United States of America

10 9 8 7 6 5 4 3 2 1

ISBN 0-13-065565-1

Pearson Education LTD.
Pearson Education Australia PTY, Limited
Pearson Education Singapore, Pte. Ltd.
Pearson Education North Asia Ltd.
Pearson Education Canada, Ltd.
Pearson Educación de Mexico, S.A. de C.V.
Pearson Education — Japan
Pearson Education Malaysia, Pte. Ltd.

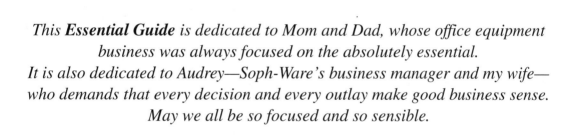

*This **Essential Guide** is dedicated to Mom and Dad, whose office equipment
business was always focused on the absolutely essential.
It is also dedicated to Audrey—Soph-Ware's business manager and my wife—
who demands that every decision and every outlay make good business sense.
May we all be so focused and so sensible.*

Contents

Chapter 17 XSLT for Adaptive Content   241

Chapter 18 XSL for Format   263

Chapter 19 XLink and Xpointer   283

Part 3
XML At Work   305

Chapter 20 XML At Work: Manufacturing   307

Chapter 21 XML At Work: Extensible Business
Reporting Language   321

Preface

The Essential Guide to XML Technologies is intended to help you understand XML and to articulate the XML story in a way that makes sense to a manager, decision-maker, or decision influencer. Not that there has been any lack of articulation about XML! XML evangelists, consultants and developers have spared neither words nor slicks to impress upon us that XML is "neat stuff," a really-nice-to-have. Marketeers furthermore have touted this or that XML tool for easier, more cost-effective management and processing of data. Yet very few have offered a sober justification for XML as a need-to-have. *The Essential Guide to XML Technologies* offers many explicit lists of XML benefits and reasons why XML makes good business sense.

The Essential Guide to XML Technologies situates XML in the information technology (IT) landscape: what is XML exactly and what kind of problems can we expect it to solve? XML is not a product or a format or a browser add-on. It is not something that you simply download and install. Instead it forms an integral part of the IT "sandwich," freeing information to move much more freely across platforms, throughout the enterprise, and between Internet-connected organizations. *The Essential Guide to XML Technologies* seeks to demonstrate how XML makes that possible.

No innovation in IT comes without a management price tag. Beyond the obvious costs for upgraded tools and data management systems, there are inevitable expenses for training and job redefinitions. Although XML's most visible impact is on the data it supports, the most profound impact of XML is likely to be on information workflow. Managed correctly and with foresight, both types of impact can be favorable. *The Essential Guide to XML Technologies* is meant to help the IT manager foresee these visible and not-so-visible impacts within the organization.

The decision to launch an XML-based initiative can have far-reaching consequences for an organization, hopefully good consequences. But it would be irresponsible to delegate that decision to technicians and programmers who do not have a feel for the larger picture. So the IT manager as XML decision maker may likely be in an awkward position, needing to comprehend the specialists' arguments for XML without understanding its basic terminology and paradigms. *The Essential Guide to XML Technologies* can serve as a survival kit of essential terms and concepts—those pieces that are necessary for a sensible decision. Furthermore, the many executive-level views of XML code examples in *The Essential Guide to XML Technologies* removes any possible psychological shock of viewing "raw XML." Nothing that an XML specialist displays should now be a total surprise to the manager.

My motivation for this book began with a defining event at the first national XML meeting (Seattle," XML, The Conference 1998"). It was actually a minor incident, an exchange during the Q & A following a presentation. A printing specialist had come to the conference with the unreasonable hope that XML would solve some of his industry's intractable problems. After the attendee and presenter had each repeated themselves three times, the frustrated presenter put him down with a slightly rude remark and the printer left the room in disgust. The underlying problem in that encounter was two-fold: (1) XML had not yet been presented accurately in terms that made sense to this attendee and (2) the attendee had not yet been sufficiently informed to ask the right questions about XML. The same problem persists even now. *The Essential Guide to XML Technologies* confronts this on-going issue for the manager in two ways: (1) presenting XML in terms that make business sense and (2) helping the manager to ask the right questions.

XML is a pervasive cluster of technologies, far more than just the Next Big Thing. No one now doubts that XML is here to stay, and its scope is expanding dramatically. Because it is so far-reaching, XML represents a body of knowledge that is impossible to capture in a single book. Nevertheless *The Essential Guide to XML Technologies* should provide the reader with a satisfying sense of having gotten the big picture.

I sincerely hopes that the conversation begun in this book will continue. Feel free to contact me at RonT@Soph-Ware.com. Tell me what's going on in your IT workplace.

Acknowledgments

I decided from the outset that this book should not simply *include* examples. It should *feature* them, and the examples should be convincing.

For the news items helping to explain the *Really* Big Idea in Chapter 3, I am indebted to the Associated Press, the *Los Angeles Times*, and the *Spokane Spokesman-Review*, whose material is used with their kind permission.

Tom Watkins (Telect, Inc.) provided me with live bill of materials data for manufacturing, which I adapted for use in "XML at Work: Manufacturing."

Rolly Chambers (Smith, Currie & Hancock, LLP, North Carolina) is the co-author of the proposed Legal XML court document standard and creator of several of the sample documents now posted at the Legal XML site. Rolly serves as co-chair of the Legal Workgroup of Legal XML and provided invaluable assistance in obtaining and making XML legal documents perform properly for the chapter "XML at Work: Law and the Courts."

James Droscha (Legislative Internet Technology, State of Michigan), provided live XML source code behind the Michigan Lemon Law, also showcased in "XML at Work: Law and the Courts."

Eve Maler (Senior XML Standards Architect, Sun Microsystems XML Technology Center) is the co-editor of W3C XML 1.0, XLink 1.0, and XPointer 1.0. Eve offered a brief review of my first draft of "XLink and XPointer." I'm also indebted to Eve for once passing along the personal advice (originally from H. H. Munro) that "a little inaccuracy sometimes saves tons of explanation." She bears no responsibility for any possible inaccuracies (which I really tried to avoid!)

My thanks also to Altova GmbH & Altova, Inc. for XML Spy, the tool used to edit and validate the XML files appearing throughout the book.

I thank my editor Mark Taub (Editor-in-Chief, Prentice Hall PTR, Computer Science), who sensed immediately that the *Essential Guide* series would be an appropriate home for a book that tries to level with managers and decision makers.

My profound gratitude to Peter Gregory (CISSP, HartGregory Group Inc.) for his careful reading and insightful review and comments.

Mary Sudul (Production Editor, Prentice Hall PTR) provided invaluable direction in proofreading and layout, enforcing a consistency in look and feel that otherwise would never have been.

And special thanks to Kristen Cornelis of Soph-Ware Associates, Inc. who transformed the manuscript from various formats and media into FrameMaker+SGML.

Part 1

Major Themes

Introduction

In this chapter...

They Said It...

But hold—don't I forget my manners?
To introduce the Stranger (what else indeed
have I come for?) to thee

Walt Whitman: Song of the Exposition

WHO ARE YOU? ....

First things first. Before we dive into this book, let's clarify its purpose and intended audience.

This is a book about essentials, but not in the sense of Extensible Markup Language (XML) tagging rules or how-tos for creating Web pages. You have well over a hundred titles dealing with XML to choose from, and many of those do a creditable job of teaching XML basics. If you have paged through this book, you will have seen many samples of markup and some striking examples of XML for the Web. But these are meant primarily to underscore the business case for XML, not to teach you how to code it.

In this book we assume that you are a decision maker. This is not a how-to-code-XML book for developers, although it will help developers who need to understand big-picture XML concepts. You may be deciding personally whether or not to invest energy into becoming an XML professional, adding to your skill as a programmer or database administrator (DBA). Or you may be a fact gatherer, charged by your organization to help management decide the next safe steps for a proposed XML initiative. You may be a manager who senses that XML may be more than just a Next Big Thing. Whatever your role, you insist on moving quickly beyond the hype of XML. You have seen more XML-as-silver-bullet infomercial pieces than you can count. You are ready to ask whether XML represents a true value proposition in your organization. Can XML help increase revenue and/or reduce expenses?

THIS BOOK IS DISTINCTIVE BECAUSE ....

If you are browsing in a bookstore, you have already seen dozens of XML titles sharing shelf space with this book. So why this XML book on essentials?

Business value vs. "neat stuff." Managers and decision makers can become just as excited about new technologies as developers can. The big difference is that a manager's excitement over XML will be based on the technology's ability to solve problems, increase revenue, or cut costs, or all of the above. The XML developer, on the other hand, is (rightfully) excited about XML purely as neat stuff. This book attempts to highlight the business value of XML, so there is a prominent bulk of discussion of management issues and a noticeable lack of attention to technical detail.

Articulation of XML's value. It is very difficult to read the XML specification or to attend an XML professional conference—even in the management track—and to deduce the business potential for XML. It is even more difficult for a manager, now convinced of XML's value, to articulate that value to the rest of the organization. Many of the chapters therefore include explicit lists of business benefits for the various parts of XML.

Style of Presentation. XML was originally proposed as a simplifying technology. Yet most outsiders would rate a conversation between XML specialists as somewhere between off-putting and terrifying. This book attempts to explain XML using plain English. That often means that there are long paraphrases, "fluffy" passages, and more bulk than a developer can tolerate. But the language also attempts to be *accurate*. The intention for this approach to explaining XML is again to help a manager understand and articulate the value of XML.

Code Listings as Confidence Builders. This book includes thousands of lines of XML markup. Most of it is taken verbatim from working XML systems. All of it has been verified (i.e., tested for XML conformity). Each such code example supports some particular point in a chapter, but there is a larger, ulterior motive for the XML markup examples. After you have read through the Executive Walkthrough discussions that accompany many of the examples, you will have no fear of confronting raw XML anywhere. This is a strong claim, but we explain in the early chapters why it is true. The larger purpose of these examples is therefore to help you address XML issues with the authority that can only come with hands-on familiarity with XML itself.

"Unedited" Workplaces. There are many case studies and workplace examples in this book. We have insisted that our XML cases be real (or at least convincing) because miniature textbook examples invariably convey a false sense of simplicity. XML does, in fact, offer *straightforward* solutions, but no project of real-world scale is ever *easy*. We intentionally present code examples that include very messy detail, sometimes even left unexplained.

Right Questions. XML began as a consortium of information providers and vendors who expressed the need for XML in well-articulated pain statements. But much of that original concern has become muffled by the sheer bulk of technical discourse. We have therefore attempted to restart executive-level thinking by posing large questions about XML and its potential. The first chapters' titles are cast as questions. And we conclude the book with yet another set of questions. We maintain that because XML has the answers, the technology deserves a legitimate and major role in the information workplace. We also use the question as a means of deducing why this or that part of the XML specification is significant.

Unmasking the Hype. An XML advocate within a provider company is frequently called an "XML evangelist," so it is understandable that a good share of the marketing literature, white papers, break-out tutorials, and trade publication overviews will have a high density of hype about XML. We hope that this book convinces you that many of the promises you hear about XML really can be realized in your organization. But we attempt—perhaps to a fault—to restrain ourselves, clarifying the exact role of XML and setting realistic expectations.

ROAD MAP ....

The book is laid out in three sections: Major Themes, Core Technologies, and XML At Work. Each section has its own approach and purpose.

The first six chapters address issues that are rarely treated in XML technical discussions. We seek to resolve some of the issues that are of little concern to developers. What led to the development of XML? What is the real problem that XML was designed to solve? Why is XML so critical to Web-based information? What is so revolutionary about plain text marked up with angle bracket tags? And the most frequently asked question: What is the difference between XML and HTML (the markup language for browsers)? By articulating to your organization some responses to these questions, you will already have addressed some fundamental concerns about this new technology.

The next 13 chapters are about core technologies of XML. We do not claim that our treatment is technically balanced and complete. We do claim that these members of the XML family of specifications each represent some aspect of a convincing value proposition. The many examples and minicases are taken from the real information workplace. And we hope that you find these to be interesting. But more than that, we hope that each chapter's summary of benefits will help you identify cost-effective XML solutions for your organization.

The next five chapters are case studies, vignettes of XML in actual settings. XML is a key player in each of these workplace exhibits, not because it is neat stuff but because it is helping to solve business problems in a convincing manner. Furthermore, these cases demonstrate that a large part of a successful XML initiative is the role of the information workers in the workflow.

As a decision maker, you may prefer to concentrate first on panoramic views, like those in the first section. Or you may first need a grasp of the technologies themselves. Or perhaps you would like first to observe XML at work. Whatever your approach to fact-gathering, follow your own inclination. The sections are written so as to be read in any order you wish. In fact, we strongly urge you to go immediately to the last chapter ("Ten Questions You Should Ask About XML") in order to see what you as a manager can expect to gain from this book.

The book will equip you—as a decision maker or influencer—for a journey. It will show you the mountain and the routes for ascending it. It will help you to decide whom to bring with you, what to take along, and what obstacles may beset you.

1 Why XML?

In this chapter...

They Said It...

Through thy Idea—lo! the immortal Reality!
Through thy Reality—lo! the immortal Idea!
Walt Whitman: "As a Strong Bird on
Pinions Free" (Leaves of Grass)

OVERVIEW ....

Extensible Markup Language (XML) did not simply emerge because it was "neat stuff." In 1996 within the Worldwide Web Consortium (W3C) decided that Standard Generalized Markup Language (SGML) was the best starting point for a simplified methodology of serious Internet information exchange. The company representatives were explicit in stating XML's reason for being. And the agenda for developing XML was clear. The W3C goals for XML represent a strong business case for XML, and the dominance of the Web is yet a further motivation.

The Need for XML

The title of this book might well have been *Why XML?* The second unit ("Core Technologies") presents a value proposition for each major piece of the XML specification. Each of these XML technologies demonstrates that it now makes sound business sense. So that makes XML worth your serious consideration.

But even before the technologies and before the release of the W3C's first draft of the specification, a large body of electronic information players not only envisioned a need for XML, they felt it. Section 1.1 of the initial draft has proven to be a consistent restatement of that need felt by the entire XML community.

W3C AGENDA FOR XML ....

The original XML Working Group W3C in November 1996 drafted a 10-item list of goals for XML. They are all cast as imperatives: "shall be," "should be," "is to be." So perhaps we should refer to them as the X Commandments. That list is part of the actual XML specification.

The mission of the working group was not to develop yet another markup language. Instead its members were driven by two over-arching considerations:

1. A decision to build as much as possible on the experience, lessons learned, and large volume of content already produced with SGML.
2. A belief that the Internet would be the pervasive infrastructure for moving all electronic content.

True, SGML has not been widely embraced by the commercial world. But serious content providers everywhere have recognized in SGML the compelling notions of markup. All content is represented as plain text. Humans can read it. Even unsophisticated software can process it. And most important for the commercial world, any variety of computer can access it. By 1996 SGML represented a major publications technology investment for the U.S. Department of Defense (DoD) and certain industries (aircraft in particular).

By 1996 the Internet had become the infrastructure that was bound to drive the delivery of electronic content technology. The same benefits that SGML had long demonstrated for easy dissemination now became crucial for the exploding content of the Internet.

But the various SGML publishing initiatives and the Internet had already made it clear that widespread success would depend more on human factors than on technology. This is amply demonstrated in the goals for the XML Working Group, the mechanisms for W3C's work, and the actual history of XML. People create content. And people must edit, share, and maintain that content.

W3C GOALS FOR XML ....

The W3C's original goals for XML as well as the current practices of creating and moving XML reflect a new politics of information. In at least seven of these goals, people issues are dominant. Since we are focused primarily on this softer side of XML, we offer a brief statement of benefit at the end of each discussion of goals.

   1. *XML shall be straightforwardly usable over the Internet.*

This may be the first time you have ever seen the word "straightforwardly." The term is used frequently by technologists who would say "easy" to one another but not to a supervisor or customer. "Straightforwardly" means roughly, "We now have all the pieces on the bench, and we know precisely in our heads how it should all work." For XML, straightforward usability over the Internet does not yet mean "directly to a Web browser." A Web content provider cannot publish just any XML content without other supporting technologies, as we shall see.

The original XML working group had agendas in mind that may have changed somewhat. And the history of XML-to-the-browser has turned out to be somewhat bumpy. Nevertheless XML is indeed made-to to-order for the Internet. First, XML markup makes content recognizable by Internet-connected partners, regardless of computer and software platforms. Much of this book focuses on XML as the ultimate platform neutralizer for content.

XML also participates in supporting the Internet itself. Within the more local layers of Internet activity, XML serves as plumbing. It is common engineering practice for separate software modules to use XML for communicating with one another. One such open standards initiative is XML-RPC. When one software module requires the resources of another module, it has long been an engineering design practice for the consumer module to issue a remote procedure call (RPC). XML makes that strategy more open. With XML-RPC the messaging between those modules consists of tiny XML documents. In this way it is more likely that a software integrator can more easily use software components from different vendors.

Electronic business Extensible Markup Language (ebXML) is an international initiative that is well on schedule toward enhancing international trade. One important component of ebXML is a system-level messaging specification for transfer, routing, and packaging. These are functions that originally were viewed as part of Internet protocol.

With applications like these, XML enables separate software components and widely separated and heterogeneous computers to talk to one another across large global networks. It is only a slight exaggeration therefore to say that the Internet is XML. This goal has been a self-fulfilling prophecy.

Benefit: As XML my content is already that much closer to being Web- and Internet-ready. Consequently my development costs are reduced. Additionally, because XML content is open, my investment in Internet-based XML is preserved.

2. *XML shall support a wide variety of applications.*

SGML is the basis of XML. We discuss this at greater length in Chapter 2. The "G" of SGML is a deliberate and comprehensive design principle that guarantees that SGML can work for all structured information. (Much of this book, in fact, was written using an SGML-enabled word processor.)

The actual track record of SGML demonstrated that it fared well in certain sectors of the electronic information world. One early adopter was the U.S. Internal Revenue Service (IRS). Another notable player is the DoD, which ordered the use of SGML to facilitate electronic commerce with the hope of streamlining its massive acquisitions procedures. The name of that initiative was Computer-aided Acquisition and Logistics Support (CALS), later changed to Continuous Acquisition and Lifecycle Support. As CALS has broadened to the commercial sector, the title has changed to Commerce At Light Speed. CALS, as an SGML application, is still primarily a technology for electronic commerce. Another notable application of SGML is the very large specification developed and enforced by the Airline Transport Association. The ATA standard supports the manufacturing, operation, and maintenance of commercial aircraft around the world.

The planners of XML wanted to make certain that XML continued the tradition of supporting information of every variety. But they needed to see that variety expand dramatically. To make sure this was accomplished they sought every means of keeping the language as simple as possible. The strategy with XML is not to change your business practices to fit an information standard. Rather it is to provide a building-block language that allows you to extend it in ways that fit your existing business practices. This has always been the philosophy of SGML, but it was spelled out more forcefully with XML. The goal of "wide variety" expresses the hope that information designers from any industry can easily form a consortium, using (extending) XML to invent a language that fits.

In order for an industry or interest group to establish the sort of information exchange that XML can support, there is typically a very run-up effort for meetings, standards drafts, protocol definitions, and finally, the full definition of a markup language. In spite of very high front-loaded costs, there are dozens of major XML initiatives underway. Table 1.1 is only a tiny sample of XML-based initiatives. This sample offers a hint of the variety of applications possible.

Table 1.1   A sample of XML-based initiatives

Language	Full Name	Application/Arena
XBRL	eXtensible Business Reporting Language	Financial reporting, including EDGAR filings to the SEC
WML	Wireless Markup Language	Wireless Application Protocol (WAP) Forum
NewsML	News Markup Language	Creation, transfer, and delivery of news
NLMCommon DTD	National Library of Medicine Common document type definition	Support of upgraded services of MEDLINE at National Library of Medicine
FpML	Financial Products Markup Language	E-commerce activities in the field of financial derivatives.
CIDX	Chemical Industry Data	Buying, selling, and delivery of chemicals

Benefit: The broad variety of maturing, industry-specific applications assures me of a shorter learning curve and decreased risk of failure of my XML-based initiative.

3. *XML shall be compatible with SGML.*

In most of the 85+ books on XML, SGML typically makes a cameo appearance as somewhat of a historical relic. SGML is historically significant for XML, but there is more to SGML's role than that. Had it not been for over a decade of serious SGML activity, XML probably never would have happened. On its own XML could never have attained the fast-track maturity that it now enjoys. (The first draft of XML was released at the November 1996 SGML meeting in Boston.) So while SGML is related historically to XML, it is more than a parent. In the mathematical sense, XML is a **subset** of SGML. We will take up the meaning of that statement in Chapter 2.

In order to view the entire XML movement effectively, it is absolutely erroneous to conclude that first we had SGML, and later XML came along. These are not separate initiatives, as we have said. To view them as separate movements can impair our perception of XML's own maturity and robustness.

There exists a significant investment in SGML legacy content within many organizations. After all, the promise of SGML was that its markup would persist for millennia and still be readable after every current vendor had long since left the marketplace. XML provides for these organizations an orderly migration path to the future. But a potential adopter of XML, even one with a large SGML store, needs to be clear about the relationship.

The precise relationship between XML, SGML, and the many hundreds of MLs now in existence are baffling to the newcomer. It makes due diligence more difficult. And journalists' constant misuse of terms hinders fact-gathering even more. Assuming that one of the reasons you are reading this book is to clarify these differences, we feel that it is important to get these distinctions right. We feel that so strongly that we dedicate an entire chapter (Chapter 2) precisely to this topic.

In articulating the purpose of XML, the XML Working Group did not discard any of the beneficial features of SGML. In fact, most of the new appeal of XML comes from extensions of features that were part of SGML all along.

XML is not some sort of hostile intellectual takeover of the markup world from SGML. Quite the contrary, XML is a clear affirmation that markup technologies are here to stay.

Benefit: XML, as a follow-on to SGML, is in reality a 15-year-old, proven cluster of technologies. This maturity of markup technologies mitigates our risk of failure and false starts.

4. *It shall be easy to write programs which process XML documents.*

Since XML is plain text, then an XML processor should be (at least partly) only a text processor. It should not require you to reinvent the likes of Microsoft® Word in order to interpret and process an XML document. On the other hand, the choice of easy was somewhat misguided. (They used easy for data creation, which is probably acceptable.) The concept of easy does not combine well with programming. It is indeed easy to concoct half-page examples. We include many in this book. It is quite another matter to develop large XML-based systems to accomplish genuinely useful work.

On the other hand, five years of history has shown the requirement to be largely fulfilled. This is because XML is by definition *structured*. (We dwell on this in Chapters 3-6.) That automatically makes it a good fit for object-oriented (OO) programming languages and for the many scripting languages in use for rapid systems deployment. And since XML is plain text throughout, that greatly eases the learning curve for developers of XML processing software. This requirement statement is a backhanded plea for the programming apparatus supporting XML also to be kept simple, within the skill set of average IT organizations.

An aside regarding documents: The XML working group may have used the term documents, but XML was destined from the start to go far beyond traditional print products. Documents in the XML specifications (and in this book) refer to electronic content of every type and medium.

Benefit: Because XML content, no matter how daunting it may appear to a newcomer, is and always will be *plain* text. There is no possibility of a single vendor's thwarting our ability to author and manage XML. This open systems approach guarantees our freedom always to select freely among vendors of our choice.

5. *The number of optional features in XML is to be kept to the absolute minimum, ideally zero.*

The phenomenon of feature creep is well understood and properly feared by every product manager. Every product that is in wide use must be tightly controlled, offering only those features that will enhance its survival. The same is even more true for an open standard. But XML is not an International Organization for Standardization (ISO) standard, so it does not enjoy the protection and control of a standard. XML therefore could have been threatened by many assaults to accommodate this or that technological opinion or vertical industry. Instead of features, the W3C has fostered the growth and maturity of XML by engendering new and separate working groups' initiatives.

The core XML standard is mature and intact. As later chapters will demonstrate, when an industry or group wishes to add features to a particular XML markup language, that only requires extensions. Designers using ebXML for example may elect to add significant facilities for security. XML is designed precisely to accomplish that-add features to the particular language (here ebXML) without requiring any change whatsoever to XML itself. Pain-free extensibility is what XML is all about.

Benefit: The investment in an XML application is safe, because there is virtually no risk of an XML application's becoming obsolete.

6. *XML documents should be human-legible and reasonably clear.*

At first glance this seems to be a curious requirement, somewhat out of place in the highly structured world of XML. It is quite at home in the world of software engineering, where human programmers constantly access code. And it is, of course, a nice thing for all documents to be clear and legible to humans. But why is this nice-to-have a need-to-have in XML? And what are the actual determiners of XML content's appearance?

First, the human-readable requirement has been part of open systems markup all along. So this is not something that just occurred to the XML designers. XML is for the consumption of computers, processors that must render it, transform it, segment it or do whatever is appropriate. But XML content must be visible and readable by humans at every stage of the information food chain: editors, designers, programmers, authors, and at times even end users. This shortens the learning curve and makes troubleshooting easier (imagine if you needed to have a tool just to read the characters in an XML file).

Second, how clear and by whose standards? There are three main contributors to XML:

1. Information architect, the designer of the content's *structure*
2. Database specialist, the manager of the content's *storage* and *retrieval*
3. Stylist, the packager who typically determines the content's *appearance*

In a perfect world, each of these functions would be kept strictly separate from the others, and the marked-up content would reflect that orderly separation. In actual practice, all three activities converge, often with unpleasant results. XML files for real business frequently are a nearly unreadable mixture of pointy-bracket markup, database language directives, and styling detail. Each specialist's (or group of specialists') native expression has become part of the markup. The result is that XML in actual practice may be nearly illegible and far from clear. Nothing that accomplishes useful work in the real workplace is going to be *easily* readable, clear, and legible. Consequently, much of current markup practice generates documents that are anything but human-legible and reasonably clear.

Third, it is now common for massive amounts of XML content to be created not by humans but by e-commerce servers and other computers within some automated workflow. As we will see in Chapter 4, the computer views its payload in a manner that is blind to human legibility. And since machines, not humans, are generating an increasingly large proportion of XML content, it may be reasonable to expect legibility and clarity. There is little hope that content created in that way can ever meet the standard of easy human legibility.

On the other hand, XML content, because it is structured, is predictable. That in itself is a strong contributor to legibility. You will be viewing much XML source directly throughout the book and will very soon be able to get a strategic grasp of any XML content.

Benefit: The skill set required for reading XML content is minimal and therefore less costly. This open accessibility to human-legible content means that professionals from all disciplines can feel at home with the same XML content. That eliminates much of an on-going need for expensive specialists and technology transfer.

7. The XML design should be prepared quickly.

The design of XML did in fact proceed quickly, resulting in version 1.0 of a full recommendation as XML 1.0 in February 1998. The W3C is an workplace consortium that issues *recommendations*, not a representational body that votes on *standards*. The process for XML (the core specification) was the same as for all of the W3C's 45 specifications. The milestones (Recommendation Track) for a formal process of moving from draft through to final released recommendation are as follows:

- *Working draft.* Chartered work item of a working group, representing work in progress and a commitment by W3C to pursue work in a particular area.

- *Last call working draft.* Special instance of a working draft, considered by the working group to fulfill the relevant requirements of its charter and any accompanying requirements documents...a public technical report for which the working wroup seeks technical review from other W3C groups, W3C members, and the public.

- *Candidate recommendation.* Believed to meet the relevant requirements of the working group's charter and any accompanying requirements documents...an explicit call for implementation experience to those outside of the related working groups or the W3C itself.

- *Proposed recommendation.* Believed to meet the relevant requirements..., to represent sufficient implementation experience, and to adequately address dependencies from the W3C technical community and comments from previous reviewers.

- *W3C recommendation.* End result of extensive consensus-building inside and outside of W3C about a particular technology or policy...appropriate for widespread deployment and promote W3C's mission.

XML in fact became a recommendation in a very short time. But not all of the related family members of XML were that straightforward. The thorniest area of XML has been in *styling* (how XML content should finally look or sound). This is predictable, because it impacts browsers, programming practices, and established methods for expressing style.

Benefit: The speed of XML's reaching W3C recommendation status meant that the workplace could begin conducting real business in only one year beyond the first draft.

8. The design of XML shall be formal and concise.

You are not likely to read many of the formal specifications that comprise XML recommendations. But you can always be sure that the specification exists, when clarification or appeal is necessary. Since every portion of XML is formally defined, a software developer can rely on the specification as a design document.

The design, as expressed in the specification, has its own formal language. That language is the same for all of the specifications for the XML family.

The first edition of version 1.0 (February 1998) was only 29 pages. The second edition (October 2000) had grown to 54 pages, still a modest size for the formal definition of a language.

Benefit: Thanks to the conciseness of XML, it is economically feasible even for small organizations and trading partners to develop XML-based systems.

9. *XML documents shall be easy to create.*

This objective is a worthy legacy of the SGML standard. Creating XML content is indeed easy, because we are dealing with plain text, as always. So in theory, creation is possible with even the lowest-grade text editing tool, running on any computer. But the nature of creating *structured* content for complex content makes a structure-aware editor almost mandatory, as it is for HTML. As we have observed for the first objective, easy should probably read straightforward.

Benefit: Thanks in part to the flat (format-free) nature of XML content (documents), the skill set requirements for data entry, editing, and management is minimal. The arrival of reasonably priced and powerful XML editors has driven the cost of entry even lower for the potential XML player.

10. *Terseness is of minimal importance.*

This caveat originates from software engineering. There it is sometimes considered a virtue to write efficient computer code (i.e., as few lines as possible) to accomplish something. The down side of terseness in computer code is generally that it makes the code unreadable by all but the writer and very few others. With the likelihood of commingled XML markup, HTML, JavaScript, and other scripting within a single file, XML likewise can become terse. For serious, reusable XML content, that practice is not only of minimal importance, but it is unacceptable because it prevents the human-legible and reasonably clear objective.

Actual XML content, at least as Web page source, is anything but terse. It is evident in XML Schemas (the means of representing XML document types using XML itself). It is evident in expressions written for Extensible Stylesheet Language Transformations (XSLT). Fortunately, there is no penalty for this because of increased processor speed and decreased memory costs, both for disk and RAM.

Benefit: The verbosity of XML is its own best guarantee that XML content will readily expose itself for maintenance and management.

ISN'T THE WEB ANOTHER STRONG MOTIVATOR FOR XML? ....

Besides the W3C's own stated motivations for XML, the role of the World Wide Web has been dominant. There are two reasons for this.

First, the Web is an arena for dynamic content. No longer limited to hand-crafted pages, the Web is the medium for content undergoing constant and frequent change. Web-based financial information must reflect complex and far-reaching changes that occur on a minute-to-minute basis. Live electronic commerce (e-commerce) by its definition is about commodities whose pricing and terms are likewise in constant flux. The various nontext media items we see and hear on the Web are also constantly updated: video capture of traffic conditions, weather maps, audio files of hourly news. Even static Web sites run rotational substitutions of images in order to capture the visitor's attention. Customers and trading partners now expect their sessions to be personalized, retaining a history of transactions and maintaining a security profile for personalized access. All of these instances of dynamic content are driven by add-on intelligence, the software that Web designers must write and integrate software to manage content. That software demands a notation that (1) is friendly to Web programming languages (typically **scripts**) and (2) fits in easily with the Internet's layers of transmission **protocols** (definitions of how to move information across the Internet). XML has proven to be the perfect fit on both counts.

Second, the obvious and dominant front-line player in the Web food chain is the browser. If the out-of-the-box software in the browser could not deliver the text, audio, and video in the way the creators intended, the Web would only be a nice concept. The fact is that every browser product has come with the intelligence to process scripting languages and to recognize structured markup (text with pointy-bracket tags). The on-going question in browser development is how smart the browser must be about content markup. Fortunately, there is a Hypertext Markup Language (HTML) that was invented solely for Web delivery. All browsers are native speakers of HTML. HTML has been a strong determinant in the development of XML as a transformer of its own content. If the vast and growing store of XML content is ever to reach the Web user's screen, printer, telephone, or player it must somehow be transformed into HTML so that standard browsers can deliver it. We call this transformation **down translation**, because it reduces XML content, no matter how complex, to HTML.

But the dynamic between XML and browsers goes further. XML-based providers continue to express their need for XML-native browsers. They envision a translation-free delivery that preserves all of the intelligence and personalization of the original XML. On the W3C side, there are several instances within the specifications that seek to accommodate browsers as they are. At this moment the issue of delivering XML-as-is, is not totally resolved. But the status is that browsers can accomplish it in only in a very restricted manner. In Chapter 16 we will demonstrate exactly what a browser can do with XML on its own and how XML as a translator of its own content can down translate to HTML.

So there are compelling reasons to say that XML is a Web technology. It is the dominant player in storing, managing, and aggregating Web content. And it is a powerful contributor to preparing that content for delivery. One commonly heard conclusion is: "Since browsers cannot display XML directly, I should not invest in XML for Web delivery." That statement contains both a half-truth and a serious lack of business judgment. XML, aided by its own built-in transforming power, delivers content quite nicely on the browser. And given the progress of browser technologies, the commitment of technology providers, and the specifications emerging from W3C working groups, it seems inevitable that XML on the Web will become even more straightforward and even more of a sound business strategy.

SUMMARY ....

XML did not originate in a vacuum. It built on the successes and lessons learned from SGML and in that respect was a mature technology from the start. The stated goals of XML articulate an entire business case for structured electronic information. They also spell out warnings of how an XML strategy could go wrong. Our association of XML with the Web is no accident. The Web has been a driving force in the development of XML from the start. In turn XML is a strong determinant in the development of Web browser technologies. XML for agile and portable content and XML for the Web is now an established fact. Whereas HTML is an adequate vehicle for delivering Web pages, XML is a robust techmology for total content definition and management.

2 What's the Difference Between...?

In this chapter...

They Said It...

Come Sir, Arise! Away! I'll teach you differences.

William Shakespeare: The Tragedy of King Lear

It is impossible even to discuss XML intelligently without understanding clearly the distinctions among the many markup languages. These languages are cited in technical news and industry reports, and their proliferation has caused serious misunderstanding among potential XML adopters. Six terms will help articulate the differences. It is essential to view markup languages as a family and not simply as a random succession. Properly armed with an accurate perception of the XML landscape, a manager is in a much better position to assess the potential value of XML within his or her organization.

DECISION MAKER'S PROBLEM.................................

For the serious evaluator of XML, the markup language landscape seems noisy and contradictory. Markup experts and proponents tell of a healthy evolution in markup languages. They are optimistic about the future of XML, although they most often fail to address the business side of markup. But those looking in from the outside may only see a chaotic series of noisy promises, failed attempts, retries, and yet more promises.

The history of markup languages may only seem to be an academic topic. But understanding that history is critical to the process of evaluating XML. The key to getting the history straight is to understand that markup languages constitute a family and not just a haphazard, Darwinian evolution. Failing to understand the straightforward relationship among members of the markup family is one of the biggest barriers to acceptance of XML by decision makers. Understanding this relationship is a fast-track method of understanding the key concepts of XML at the executive level.

SNAPSHOT OF THE TERMINOLOGY CHAOS............

The worst culprit in the confusion over markup languages is the word "language" itself. To compound the problem, writers often attempt to explain XML by appealing to the terms dialect and vocabulary. As clever as these may be, analogies with human language are likely only to confuse the matter. (Analogies are useful, so we too will offer an analogy, though not based on human language. We only hope that ours is more helpful.)

Another factor in the confusion is HTML. HTML has been in wide (global) use for years on the Web. XML has not displaced it and probably never will. So HTML seems to be a clear winner. Behind that reasoning is a serious misunderstanding of the nature of each language.

It has further confused decision makers to learn that XML is a successor to SGML. From that it is too easy to deduce that SGML was tried, that it failed, that XML (having displaced SGML) is a second try, and that it too may fail. This has been a widespread misconception, again based on faulty logic.

LOOK AT ME FIRST ....

Figure 2.1 is a diagram that situates various languages, a word which has two different meanings, each very important for the XML evaluation process.

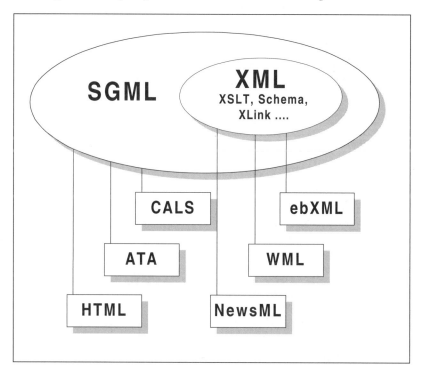

Figure 2.1 The language picture

A Slightly Unorthodox Analogy

Let us suspend the discussion about languages for a moment with an analogy that should help clarify the landscape. Let us consider SGML (the large ellipse in Figure 2.1) as a top-of-the-line box of Lego Blocks®. With that kit we are able to build interesting and complex houses, cars, figures, and stick figure people, some battery powered and remotely controlled. We call some of our creations CALS, ATA, and HTML.

XML (the smaller ellipse) is a Lego Blocks starter kit. But there are accessory kits available for XML, kits that you will need for building anything of any usefulness. There are already a number of these accessory kits available: XSL, XSL Schema, Xlink, and more. The Lego Blocks company is producing still more such accessories. With XML and its accessories you can build things just as large and as interesting as you can with the SGML set, the "big kit." Some of the more notable projects built with XML are ebXML, WML, and NewsXML.

The lesson of this little tutorial is that the "L" in -ML does not always stand for "language." In the case of SGML and XML it stands for "Lego." All of the other items in our diagram really are languages (or initiatives based on languages).

Then what exactly are SGML and XML... really? They are not the markup languages that accomplish actual work. Instead they truly are the "building blocks" of the languages. The technical term for that is metalanguage. So the proper way to describe SGML and XML is that they are metalanguages, serving exclusively as constructors of languages.

XML as a Subset: The Inner Ellipse

A moment ago we referred to XML as the smaller kit of blocks. The technical way of expressing that is to say that XML is a subset of SGML. Note that being a subset means that its "pieces" come from the larger set (SGML in this case). It does not mean that SGML came first, had its chance, and then was replaced by XML. Both metalanguages have their place. And both coexist very nicely today.

Applications of SGML and XML: Markup Languages and Instances

There are six markup languages in our family diagram. These are the labeled rectangles. These are only six of hundreds of existing markup language applications. In Chapter 1 we described five of these languages briefly, mentioning the particular purpose of each.

The notable item among the applications is HTML. HTML is indeed a markup language whose specification is thoroughly SGML. But it is only a single application.

What about the millions of HTML Web pages? To finish off our "terminology toolbox" we call these instances. An HTML file is an instance of HTML, as are the millions of other HTML files in existence. All of the XML examples that we will view in the book (the ones with .xml as the file name's extension) are instances of some XML or SGML language.

Terminology Wrap-up

In the preface we promised that this would not be a book about arcane aspects of XML. We also promised that specialized terms would be kept to an absolute minimum. This brief chapter has sought to concentrate on the absolutely essential terminology required by decision-makers and potential adopters. We cannot read this book or any management report or executive summary of XML without a clear idea of what XML really is. As a final pass over this cluster of essential terms, here is a condensed summary (with apologies to Lego!). By this time it should make perfect sense.

1. SGML is an ISO standard, the "big box of Legos®" used to create markup languages. We call this "language Legos kit" a metalanguage.

2. HTML is but one of the possible markup languages created with SGML. Technically speaking, HTML is an SGML application. So are the languages defined by the CALS initiative from the ATA. The markup languages themselves are like the various toys you create with Legos.

3. XML is the work of the W3C and is a recommendation, not technically a standard. XML will never be a standard in the way that SGML is, but it can be just as useful.

4. XML is a subset of SGML (a smaller box of Legos, making it easier for us to create markup languages. FinML (for the financial industry) is an XML language. So is WML (Wireless Markup Language for wireless devices), NewsXML (for creating and delivering news content), and thousands of other markup languages.

5. XML includes other W3C recommendations, including eXtensible Style Language Transformations (XSLT, for transforming XML content from one form to another), XML Schema (for describing XML content structure using XML iteself), and XLink (for non-invasive location of XML content).

TEN QUESTIONS ABOUT XML THAT A MANAGER SHOULD ASK..

We have attempted to correct some misunderstandings about XML that are the result of poorly understood terminology. All too frequently, managers and decision-makers find themselves trying to answer the question "Should I adopt XML or not?" Our discussion should have demonstrated that this is a meaningless question, based on a poorly-explained and half-understood technology. With a better grasp of basic XML concepts, it should be easier to detect some of the common misinformation that we read concerning XML. And having done that, we are in a better position to ask some of the questions that a potential adopter should ask about XML. There are surely more, but at least we can now use sensible terminology to begin thinking accurately about the business side of XML:

1. How many XML industry-related applications (with their own markup languages) are developed to the point of conducting real business? In other words, has the overall number of XML applications reached critical mass?

2. Does the currently-available suite of XML specifications (Schema, XSLT, and the rest) allow us to define an application that fits our organization or industry?

3. Does there exist an XML application (with its own markup language) for our industry? If so, does the application fit well enough with our business practices to deserve further investigation?

4. Is there a sufficient selection of XML tools available to support our industry's proposed (or adopted) XML application? That is, can I expect to conduct real business in XML using moderately priced and trainable skill sets, or must I rely on expensive consulting?

5. Does there exist a sufficient variety of training materials for the XML application in our industry to make an initiative feasible at this time?

6. For the XML initiative currently underway for my industry, how far along in the approval process is the proposal for the actual markup language (the -ML)? In other words, what kind of lead time do I have for getting my organization ready?

7. I want us to walk, and then run, before we fly. So how much would it cost my local organization to launch a modest XML application as a feasibility project, including its own special-purpose markup language?

8. What sort of up-selling and reallocation of resources is necessary for existing applications (NewsXML, ebXML, and the scores of others) to get

off the ground? My management will never buy into XML for its own sake. Adopting technology because it is cool is no longer cool. The same certainly had to be originally true for all of these initiatives.

9. How exactly might an XML application (including a markup language) result in cost reduction or cost containment for our organization? Is there a possible return on investment (ROI) for an XML application (e.g. increased sales)? Is there a danger that XML might only fuel a runaway initiative that erases our original value proposition for XML?

10. How exactly should our organization budget for an XML initiative? Is the front-loaded cost to be charged directly against projected savings? Are those savings likely to be realized within certain cost centers, or must we wait to determine that when the actual results show up on our balance sheets? Are we properly measuring our information processing costs today so that we even recognize any real savings?

SUMMARY ....

Understanding some key terms and relationships among key XML concepts enables us to make sensible management decisions about XML. Trade publications and even live trade shows may offer little help. Viewing XML and its applications (markup languages) within a proper framework allows us to ask the important management questions. When we view XML in its relationship to major business initiatives, we discover that it is more than a mere technology. It is certainly more than a set of markup rules. XML makes sense for an organization because it eases the information workflow, reduces long-term investment in information resources, and allows for a low cost of entry into many emerging technologies. Understanding XML's place in the current information landscape prepares us to ask the right questions for each organization.

3   What's the *Really* Big Idea?

In this chapter...

They Said It...

Through thy Idea—lo! the immortal Reality!
Through thy Reality—lo! the immortal Idea!
Walt Whitman: "As a Strong Bird on
Pinions Free" (Leaves of Grass)

Markup is about much more than pointy-bracketed tags. The fundamental concept behind markup is both simple and revolutionary: all content to which we can apply markup is data. Structured markup means that that data is *hierarchical*, or tree-structured. The assumption of content-as-hierarchical-data means that we can apply markup technologies consistently to every process of the information food chain.

In news reporting we find a logical structure at work to guide how journalists write and how the news is finally presented. Journalism offers an outstanding example of the separation of internal structure from final appearance. That separation is the central concept of markup.

THE BIG IDEA ....

In the World According to Markup, all content is data. That sounds simple enough, not something particularly revolutionary. A casual human observer may perceive content-as-data as simply an orderly and predictable format: layout of a page, appearance of a magazine cover, order of items in a financial report. In structured information markup, we formalize the notions of *order* and *predictability*. Once we have spelled out rules for some type of content (i.e., news), it is an easy task to convert the rules to an XML definition. That definition will then apply to all content of that type.

In this demonstration we will look closely at news stories, noting their underlying order and using that order to deduce an actual XML markup language for representing all new stories. Using that XML markup we then apply transformation scripts to render the news in entirely different formats.

Logical Structure: Journalistic Prose

We immediately recognize and interpret the familiar format of journalism. Figures 3.1–3.3 show the lead paragraphs from three news stories that appeared in one week:

Fiery Mir plunges into South Pacific
Russian spacecraft breaks into pieces after re-entry

Associated Press

KOROLYOV, Russia

The Mir space station returned to Earth in pieces this morning, ending its 15-year, 2.2 billion-mile odyssey with a fiery plunge into the South Pacific, Russian space officials said.

Figure 3.1 An Associated Press report

Fed cuts rate; stocks fall
Central Bank targets economy not Wall Street

By Peter G. Gosselin, *Los Angeles Times*

WASHINGTON

The Federal Reserve cut a key short-term interest rate half a percentage point to 5 percent Tuesday in a drive to keep economic growth—but not necessarily the stock market—from falling further.

Figure 3.2 A story, with art, from the Los Angeles Times

Cocaine smuggler faces life in prison
Colombian found guilty of seven federal charges

By Kevin Blocker, Staff writer [Spokane *Spokesman-Review*]

A federal jury found a Colombian drug and counterfeit money smuggler guilty Thursday of seven federal charges that could send him to prison for the rest of his life.

Figure 3.3 A report from Spokane, WA

Like all proper journalistic prose, these excerpts demonstrate what we learned as reporters for the school newspaper: tell *who*, *what*, *where*, and *when* by the end of the opening paragraph. The style sheets of the *Los Angeles Times* and the *Associated Press* still demand the same. Journalists never deviate from this principle. Newspaper journalism style is not simply a nice-to-do. It is a must-do.

But why? News publishers are not simply stylistic bigots. There is a fundamental reason why things are the way they are. Let us first transform these news pieces to a pseudo-database format with rows and columns as shown in Table 3.1.

Table 3.1   Table rendition of news stories

Domain	International	National	Local
Headline	Fiery Mir plunges into South Pacific	Fed cuts rate; stocks fall	Cocaine smuggler faces life in prison
Capsule	*Russian spacecraft breaks into pieces after re-entry*	*Central Bank targets economy not Wall Street*	*Colombian found guilty of seven federal charges*
Byline		Peter G. Gosselin	Kevin Blocker
Affiliation	*Associated Press*	*Los Angeles Times*	*Spokesman-Review*
Origin	KOROLYOV, Russia	WASHINGTON	SPOKANE
Date	March 23, 2001	March 20, 2001	March, 21,2001
Lead	The Mir space station returned...	The Federal Reserve...	A federal jury found...

The publisher of Spokane *Spokesman-Review* enforces a style sheet that invariably results in stories that will fit perfectly into this table. But rendering the stories as a table is more than just an exercise in style analysis. By transforming running prose to a table, we have forced a number of things to the surface:

1. The same who-what-where-when rule is indeed enforced, even in professional journalism. But in practice, depending somewhat on the publisher, these four requirements are enriched. Here there are eight. All but one of these items are invariable requirements for this publication.

2. The requirements for the writer are invariable, regardless of the beat (international, national, or regional). You are an employed writer, not an author that may take liberties with the publisher's style sheet.

3. The order of the items (including their placement in the actual page layout) is uniform and invariable.

4. When the date of the event is within the past six days, it is proper to use the day's name (Tuesday, Thursday, this morning) rather than the full date.

5. The publisher allows for the byline (writer's name) to be optional. But this exception to the rule is itself a formal, invariable rule: The byline is optional *if and only if* the source is a syndicated news feed (e.g., Associated Press, Cox News Service, *New York Times*) or if the received piece did not contain a byline.

6. Exception rule for publisher's identity: Staff Writer following the byline means *Spokesman-Review* by implication.

Invariable list of items. Invariable requirements. Invariable order and layout. Invariable rules (even rules of exception). What is the value of all this harsh invariance anyway? For one thing, it makes life much easier for the editors— news editors, copy editors, layout editors, and everyone else involved in the workflow of the newspaper. But the most important player in this communication flow is the reader. An *invariable* set of rules for creating the news pages means that every item of a story's opening is *predictable*. You know what each item is, partly because of its placement on the page and partly because of the order of the items. Furthermore you not only can *predict* the items in a news story, you *expect* it. Or at least, if some of that order were missing or broken you would be irritated.

Journalistic prose is distinct because it is constrained. Those constraints are spelled out in the publisher's style sheet. The constraints result in a huge communications payoff for you, the consumer. You can interpret news from the opening segment alone in a very efficient manner. And how is that possible? Have you ever seen the style sheet (a fat manual, actually) that your local newspaper uses? When you read a news piece do you deconstruct it, transforming it into a table like our example? Surely you don't. Yet somehow you have *inferred* the style of your newspaper—including the list of required items, their order, and the rules of their inclusion and exclusion. Just to extend this discussion one more step, when you read your local newspaper you are an *inference engine* for its content. With or without a table, you automatically drop each item into its proper slot.

Another way to say invariant or predictable is structured. It appears that the lockstep compliance with a style sheet and our neatly organized table are sufficient proof that journalistic style is indeed structured.

But structure has bought us even more, as the following procedure demonstrates. If we simply **select** Table 3.1 (as I did when authoring this chapter) and **paste** it into a spreadsheet, the spreadsheet program immediately recognizes the table as a near-native and happily receives it as a spreadsheet.

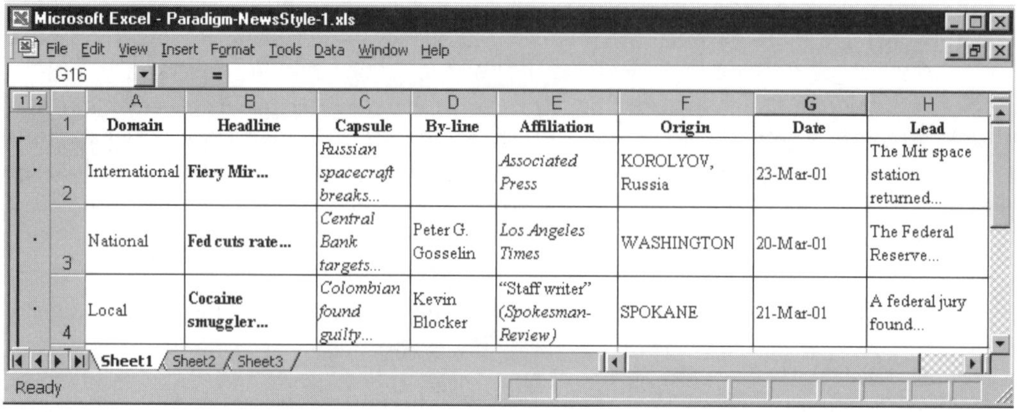

	A	B	C	D	E	F	G	H
1	**Domain**	**Headline**	**Capsule**	**By-line**	**Affiliation**	**Origin**	**Date**	**Lead**
2	International	**Fiery Mir...**	*Russian spacecraft breaks...*		*Associated Press*	KOROLYOV, Russia	23-Mar-01	The Mir space station returned...
3	National	**Fed cuts rate...**	*Central Bank targets...*	Peter G. Gosselin	*Los Angeles Times*	WASHINGTON	20-Mar-01	The Federal Reserve...
4	Local	**Cocaine smuggler...**	*Colombian found guilty...*	Kevin Blocker	"Staff writer" (*Spokesman-Review*)	SPOKANE	21-Mar-01	A federal jury found...

Figure 3.4 Table 3.1 as a spreadsheet

Table 3.2 is the same information, this time copied back from the spreadsheet program.

Table 3.2 Sorted data (by date, newest first)

Domain	International	National	Local
Headline	Fiery Mir plunges into South Pacific	Cocaine smuggler faces life in prison	Fed cuts rate; stocks fall
Capsule	*Russian spacecraft breaks into pieces after re-entry*	*Colombian found guilty of seven federal charges*	*Central Bank targets economy not Wall Street*
Byline		Kevin Blocker	Peter G. Gosselin
Affiliation	*Associated Press*	*Spokesman-Review*	*Los Angeles Times*
Origin	KOROLYOV, Russia	SPOKANE	WASHINGTON
Date	23-Mar-01	21-Mar-01	20-Mar-01

Table 3.2   (Cont'd) Sorted data (by date, newest first)

Lead	The Mir space station returned...	A federal jury found...	The Federal Reserve...

Granted, the word processing program did convert the spreadsheet to a table. And at first glance there might not seem to be anything spectacular about a spreadsheet whose cells contain only textual data. We performed this little exercise in order to demonstrate first that our structured text, once rendered as a table, became *data*. With no further doctoring, the structured text now behaves as genuine spreadsheet data with lettered columns and numbered rows. As spreadsheet data we are able to sort the stories by date (earliest first). The spreadsheet is easily able to export the sorted data back to a table (see Table 3.3).

Table 3.3   Sorted data (by date, oldest first)

Domain	National	Local	International
Headline	Fed cuts rate; stocks fall	Cocaine smuggler faces life in prison	Fiery Mir plunges into South Pacific
Capsule	*Central Bank targets economy not Wall Street*	*Colombian found guilty of seven federal charges*	*Russian spacecraft breaks into pieces after re-entry*
Byline	Peter G. Gosselin	Kevin Blocker	
Affiliation	*Los Angeles Times*	*Spokesman-Review*	*Associated Press*
Origin	WASHINGTON	SPOKANE	KOROLYOV, Russia
Date	20-Mar-01	21-Mar-01	23-Mar-01
Lead	The Federal Reserve...	A federal jury found...	The Mir space station returned...

This exercise has also demonstrated another important property of data: that it can be easily transformed from one format to another. The transformation from table to spreadsheet to table is an example of a "round trip," a common validation test for data transfer. Just to prove further that this is data that we can truly manipulate like other data, we re-sort the "news archive" by date, this time most recent first, and again round-trip it back to a table, Table 3.4:

Table 3.4   Sorted data (restored to original form)

Domain	International	Local	National
Headline	Fiery Mir plunges into South Pacific	Cocaine smuggler faces life in prison	Fed cuts rate; stocks fall
Capsule	*Russian spacecraft breaks into pieces after re-entry*	*Colombian found guilty of seven federal charges*	*Central Bank targets economy not Wall Street*
Byline		Kevin Blocker	Peter G. Gosselin
Affiliation	*Associated Press*	*Spokesman-Review*	*Los Angeles Times*
Origin	KOROLYOV, Russia	SPOKANE	WASHINGTON
Date	23-Mar-01	21-Mar-01	20-Mar-01
Lead	The Mir space station returned...	A federal jury found...	The Federal Reserve...

Unlike the calculus, there is no Fundamental Theorem of markup technologies. But if there were it would read:

> # Content that is *structured* is content that is *data*

Or to state it a bit more informally, content that is structured needs only a nudge of some kind to turn it into useful data. The nudge we chose was to copy-paste the Word table into Microsoft® Excel.

Now that we've demonstrated a content-to-data methodology, two questions deserve a response:

1. So what?
2. Other than as tables or spreadsheets, how can we represent content-as-data?

We will answer the first question by demonstrating that this structured data, rendered as XML, is portable (i.e., non-proprietary and open) and that it can readily be prepared for delivery in a variety of formats.

The second question is important because we are certain that it's impossible to rely solely on tables and spreadsheets for moving data as freely as we'd like. The table format we used for representing the three news stories is built in (and *locked* in) to Word. The spread sheet that was part of our round trip exercise is Excel, likewise a proprietary format. In fact, it will be impossible to represent our data in *any* format at all, if we want the data to be truly and totally open and transportable.

The whole point of markup technologies is to get us free from the limitations of proprietary formats. So where it is necessary to select data handling tools, we demand the freedom to select whatever tools we wish from whatever vendors we choose. We need a data representation that is accessible enough for us to create our own tools, where that's necessary. The representation must also preserve the *structure* of our data.

COMPUTER-RECOGNIZABLE CONTENT ....

We now apply a black box transformer that blindly accepts spreadsheet data and transforms it into XML markup notation. Here is what the XML transformer produces:

```
<?xml version = '1.0'?>
<archive>
   <article>
      <domain>International</domain>
      <headline>Fiery Mir plunges into South Pacific</headline>
      <capsule>Russian spacecraft breaks into pieces after re-entry
       </capsule>
      <by-line></by-line>
      <affiliation>Associated Press</affiliation>
      <origin>KOROLYOV, Russia</origin>
      <date>23-Mar-01</date>
      <lead >The Mir space station returned...</lead >
      <href>http://www.ap.org</href>
   </article>
   <article>
      <domain>National</domain>
      <headline>Fed cuts rate; stocks fall</headline>
      <capsule>Central Bank targets economy not Wall Street</capsule>
      <by-line>Peter G. Gosselin</by-line>
      <affiliation>Los Angeles Times</affiliation>
      <origin>WASHINGTON</origin>
      <date>20-Mar-01</date>
      <lead >The Federal Reserve...</lead >
      <href>http://www.latimes.com</href>
   </article>
```

```
<article>
    <domain>Local</domain>
    <headline>Cocaine smuggler faces life in prison</headline>
    <capsule>Colombian found guilty of seven federal charges</capsule>
    <by-line>Kevin Blocker</by-line>
    <affiliation>Spokesman-Review</affiliation>
    <origin>SPOKANE</origin>
    <date>21-Mar-01</date>
    <lead >A federal jury found...</lead >
    <href>http://www.spokesmanreview.com</href>
    </article>
</archive>
```

We are disregarding the internals of the black box transformer. We are interested only in what this latest rendition of the weekly news tells us about XML *markup*. For now, some simple observations:

- Instead of column headers to describe the contents of items that we saw earlier, there are now pointy-bracket tags: **domain**, **headline**, **capsule**, etc.

- Wherever there is an opening tag (e.g., **<headline>**) there is always a corresponding closing tag (e.g., **</headline>**).

- Even where there is no information between a tag pair, there is still a tag pair (**<byline></byline>**) in the Associated Press article.

- Each separate news piece, including all of its data items is wrapped within an **<article>...</article>** pair.

- The entire package of this week's news pieces is wrapped within an **<archive>...</archive>** pair.

- This rendition is clearly not a word processing or page designer format! It is far less attractive than the original boxed exhibits above. In fact, from a page layout standpoint, it is downright ugly. It is definitely less pleasing than the table rendition. While it is readable, it is something more fit for a computer than for the general news reader.

- The rendition, which is not a format, is in fact simply plain text.

- The cryptic first line tells us (and probably a computer) that this is an XML rendition.

- The tag names are case sensitive (lower-case or upper-case is consistent in the tag pairs).

- There is nothing specific about how any of this information should finally appear (on a Web page, on a printed news page).

And what can a computer can do with markup? For now, here are two demos, shown in Figure 3.5. First, if we use Microsoft® Internet Explorer (v. 5.5, including its XML parser) to **open** this markup file directly, the browser obliges with the following:

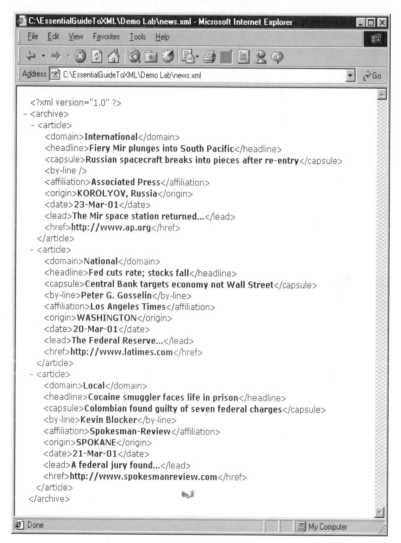

Figure 3.5 The full version of the news summary

Figure 3.5 is a slightly more pleasant layout of XML notation, requiring no black boxes other than the intelligence of Internet Explorer to recognize that this is XML. But IE provides us more. The "+" and "−" symbols are in fact smart expand/rollup buttons that allow us to view the select and view the various embedded levels of content. So if we click on "–" for the entire **<archive>**, IE displays the screen in Figure 3.6.

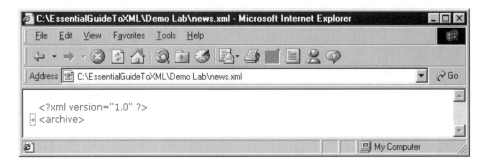

Figure 3.6 The archive condensed

By pressing the "+" button on **<archive>** and by pressing various expand/rollup buttons within this XML package, we can produce selective views as shown in Figure 3.7.

Figure 3.7 Selective views

So without any special viewing software other than IE, it is possible to view and manipulate raw XML. True, this is still just XML notation and only a slightly pretty format, though a little more pleasing than our first raw listing. But with just this brief viewing with IE, we have seen that markup enables our content to behave like data. It can now shake hands with the computer.

Figure 3.8 is yet another view of exactly the same news data. This time we preprocess the XML before asking IE to open it. Whether we use the term reuse, recycle, or re-purpose the point is that we always leave the original marked-up data in its original form. And this time, after we've done some preprocessing, the appearance and general smartness of the view is considerably improved.

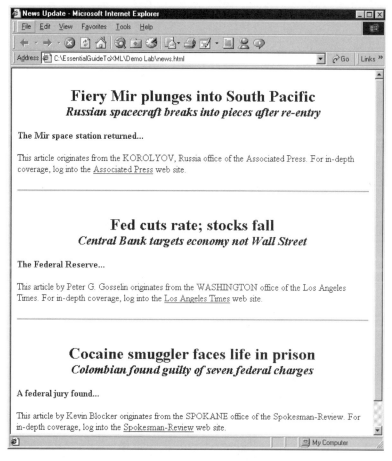

Figure 3.8 A view after preprocessing XML

We have not touched the original XML markup version of this information. The original data is still precisely in the state that we left it. But this time we have used that data to create an HTML Web page.

Apart from the steadily improving appearance of the screens, what has this series of views demonstrated to us? In addition to the observations earlier, here are some conclusions about markup in general:

- Even though markup is not as *attractive* as final page layout in a newspaper or magazine, it is still humanly *readable*.
- Once we have information in markup form—reduced to plain text and properly tagged-we can reuse that information as is.
- The workflow connected with markup information involves laborsaving tools. In this chapter we only mentioned some of these in passing, sometimes calling them "black boxes." Internet Explorer with its built-in XML recognizer, is one example of such a tool for XML.
- *First* we make sure that the information is accurate and structured, using some markup scheme that the computer can understand. *Then* we deal with its appearance. While both of these areas are critical, they are separate activities.
- In a perfect markup world, an organization applies this separation of activities-content structuring and rendition—rigorously to its creation and maintenance workflow.

AUTHOR'S (EMBARRASSING) LESSON LEARNED .....

In Figure 3.8, after finishing the tables and graphics for this chapter, I discovered that I had misspelled "re-entry," having typed "re-intry" instead. I had committed this critical blunder in Table 3.1. And the error of course had rippled through the remainder of the entire chapter. In the old days of traditional writing and page layout, such an error might have entailed much handwork to touch up each of the screens, tables, views, and other exhibits sprinkled throughout the chapter. But happily, because we are in fact demonstrating markup, the fragment in which I committed that error was part of a systematic markup workflow. I merely had to correct that misspelling once and then run the various automatic transformation utilities again. This is but a trivial example of the principle referred to as write once, propagate everywhere. The same piece of marked up content is reused, recycled or repurposed possibly to a very broad array of media, devices, and audiences. The maintenance savings for this information strategy are obvious.

SUMMARY ....

Information that is structured can be transformed to XML data. Once it is rendered as XML, we can apply XML tools and programs to the data to accomplish anything we wish: edit, store, access, locate, manage, exchange, transform, or deliver. All XML data is *hierarchical*. This means that it is tree-structured. Content-as-hierarchical-data means that we can apply XML markup technologies consistently to every process of the information food chain. That process may be as straightforward as on-the-fly conversion to HTML. Or it could be as complex as generating a personalized, downloadable parts catalog for an OEM customer in PDF format.

4 How Does XML Solve the Digital Problem?

In this chapter...

They Said It...

> *This poor ignorant Monarch...was persuaded*
> *that the Straight Line which he called his*
> *Kingdom...constituted the whole of the*
> *world....Not being able either to move or to see,*
> *save in his Straight Line, he had no conception*
> *of anything out of it.*
>
> Edwin A. Abbot (1838-1926), Flatland

Digital information operates strictly in "Line-land,"[1] a one-dimensional universe that views objects one item at a time—one character at a time in the case of XML. Digital content (ones and zeroes representing everything) is good because it guarantees that the content cannot easily be corrupted. Open systems content is good because it guarantees that information cannot be trapped in proprietary formats. Open digital content is therefore doubly good because we can store, transmit, and receive it reliably in a vendor-free manner. But because every part of the digital transmission plumbing is one-dimensional, it impacts workflow in some fundamental ways. The transmission and exchange process force us constantly to deconstruct and then reconstruct content. XML, with its accompanying technologies, is the ideal approach for this deconstruct/reconstruct process.

WHY DIGITAL? ....

If you are a serious reader of this book, you are already convinced that digital is good. You already know that human-readable pages, pictures, film, or faxes can deteriorate over time. You already know that by reducing pages, images, or sounds to strings of ones and zeroes they have a much greater chance of survival. It is extremely easy for any digital computer to store ones and zeroes on magnetic media of any variety. Once stored, the content is secure. Digital content is content that is secure—secure in the sense that it will not deteriorate over time.

---

[1] This one-dimensional world is the creation of Edwin A. Abbot (1838-1926), author of the science fiction classic *Flatland: A Romance of Many Dimensions,* 6/e (New York: Dover Publications, 1953). This is a must-read for anyone with a vested interest in computer-based information.

WHY OPEN SYSTEMS? ·····································

Every word processing and page processing storage format is digital by definition. The problem with just-digital is that a digital storage format is liable to be proprietary. Most word processed documents on the planet—including their embedded tables, graphics, and audio clips—exist in proprietary digital formats. We and the document are therefore captives of the vendors and their technologies. The ticket to freedom for us and for our digital content is a strategy of representing all of that content in some vendor-independent notation.

Open systems content is content that is transportable, easily exchangeable, reusable, and—because it is digital—least likely to deteriorate over time. But those are XML evangelistic statements you already have heard. And you probably believe them or you wouldn't be reading a book on XML.

SO WHAT'S THE PROBLEM? ·······························

As we shall see in Chapter 5, XML information is content on the *move*. While much of this book will deal with how to write and edit XML information, there is also a fundamental issue of how to move it. You and your organization must learn how to create and manage XML information. Fortunately, the XML specification itself has already solved the problem of its transmission and exchange.

Conversely, don't go to the trouble of converting data to XML if it is going to just sit there. There are more efficient ways to store data in place.

If there is a downside to digital information, even open systems digital information, it is the nature of the channel (the plumbing) required to move it or even to read it. While the current technology of the digital computer is vastly improved over those of 30–40 years ago, it still must process strings of ones and zeroes. Because we humans readily perceive a document of text, tables, and graphics as whole (two-dimensional) pages, it is almost impossible for us to imagine the computer's view of the digital world. In that dimension-challenged world, a page—a two-dimensional object—must be stored, retrieved, and transmitted as a one-dimensional string, regardless of how it may appear on the screen (see Figure 4.1).

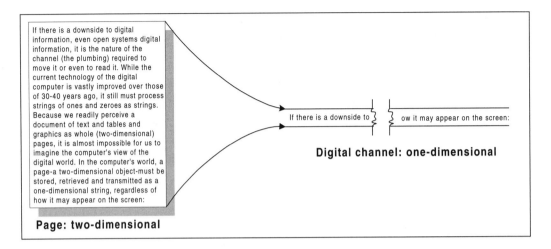

Figure 4.1 Deconstruction: Translation of two-dimensional page to one-dimensional channel

The computer may be able to read and process that string by clustering the ones and zeroes into units that make up characters. But clustered or not, the string is still a one-dimensional object of characters.

At the input end, there must be some form of systematic deconstruction. Some intelligent mechanism must reduce the page to a single-dimensional string in preparation for its digital transfer.

Likewise, in order for that digitized page to be useful to the recipient, something must "undigitize" that string, restoring the page to its two-dimensional form. In other words, some intelligent mechanism at the receiving end must reconstruct the original page from its digital representation. That would be like flipping Figure 4.1 horizontally (see Figure 4.2).

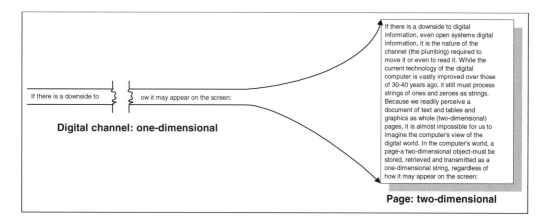

Digital channel: one-dimensional

If there is a downside to   ow it may appear on the screen:

If there is a downside to digital information, even open systems digital information, it is the nature of the channel (the plumbing) required to move it or even to read it. While the current technology of the digital computer is vastly improved over those of 30-40 years ago, it still must process strings of ones and zeroes as strings. Because we readily perceive a document of text and tables and graphics as whole (two-dimensional) pages, it is almost impossible for us to imagine the computer's view of the digital world. In the computer's world, a page-a two-dimensional object-must be stored, retrieved and transmitted as a one-dimensional string, regardless of how it may appear on the screen:

Page: two-dimensional

Figure 4.2 Reconstruction: Translation of one-dimensional channel to two-dimensional page

And It Gets Even Worse!

We can easily imagine transforming letters on a page to ones and zeroes. Likewise, transforming a graphic to ones and zeroes is commonplace and straightforward to understand. Figure 4.1 suggests those transformations. But there is much more on a printed page than just symbols and pictures. The page itself has an overall style design: width, margins, fonts, faces, placement of page numbers, spacing of all kinds.

In order for a properly styled page to be digitized and subsequently reconstructed, it is necessary to encode all of the styling information as well. Proprietary systems typically commingle the styling data with the textual content. The open systems approach dictates that styling data be kept separate from content. But separate or not, some mechanisms must also deconstruct and then reconstruct a page's styling.

This all sounds very theoretical, interesting perhaps, but not terribly useful. Worse, this multiple deconstruct-reconstruct process hints at outrageous budgeting requirements for open systems technologies: complex software, high-powered computing, expensive new skills sets, radically redesigned workflow, long-deferred payback.

SO WHAT'S THE SOLUTION?...............................

By addressing six key problem areas, we spell out six requirements for the design for a digital exchange system that makes sense. And in doing that we also suggest six of the fundamental reasons that XML came into existence:

1. Documents must be grouped in such a way that the system can deal with them as classes or types.

2. All content—regardless of media—must be reducible to some system of fragments in order for the system to manage it and to move it digitally.

3. The level of computer intelligence required to deconstruct and then re-construct the content must be minimal.

4. Like the content we expect to share, the intelligence for deconstructing-reconstructing must likewise be easily sharable among a wide class of computers.

5. The content we expect to process must be structured. Specifically, it must be hierarchical data.

6. The logical structure of the content must be maintained separately from its physical appearance. We must disallow the messy commingling of logical structure with styling information.

CONTENT AS CATEGORIES ....

No serious professional (except an academic researcher) would hope to fund the de-velopment of a pure inference engine. Such a system would accept *any* document, no matter how novel or unique, and somehow magically determine its genre, its lan-guage, and every detail of its content and style.

The goal of practical information publishing technology is to focus rather on specific *types* of content: repair manuals, maintenance manuals, policy manuals, rate tables, industry-specific regulations. E-business developers likewise focus on specific types of content: purchase orders, invoices, receipts, receiver reports, bills of materials, and various accounting document types. This modest goal of developing a system and workflow for a particular type of content is entirely doable.

XML is designed specifically to deal with classes or types of content. As we shall see in Chapter 5, XML treats these classes in much the same way that human language supports large communities of speakers. We dedicate Chapters 10 and 11 to XML's descriptions of document types. These are powerful tools for supporting an almost in-finite number of industry-specific documents in a very simple manner.

Reducing content to manageable fragments is necessary for digital processing and transfer. But simply chopping a file into arbitrary lengths would accomplish very little. Instead, the process requires some systematic method for segmenting the con-tent in the first place.

XML deals in logical units called **elements**. These are the basic building blocks that constitute all members of a given class of documents or media. By providing a segmentation scheme from the start, XML automatically assists with its own digital transfer.

XML also deals in physical units, the units that we most commonly think of in file management systems. The XML name for these is **entities**. We will take up entities in Chapter 12.

Minimal Intelligence of the Processor

Electronic content is by definition content that must be processed by computers. The processor speeds and storage capacities of computers have improved dramatically, but a computer out of the box still has no specialized knowledge about an application like content management and transfer. We demand a content workflow that relies on computers to deconstruct, transmit or transform, and then reconstruct content flawlessly. Yet we must insist that the intelligence required for this processing be absolutely minimal. At best we would hope that effective e-content processing is possible on a computer costing less than $1,000. We would also hope that the required software would cost next to nothing.

Thanks to the effort of many work groups, XML is able to accomplish all of the steps in its workflow with a minimum investment in software. And thanks to the array of freely available tools and for-purchase editors now supporting XML, the task of managing and moving e-content is within easy reach of any organization.

Portable intelligence

In almost every real-world case, e-content is exchanged among organizations with different computers. So it would do us little good if all of the software required for e-content processing were written for only a single platform or operating system.

Some key areas of the XML specification that support transfer and transformation of e-content are designed intentionally to be totally platform-independent. And most of the XML support tools available likewise are programmed to be easily installable on any platform.

CONTENT AS STRUCTURED DATA ....

XML, as part of the legacy of markup technologies, insists on structured data. In fact, it insists on hierarchical (tree-structured) data as its native form. Consider once again the XML representation of an archived news story from Chapter 3:

```
<archive>
   <article>
      <domain>International</domain>
      <headline>Fiery Mir plunges into South Pacific</headline>
      <capsule>Russian spacecraft breaks into pieces after
         rentry</capsule>
      <by-line/>
      <affiliation>Associated Press</affiliation>
      <origin>KOROLYOV, Russia</origin>
      <date>23-Mar-01</date>
      <lead>The Mir space station returned...</lead>
      <href>http://www.ap.org</href>
   </article>
      :
      :
      :
</archive>
```

Reading the markup in plain English, we would say "An archive *contains* an article, followed by as many articles as there are in this archive." Then we would move inward and say, "An article *contains* a domain, followed by a headline, followed by a capsule, followed by an optional byline, and so on." This container-contained relationship is easy to depict with an indentation scheme, just as we have done. But for a one-dimensional channel, it would be a challenge to convey indentation, were it not for XML's balanced tags.

As we shall demonstrate in Chapter 5, XML allows for a deconstruct-reconstruct process of a document that loses nothing of the document's original structuring information.

SEPARATION OF STRUCTURE AND APPEARANCE ...

It requires a new way of thinking for us to conceive of documents, records, or audio files without their styling information. Yet that is just what XML demands. On the other hand, XML is extremely concerned about appearance and style. The innovation of XML is that is defers the styling of a document, report, or audio output until after it has processed the core content. Again, XML does not *disregard* style. It simply *separates* style from logical structure. Chapter 18 describes XSL-FO (Extensible Style

Language-Formatting Objects), an XML specification devoted largely to the page lay-out of XML documents.

SUMMARY ....

The digital problem for digital information is that all of the structural and styling in-formation must somehow be reduced to a series of elementary units in order for us to transmit it. And once received, it must then be reconstituted (reconstructed, restored) to its original form. The requirements for a system to accomplish that are major. For-tunately, XML was developed precisely to solve this problem.

5 XML as Workflow

In this chapter...

They Said It...

Antonio. *I'll teach you how to flow.*
Sebastian. *Do so. To ebb... Hereditary sloth
instructs me.*

William Shakespeare, The Tempest

XML is about workflow. We (or computers on their own) create XML content. Then we store it, search it, retrieve it, transform it, process it, reorganize it, transmit it, and format it. This workflow is a constant process of encoding the content in some way so that the recipient can decode and use it. In that regard, XML workflow is very similar to human language. Both are intended to convey information. And both rely on a set of rules to determine what is proper, what can be accurately understood by the recipient. We call the set of rules for human languages a **grammar**. Similarly we apply grammar to XML to demonstrate that rules provide a simple and effective way to express and convey electronic content. Moreover, just as for human communication, real publication and real e-business often require translation. We must provide for the exchange of content among entirely different XML languages. XML as a metalanguage allows for straightforward XML-to-XML communication and translation.

ELECTRONIC CONTENT: CONTENT IN MOTION .....

Whatever your role in information technology, you are in the business of *moving* content. You may move it in and out of storage. You may disseminate that content, publishing it across a wide enterprise and beyond. You may move it in place, transforming it from one form to another. You may work with e-business trading partners to make their business information flow safely between manufacturer and wholesaler, for example. Or your e-business may involve content that moves between supplier and customer.

Content in Motion Overcomes Boundaries

In any case, electronic content is not a closet experience. No one except a pure researcher is interested in content that goes nowhere. And every practical movement of content entails crossing a *boundary*. It may be a boundary of space—disseminating a complex policy manual from several source archives to a global organization. It may well be a boundary of hosting platforms—sharing purchase history information among hundreds of entirely different computers. It may be a barrier of time—archiving nuclear waste information in a manner so as to assure that it will be readable five centuries from now, regardless of future technologies. Creating, storing, and retrieving content is the primary mission of the information professional. But helping that content to move effectively across boundaries is a nobler and more challenging mission.

XML IS COMMUNICATION...................................

Information in motion across boundaries. This is only a slight paraphrase of the process of *communication*. The same dynamics and problems we encounter with everyday communication—spoken, written, and pictorial—are those we confront in moving electronic information. Understanding the communications model of sending and receiving information will help us to realize why XML for electronic information was a solution waiting to happen. Figure 5.1 depicts the life cycle of a spoken message.

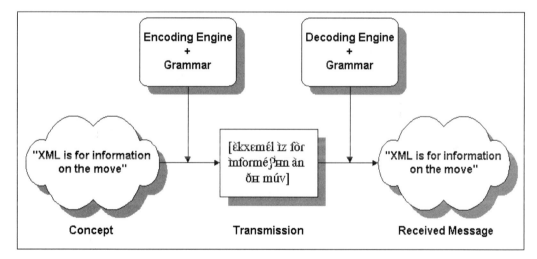

Figure 5.1 Human communication process

Figure 5.1 hides enormous complexity. In reality the chain of events is much more complex than the picture suggests: more milestones, more layers, more stages of translation. But the significant point for our discussion is that both the speaker (the one formulating a concept and uttering physical sounds) and the hearer (the one recreating the original concept from the physical sounds) rely totally on a single *grammar*.

This process is automatic for native users of a shared spoken language. But unconscious or not, some strong and uncompromising assumptions (principles) are at work:

1. *Encoding* and *decoding* are separate and critical steps in the communications path.

2. Both the speaker and the listener share a well-learned and deeply ingrained set of *rules*. We call that set of rules a *grammar*.

3. Once a message is encoded, it is almost immaterial how you choose to *transmit* it: sound waves between you and the listener, telephone, audio tape, or digitized sound. Whatever the boundary—distance, time, delays, interruptions—you can select an appropriate transmission method to transcend it.

4. The communications process is successful if and only if the received and reconstructed message (right cloud) is the same as the sender's original concept (left cloud).

To change the scenario only slightly, consider the case of an electronics manufacturer who must communicate content to a network of distributors. But in this case the manufacturer is communicating not an idea but business-critical supply chain information: bills of materials (describing the components of infrared sensing devices), purchase order receipts, and shipping and billing information, for example.

Or consider the problem of the large utilities company that must frequently update and re-publish regulations received from state and federal agencies. Again, the content is not a set of ideas but large volumes of highly structured regulations and numeric data.

We can easily sketch an XML methodology for accomplishing either of these tasks. For the moment, we'll disregard most of the internals of XML. Study the following communications workflow, this time for structured information. Figure 5.2 is a car rental record.

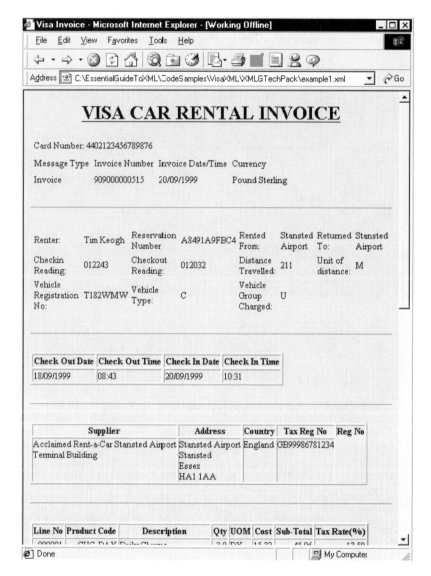

Figure 5.2 Web page rendition of car rental invoice

But in order to produce that end result, there is a significant XML workflow (see Figure 5.3).

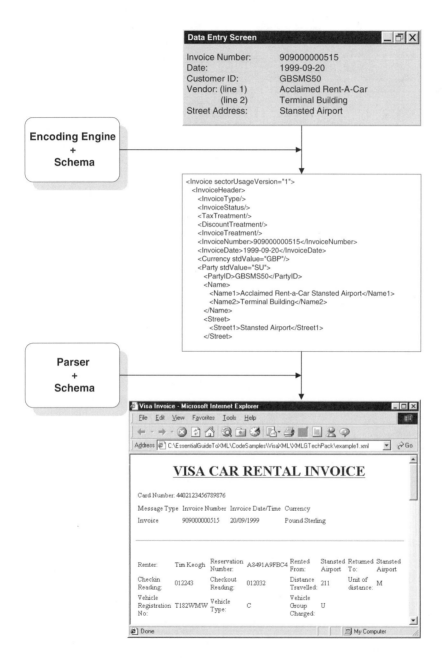

Figure 5.3 XML Workflow for credit card invoicing system

Once again, some underlying assumptions:

1. Encoding (the record into XML) and decoding the record are separate tasks.

2. For some XML-based business, there may not appear to be separate record-to-XML and XML-to-final-form steps at all. The originator (here, the data input and capture software) may simply create the invoice record as XML from the outset. Likewise the receiver (here, Web browser) may access the XML record directly. But visible or not, the same workflow happens, on the fly in this case.

3. Whether or not a transformation is involved, a shared set of rules (schema in Figure 5.2) defines how XML applies to the record. That set of rules applies both to the sender and the receiver. Each agrees on those rules as the basis for doing business.

What is this set of rules (grammar)?

We have stressed the importance of a grammar in natural language communication. Similarly we stress the central role of XML rules—an XML grammar, actually—in making XML work. We call this set of rules an XML schema. But what, in the simplest terms possible, is a schema? There are two components of a schema, and they are the same as for the grammar of a human language:

1. An inventory of the parts and pieces available to a user.

2. A set of rules describing all of the ways that a user may "legally" assemble those parts and pieces.

For English, the grammar specifies components like noun phrase and verb phrase. "Valerie" and "the driver of the tan Jaguar" are each instances of noun phrases. "Failed to stop at the intersection" and "was issued a citation" are each verb phrases. Here is a simple assembly rule:

Sentence = Noun Phrase + Verb Phrase

This tells us that we may use either of the noun phrases and either of the verb phrases to produce four acceptable English sentences:

1. Valerie failed to stop at the intersection.

2. Valerie was issued a citation.

3. The driver of the tan Jaguar failed to stop at the intersection.

4. The driver of the tan Jaguar was issued a citation.

Again, one part of the set of rules (the inventory) tells us what building blocks are available. The other set defines how we are to assemble them. Note that if we had not just two, but millions of noun phrases and verb phrases, we could create tens of millions of acceptable sentences. And we could do so with only a single assembly rule. That is, rules apply to *classes* of sentences, not to individual *instances*. Every possible simple declarative sentence of English is generated by the single rule above. As far as we are concerned, that inventory and that single assembly rule constitutes the entire grammar of English.

If you are a native speaker of English, are you conscious of grammar's determining how you form every sentence? Of course not. The point is that whether or not it is this grammar, the relatively small set of rules make it possible for you to speak and write an infinite number of well-formed simple declarative sentences.

What does the rule set for an XML language describe? Here is the answer in two parts, and we shall revisit this two-part list over several chapters:

1. All of the possible *elements* in that language.
2. All of the possible tree-structured *arrangements* of those elements in the language.

In an XML language for automotive manufacturing, the possible elements for a wheel assembly may include wheel, rim, tire, brake kit, cylinder, caliper, drum, disk, and many thousands more. The tree structure would dictate that a wheel contains certain sublements, including brake kit. Brake kit in turn would contain the sublements cylinder, caliper, and so on. Just as a physical brake cylinder kit contains several physical parts, the XML element brake kit would contain several XML subelements.

In the XML publishing world, the elements of a large publication—ManualSet, for example—may include elements familiar to us all along: volume, introduction, table of contents, list of figures, chapter, section, paragraph, illustration, table, appendix, index. And again, the structure rules would define exactly which elements contain which other elements.

This two-part list

1. An inventory of elements.
2. Rules describing how elements contain sublements.

This is a good working definition of an XML schema. In Chapters 7-12 we will expand on the essentials of the schema. It represents the intelligence of XML smart content, the added value that turns information in a quantifiable asset.

In English an inventory of phrases plus a small and concise set of rules can account for a nearly infinite set of acceptable sentences. We call each of those sentences well-formed because they conform to the rules. And we don't need a new rule for each sentence. Similarly, in an XML language a small inventory of elements and a limited set of structuring rules (i.e., a single schema) could conceivably provide everything that an entire industry needs to do business. Too good to be true?

XML AS THE TOTAL SOLUTION: REALITY CHECK ....

In a perfect communications world we might all agree on a universal language based on a grammar that we would all agree to master. (That's been tried and without much success—remember Esperanto?) So in the real world of living human languages, how do we manage to communicate at all?

Suppose that a speaker generates sentences that simply include new words. There is no change to the rule set (Part Two of the grammar), only to the inventory of parts. For example, the speaker may use driver of the slow-moving lorry as a noun phrase. The listener, an American totally unfamiliar with British English, may require a dictionary or some other aid to understand the sentence. In other words, the structure of the language is still intact. Only the inventory (vocabulary) has been extended, in this case to allow for British terminology. So we enhance our internal rule set, adding "lorry" and its definition to the inventory of parts. We have extended the language.

The same sort of easy extensibility is common in XML. And it is probably what most people have in mind when they think Extensible Markup Language. We can extend an XML language quite painlessly simply by adding to the repertoire of elements. The manufacturer may redesign the air brake for a line of trucks, requiring a new set of elements. But if this extension does not break the structure rules, the impact is minor. In fact, for those recipients who do not deal in air brakes, there is no impact at all.

For educational publishing, a provider of scientific multimedia training may enhance its titles by including interactive laboratory exercises in each unit. If those titles are encoded and exchanged as XML, the producer or training center need only add to the repertoire of elements. The grammar itself remains intact. We have only *extended* the language, not changed it.

So is a single XML language sufficient for operating an entire vertical industry? It would seem so. Unfortunately, a vertical industry includes many horizontal activities: accounting, legal affairs, human resources, marketing. Each of those areas may represent entirely different XML languages: different inventories of elements and different rules for how to group the elements.

TRANSLATION AND TRANSFORMATION.................

Simple extension can only go so far. An American needs to add only certain terms and a few simple pronunciation adaptive mappings in order to understand British or South African or Australian English. But to understand Portuguese or Mandarin Chinese requires more. This is not simply *extension* but *translation*. For two speakers of entirely different languages to communicate, at least one of them must have mastered two grammars. Our communications flow diagram now would includes both grammars and a translation step as part of the encoding or decoding process.

For XML-based business and publishing, the situation is very similar. An aircraft manufacturer will deal with suppliers who represent scores of different vertical industries: plastics, chemicals, hydraulics, avionics, metals, to name a few. Each of those industry groups may conceivably use a different XML grammar, including entirely different rules. In that case a supply chain transaction must include an XML translation, a grammar-to-grammar conversion of data.

SO WHAT HAS XML BOUGHT US?.........................

It might appear that our early optimism about XML as the extensible language was premature and ill-founded. Indeed it is possible to extend an XML language's list of elements almost at will, without necessarily disrupting real work (publishing or e-business). And we can similarly enhance the rules for combining elements. But tinkering with the structuring rules can be very disruptive. Conducting business across the boundary of different XML languages is similar to a Canadian manager's having to master Russian in order to operate a subsidiary in St. Petersburg. Has the promise of XML let us down?

Not at all. As we saw earlier, XML as a metalanguage enforces certain mechanisms across all XML languages. All XML languages have repertoires of elements and rules for how to combine those elements. XML as a metalanguage dictates both how to describe the repertoires and how to formulate the rules.

Why is this important? Because now we are guaranteed that we can translate in a consistent manner among all of the hundreds of XML languages, regardless of their element sets and rules. In the old days of proprietary formats (word processing, page layout, forms, tables) we had to rely on proprietary conversion software. For XML-to-XML translations, that task is routine and straightforward.

How Does XML Accomplish Translations?

If you have looked ahead in this book, you will have already seen Chapters 16 and 17 dealing with XSLT. XSLT allows for easy translation among any XML content. The Visa Web page rendition of the rental car invoice in Figure 5.2 is an example of how XSLT can transform XML data. XSLT, plus the related XML specifications that XSLT needs, provide the breakthrough methodology so long awaited in the real workplace.

SUMMARY ....

Just as human communication is all about encoding and decoding thought, speech segments, and sound signals, XML is about workflow. Unlike traditional IT technologies, XML does not merely allow for complex information workflow. It assumes it. There is constant movement within an XML system, all of it directed by underlying schemas. These are consistent sets of rules defining which elements are allowable for a particular application and how those elements may legally be combined. When an XML instance of a particular type conforms to the rules for that type, we say that the instance is well-formed or valid. The payoff for conducting business based on XML conformance is that the actual workflow for a new initiative can be defined ahead of time according to well-understood rules. While there is bound to be a learning curve, an XML workflow promises a minimum of unpleasant surprises. Thanks to XML's built-in transformation capability, the manager can be assured that XML is not simply portable in theory but reusable in practice, and for a large variety of applications.

6 XML as Knowledge

In this chapter...

They Said It...

Knowledge that sleeps, doth die
Ben Jonson: An Ode to Himself

Popular summaries of XML claim that XML "offers enriched information," that it "exposes its content more readily" to this or that process, that it "allows for more intelligent searches." If true, these benefits could be of undeniable value to an information-based organization. However, there is very little explicit language in the W3C recommendations and proposals about "information enrichment," "exposed content," or "intelligence." As potential adopters, we should look beyond optimistic claims. We should satisfy ourselves that certain XML technologies really do add these benefits to our information. We design and apply XML markup in order to store, manage, and deliver content in a consistent manner. But there is also an internal phenomenon at work. Internally, XML markup constitutes knowledge. In this chapter we focus on the knowledge-enabling aspects of XML markup: how it indeed results in greater exposure, enhanced intelligence, and more focused searches of our information.

MARKUP AS KNOWLEDGE.....................................

The most visible aspect of XML markup is the tagging scheme, which we inspected earlier. Organizations and machines create tagged data so that other organizations and machines can receive and interpret that data. So even a rudimentary XML markup scheme exposes a certain level of stored knowledge. The following small sections explore aspects of knowledge borne by structural markup alone: processing to generate knowledge added, hierarchical ordering as knowledge of relationships, computer or human interpretation of markup to assure that that knowledge is properly understood and consumed.

Added Knowledge: News Stories Revisited

The news writers and editors behind the stories we saw in Chapter 2 were following certain rules of style and structure, as we observed. Structure itself bears significant knowledge about the content it supports. But there is nothing in the printed text itself that explicitly encapsulates those rules. The stories are only print-version expressions of the rules. So all of that knowledge remained in the style book. Our task, in rendering each of those samples into XML, was to pull as much of the structural knowledge as possible into the actual content. Here is a summary of the process we applied to the three news pieces in Chapter 2:

1. With only our intuition as lay readers, we *sensed* some coherent, consistent structure in our journalism example.
2. We *articulated* that structure with a hand-created table.
   a. We *devised* the column headers.
   b. Where data was missing, we *inferred* it, based on commonly accepted rules.
3. We *transformed* the table data to machine-readable data (spreadsheet... could have been a database).
4. We *manipulated* the data.
5. We *converted* the data to XML markup.
6. We used that stored structural knowledge to *transform* the content according to page design principles.
7. We demonstrated how to *deliver* data as on-the-fly Web publication.

Every instance of content—including our news stories—therefore contains knowledge of two varieties: (1) knowledge in the everyday sense (what the content itself says) and (2) knowledge about relationships among the elements of the content. This latter type of knowledge is the focus of this chapter, the central concern of XML itself.

HIERARCHIES TO EXPRESS RELATIONSHIPS............

With step 2, we were articulating structure. And in doing so we were adding additional knowledge about the content of the news articles. We refer to data about something as metadata. The table mechanism and the markup represent metadata, data added to the news stories. Consider the marked-up XML file and the items of metadata expressed by XML. The results are displayed in Figure 6.1.

```xml
<?xml version = '1.0'?>
<archive>
    <article>
        <domain>International</domain>
        <headline>Fiery Mir plunges into South Pacific</headline>
        <capsule>Russian spacecraft breaks into pieces after
            re-entry</capsule>
        <by-line></by-line>
        <affiliation>Associated Press</affiliation>
        <origin>KOROLYOV, Russia</origin>
        <date>23-Mar-01</date>
        <lead>The Mir space station returned...</lead >
        <href>http://www.ap.org</href>
    </article>
    <article>
        <domain>National</domain>
        <headline>Fed cuts rate; stocks fall</headline>
        <capsule>Central Bank targets economy not Wall Street</capsule>
        <by-line>Peter G. Gosselin</by-line>
        <affiliation>Los Angeles Times</affiliation>
        <origin>WASHINGTON</origin>
        <date>20-Mar-01</date>
        <lead >The Federal Reserve...</lead >
        <href>http://www.latimes.com</href>
    </article>
    <article>
        <domain>Local</domain>
        <headline>Cocaine smuggler faces life in prison</headline>
        <capsule>Colombian found guilty of seven federal charges</capsule>
        <by-line>Kevin Blocker</by-line>
        <affiliation>Spokesman-Review</affiliation>
        <origin>SPOKANE</origin>
        <date>21-Mar-01</date>
        <lead >A federal jury found...</lead >
        <href>http://www.spokesmanreview.com</href>
    </article>
</archive>
```

```
C:\EssentialGuideToXML\Demo Lab\news.xml - Microsoft Internet Explorer

File  Edit  View  Favorites  Tools  Help

Address  C:\EssentialGuideToXML\Demo Lab\news.xml

<?xml version="1.0" ?>
- <archive>
  - <article>
      <domain>International</domain>
      <headline>Fiery Mir plunges into South Pacific</headline>
      <capsule>Russian spacecraft breaks into pieces after re-entry</capsule>
      <by-line />
      <affiliation>Associated Press</affiliation>
      <origin>KOROLYOV, Russia</origin>
      <date>23-Mar-01</date>
      <lead>The Mir space station returned...</lead>
      <href>http://www.ap.org</href>
    </article>
  - <article>
      <domain>National</domain>
      <headline>Fed cuts rate; stocks fall</headline>
      <capsule>Central Bank targets economy not Wall Street</capsule>
      <by-line>Peter G. Gosselin</by-line>
      <affiliation>Los Angeles Times</affiliation>
      <origin>WASHINGTON</origin>
      <date>20-Mar-01</date>
      <lead>The Federal Reserve...</lead>
      <href>http://www.latimes.com</href>
    </article>
  - <article>
      <domain>Local</domain>
      <headline>Cocaine smuggler faces life in prison</headline>
      <capsule>Colombian found guilty of seven federal charges</capsule>
      <by-line>Kevin Blocker</by-line>
      <affiliation>Spokesman-Review</affiliation>
      <origin>SPOKANE</origin>
      <date>21-Mar-01</date>
      <lead>A federal jury found...</lead>
      <href>http://www.spokesmanreview.com</href>
    </article>
  </archive>

Done                                          My Computer
```

Figure 6.1 Internet Explorer's rendering of an archive

MARKUP'S VALUE ADDED.....................................

This XML example demonstrates very simply the sort of knowledge that markup conveys about its content. It also demonstrates vividly that XML allows almost no ambiguity in how we or a computer will interpret it.

1. Arrangement (structure) of the main categories, subcomponents: **organization**. With nothing more than markup, a human reader can recognize immediately the order (inclusion and subordination) among the various elements. This is a collection called an `archive`. It consists of `articles`. Articles in turn consist of a series of yet more elements.

2. Embedding, paired tags (start, stop): **precision**. The XML tagging scheme expresses a single crisp and unambiguous role for each of the elements of the content. There is also no possibility of confusing the relationship among the elements. For example, the date and URL for one article cannot possibly be confused with those of another article.

3. Indentation of the elements: **readability**. XML documents should be human-legible according to the specification. The indented layout wherein subelements are enclosed within their parent elements aids the human reader. This may seem trivial in a brief example, but it works out to immediate savings in maintenance costs.

4. Kinds of data to expect in every instance of an archive member: **consistency**. Both the human reader and the computer that processes XML rely on the content's own knowledge about its consistent structure from article to article.

5. Sequence in which we place (input) and anticipate (retrieve) each item of data: **order**. Order is the most notable characteristic of the smart document. It imposes strict control at the front end, dictating how we create every instance (article) of a class of documents (news). The payoff at the back end is that a trading partner and her computer can be assured that every item of every instance will be in that same order.

6. Pieces of data that may be omitted: **exceptions**. XML rules express formally which elements are optional. This is a feature of an XML document's internal knowledge that cannot be easily deduced otherwise.

7. The <?xml....> tag: **identification**. The opening tag of XML-conforming content announces to a computer or human reader that it is presenting itself as a fully qualified instance of XML. This self-knowledge on the content's part is its ticket to the XML party.

8. "Well-formed-ness" of the data: **conformity**. We have already used the terms XML-conforming and XML-compliant. For XML the specifica-

tion has given us the term **well-formed**. Whether an XML instance is well-formed or not depends on information that is expressed entirely by its markup: a) Proper "nesting" of subelements (e.g. `headline` always and totally within `article`) b) Start and end tags properly paired c) Consistent use of upper and lower case in tag names.

The smart document has been an elusive and ill-defined goal for decades. For the structural aspects of a document's intelligence, XML represents an ample fulfillment of the dream.

XML AS EXPOSED CONTENT ....

The consumer of the knowledge borne by XML markup is either a human reader or another computer. In order for XML to make business sense it is important for either consumer to get its job done at a reasonable cost. That cost is determined by how visible the XML content is to its consumer. Because XML markup exposes its supported content in a consistent and predictable manner, both humans and machines can more readily exploit XML technologies. Following are but a few suggestions of the benefits of XML's exposure, both to humans and to machines.

1. Human IT manager or XML technician. If you are a part of XML content workflow you can readily view raw XML markup that may be foreign to you. And for content whose markup is somehow broken, you can readily analyze that content to determine its markup bugs. An information architect or document designer can more readily modify the structure of some class of documents to accommodate new business requirements.

2. Computer. Because XML markup is totally exposed, the computer requires only modestly priced software (off-the-shelf or locally developed) in order to process content. Exposed XML means that the software can readily detect, isolate, and interpret each data element. The software can likewise infer the structure (peer relationships and subordination among the items). It can approve or reject a piece of content as being well-formed or not. And based on the exposed knowledge about the content, it can assign specific processing tasks to closely defined data items. For example, an XML-aware layout software can handle all of the details of page layout for a publication. It can create hyperlinks, place graphics, merge boilerplate, or convert a document to some completely different type.

• Sorting on the fly, according to user's criteria.

- Searching according to user's requests.

- Converting to entirely different XML structures.

MORE INTELLIGENT SEARCHES............................

"What knowledge does XML expose?" is another way of asking, "In how many ways can we search on XML content?" If the raw XML file is stored as a database, then searching on the tag names is straightforward and efficient. No further data preparation or preprocessing is necessary. The XML knowledge of content means strictly the knowledge that is expressed by markup. We (and an XML processing system) can infer strictly from markup that Kevin Blocker is a writer for the Spokane *Spokesman-Review* and that he wrote the local news article in our suite. We know that the headline "Fiery Mir plunges into South Pacific" and the associated lead paragraph belong to a particular news piece. And we know certain other facts about each news piece. So in that limited sense, it is proper to say that searches are more intelligent with XML.

But there is an added searching capability with XML. A user may wish to approach some content in successive approximations. That is, she may wish to query the content first in some very general fashion: What are the international news stories for a particular time period? Later, she will narrow down the search: What news stories describe Russian technology? Because XML can be reorganized on the fly, the user's search software can massage a piece of content to adjust to the user's repeated queries. To achieve this, the systems architect may decide to bulk download a large span of content along with search software to run on the desktop. The user can then run the search repeatedly in any way she wishes and in any way that each result may dictate.

SUMMARY ....

XML content is smart content. We commonly think of knowledge only in terms of the actual stored content. But there are additional layers of knowledge encapsulated and conveyed by markup. Once we inject markup-borne knowledge we can then rely on it to express logical relationships among items of content. We can expect smart help from the markup itself for more refined searches. We can furthermore be assured that the consumer—human reader or processing machine—will find the knowledge to be intact and useful upon delivery.

Part 2

Core Technologies

7 Elements and Attributes to Expose Content

In this chapter...

They Said It...

EXPOSE: to make bare, denude, disrobe, divest, strip, uncover, ... betray, blab, divulge, give away, let out, reveal, tell, uncover, unveil, spill the beans, tell all.

Roget's II: The New Thesaurus

Content that can expose itself represents a remarkable information technology breakthrough for XML. An electronic document is not just a *holder* of information but is an active *revealer* of information. In order for XML content to behave with that level of intelligence, it uses the basic built-in mechanisms of elements and attributes.

NEED FOR ELEMENTS ....

In a word, documents have always been dumb. We and sometimes even sophisticated machines can read them. But the document cannot actively tell us about itself. The content cannot expose itself. In order for IT to move forward in any meaningful way, the content must be more proactive, more self-exposing, assuming more of the communications burden. The content must be "smart."

Elements at Work: Shakespeare and Purchase Order

Consider this well-known passage from Shakespeare's *The Tragedy of Julius Caesar* (Act 3, Scene 1):

Decius Brutus: Great Caesar!

Caesar: —Doth not Brutus bootless kneel?

Casca: Speak, hands, for me!

[*Casca first, then the other conspirators and Brutus stab Caesar.*

Caesar: Et tu, Brute?—Then fall, Caesar!

[*Dies.*

Cinna: Liberty! Freedom! Tyranny is dead!

Run hence, proclaim, cry it about the streets.

This passage is familiar to most English-speaking secondary school graduates. When we read it with attention, it is as if the gripping tragedy of the moment leaps out to us on its own. But of course even the finest drama does not ever leap out from a printed script on its own. The printed form has well-defined and well-learned conventions that help it along: spacing, italics (for identifying characters), separate paragraphs and left square brackets (for stage directions). These are associations that a mindless computer cannot immediately perceive on its own, even when the nicely printed page is in electronic form (as the excerpt is). By itself that passage—even though it contains widely recognized formatting information—cannot expose anything meaningful about its content.

The same holds true for a purchase order, a critical piece of business workflow (see Figure 7.1).

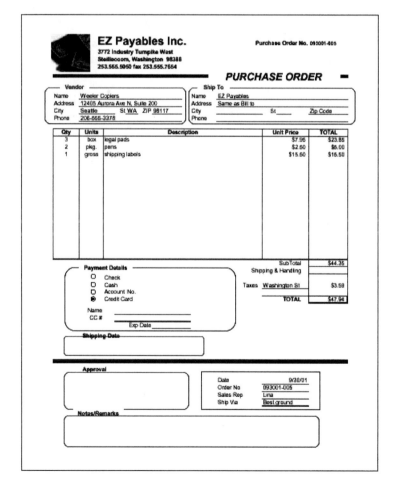

Figure 7.1 Purchase order as a printed page

The meaning of the items on a purchase order is obvious to anyone familiar with buying things within an organization. We are familiar with this only because of the learned conventions that go along with purchase orders: where the purchaser's name and address are located, where each item is described, where to find the cost per item, and where to find totals. But again, computers, because they are visually challenged, are very poor at locating things on pages and determining their meaning simply by location. It appears therefore that even rather formal content is very reluctant to expose its content on its own.

The world—even the Shakespearian community—can survive without self-exposing electronic artistic content. But electronic commerce is absolutely impossible without business documents that can expose their content clearly and unambiguously to other machines.

This XML example demonstrates very simply the sort of knowledge that markup conveys about its content. It also demonstrates vividly that XML allows almost no ambiguity in how we or a computer will interpret it.

ELEMENT AS A BASIC UNIT OF XML........................

The basic structural unit of XML is the element, the central means for self-revealing intelligence. The element is the common currency for exchanging XML information of all varieties. Together with its attributes, an XML element conveys and exposes significant internal knowledge about the structure of the content. Here and in Chapter 8 we will explore the central role and importance of elements and attributes.

How it works

The element is a unit of structural information in some content. Look again at the passage from Julius Caesar, part of a large corpus of literary materials rendered as XML and released by Jon Bozak in the period 1996-1998:

```
<SCENE>
   <SPEECH>
      <SPEAKER>DECIUS BRUTUS</SPEAKER>
      <LINE>Great Caesar!</LINE>
   </SPEECH>
   <SPEECH>
      <SPEAKER>CAESAR</SPEAKER>
      <LINE>Doth not Brutus bootless kneel?</LINE>
   </SPEECH>
   <SPEECH>
      <SPEAKER>CASCA</SPEAKER>
      <LINE>Speak, hands for me!</LINE>
   </SPEECH>
```

```
<STAGEDIR>CASCA first, then the other Conspirators and BRUTUS
            stab CAESAR</STAGEDIR>
<SPEECH>
   <SPEAKER>CAESAR</SPEAKER>
   <LINE>Et tu, Brute! Then fall, Caesar.</LINE>
</SPEECH>
<STAGEDIR>Dies</STAGEDIR>
<SPEECH>
   <SPEAKER>CINNA</SPEAKER>
   <LINE>Liberty! Freedom! Tyranny is dead!</LINE>
   <LINE>Run hence, proclaim, cry it about the streets.</LINE>
</SPEECH>
</SCENE>
```

In this passage there are four types of elements: **scene**, **speech**, **speaker**, **line**, and **stagedir**. (Obviously this is a harsh abridgement of the Scene One. The original scene is more than twenty times as long.)

And consider again the purchase order, this time rendered as XML:

```
<PurchaseOrder>
   <PONumber>093001-005</PONumber>
   <Date>9/30/2001</Date>
   <BillTo>
      <BillToName>EZ Payables Inc.</BillToName>
      <BillToStreet>3772 Industry Turnpike</BillToStreet>
      <BillToCity>Steillacoom</BillToCity>
      <BillToStateAbbrev>WA</BillToStateAbbrev>
      <BillToZip>98388</BillToZip>
      <BillToPhone>253.555.5050</BillToPhone>
      <BillToFax>253.555.7654</BillToFax>
   </BillTo>
   <Vendor>
      <VendorName>Weeler Copiers</VendorName>
      <VendorAddress>12405 Aurora Ave N, Suite 200</VendorAddress>
      <VendorCity>Seattle</VendorCity>
      <VendorStateAbbrev>WA</VendorStateAbbrev>
      <VendorZip>98117</VendorZip>
   </Vendor>
   <ItemList>
      <Item>
         <Quantity>3</Quantity>
         <Units>box</Units>
         <Description>legal pads</Description>
         <UnitPrice>7.95</UnitPrice>
         <ExtendedPrice>23.85</ExtendedPrice>
      </Item>
```

```
    <Item>
       <Quantity>2</Quantity>
       <Units>pkg</Units>
       <Description>pens</Description>
       <UnitPrice>2.50</UnitPrice>
       <ExtendedPrice>5.00</ExtendedPrice>
    </Item>
    <Item>
       <Quantity>1</Quantity>
       <Unit>gross</Unit>
       <Description>shipping labels</Description>
       <UnitPrice>15.50</UnitPrice>
       <ExtendedPrice>15.50</ExtendedPrice>
    </Item>
  </ItemList>
  <SubTotal>44.35</SubTotal>
  <ShippingHandling>0.0</ShippingHandling>
  <Taxes>3.59</Taxes>
  <TotalBillable>47.94</TotalBillable>
  <PaymentType>Credit Card</PaymentType>
  <SalesRep>Lina</SalesRep>
  <ShipVia>Best Ground</ShipVia>
</PurchaseOrder>
```

As simple strings of printed characters in their original (print-ready) versions, neither the play nor the purchase order expose any real meaning on its own. But we claimed in Chapter 6 that XML markup—plain text with pointy-bracket tags—can expose meaning, even to a computer. We will now discover exactly how XML uses elements to communicate that meaning in a consistent machine-recognizable manner. In Chapter 7 we will look closely at how attributes expose that meaning to an even greater degree.

Meaning of an Element

An XML element answers three questions about the portion of the content it represents:

1. What *kind* of content is this?
2. Where does this segment fit within the overall *structure* of the content?
3. What extra information *about* this segment has the author (or editor or publisher) added to the content?

In other words, the mechanisms of elements provide three types of information about content:

1. Element *type* information.
2. *Structural* information.
3. *Metainformation* (information *about* content).

Element types

In the following excerpt, there are three types of XML elements: **SPEECH**, **SPEAKER**, and **LINE**:

```
<SPEECH>
        <SPEAKER>DECIUS BRUTUS</SPEAKER>
        <LINE>Great Caesar!</LINE>
</SPEECH>
```

It is important to note the difference between our intuitive understanding and the formality of XML. We as theater-goers or readers only perceive "Great Caesar—" as the speech. XML on the other hand sees all of the following as the element **SPEECH**:

```
<SPEECH>
        <SPEAKER>DECIUS BRUTUS</SPEAKER>
        <LINE>Great Caesar!</LINE>
</SPEECH>
```

XML and the computer seem to have a unique way of perceiving the information universe! This is a strong hint that XML is in fact adding extra knowledge to the content, knowledge that is intuitive to us but that is nonobvious to the computer. In this case, XML tells us not only what is said, but who said it.

So what we hear as a speech ("Great Caesar—") XML understands as only a line. XML is clearly accomplishing something with markup that is beyond traditional print format. We shall spell that out shortly.

Mechanics of an Element

The formal mechanism is the now-familiar tag. Tags are common knowledge because of Web pages. If we select View Source during a browsing session we are likely to be treated with a view of the markup responsible for the current page. We recognize tags as the signature characteristic of HTML. But there are some brief formal XML issues about tags that we need to clarify:

1. Tag means a sequence of the following: "**<**", followed by the element name, followed by "**>**": **<STAGEDIR>** or **<BillTo>**, for example.

2. There are start tags, those having no "/", and end tags, those with "/" just after the "<": **<ShippingHandling>** and **</ShippingHandling>**. Tags *always* come in pairs.

3. The name of the element (the string between the angle brackets) is arbitrary, invented, and shared by the entire community that exchanges a particular document type.

4. Maintaining consistency (spelling and upper- or lower-case) for the element's name is significant.

Here are portions of the XML notation for each of the examples. Note the XML terminology we use for referring to the various aspects of an element.

Structural information

Look again at what XML calls a "speech":

```
<SPEECH>
       <SPEAKER>DECIUS BRUTUS</SPEAKER>
       <LINE>Great Caesar!</LINE>
</SPEECH>
```

For XML there is more to speech in a play than just the utterance. XML considers a speech to consist of both the speaker and the spoken line. A rather trivial example, but the notion of containment—**speech = speaker + spoken line**—is fundamental to XML. In other words, both an XML speaker and an XML line belong within an XML speech.

As a graph, here is how that XML relationship looks:

Speech

/

Speaker Line

It is possible to view this very simple structure as a tree. Speech is the root, if we agree to view the structure as an inverted tree. In later chapters, we will discover how the tree structure is central to XML. In fact, whenever we use the terms markup technologies and structure we are invariably thinking in terms of data trees. Furthermore, we extend the concept of tree to the elements themselves. Each of the elements in XML content occupy nodes on the tree.

The content-as-tree communicates both with its branching structure and with its node types. So when we see a tagged element in XML we are really learning two things about the element:

1. What *type* it is: Speech, Speaker, or Line in this case.
2. How this element is related *structurally* to other elements in this play: Speaker and Line are both subordinate to Speech in this example.

These then are two important items of information that the XML markup exposes about itself.

Metainformation

When you watch the Warner Brothers movie *The Perfect Storm*, you are experiencing *content*. When you log onto *perfectstorm.warnerbros.com*, you can learn a wealth of information about *The Perfect Storm*: meteorological data from 1991, the people of Gloucester, Massachusetts, special effects for re-creating the scenes on board the fishing vessel, and even how to receive posters. All of that information is metainformation or metadata. It is information *about* the content.

DEEPER KNOWLEDGE EXPOSURE ....

Consider the following sample from the legal world. It is an excerpt from the "Electronic Court Filing Draft Specification," drafted by the LegalXML consortium. The XML specification is to expedite information workflow through the courts.

Here is a section of the electronic envelope of a court filing, a full description of the case:

```
<Addressee>
  <Name ID="Ref01">
    <Person>
      <FullName>Margret Marly Jefferson</FullName>
      <FirstName>Margret</FirstName>
      <MiddleName>Marly</MiddleName>
      <LastName>Jefferson</LastName>
      <NameAlias MatchWith="Ref01" Type="aka">
        <Person>
          <FullName>Marty Halvorson</FullName>
          <FirstName>Marty</FirstName>
          <LastName>Halvorson</LastName>
        </Person>
      </NameAlias>
    </Person>
  </Name>
```

```
    <Address Type="Business">
      <AddressLine>New Mexico Supreme Court - JID</AddressLine>
      <AddressLine>207 Shelby Street</AddressLine>
      <AddressCity>Santa Fe</AddressCity>
      <AddressState>New Mexico</AddressState>
      <AddressPostalCode>87501</AddressPostalCode>
    </Address>
</Addressee>
```

You are already familiar with how elements and their tags appear. For example, this entire block of XML describes the addressee. There are two subelements within **Addressee**, **Name** and **Address**. But for the element tag **Name** there is additional apparatus. The document's author added some information about this particular name: an **ID** having a value of **Ref01**. In the vocabulary of XML, **ID** is an **attribute** of the element and **Ref01** is the value of that attribute. The attribute (**ID=Ref01**) is not actually part of the content. Instead it is information *about* this particular **<Name>** element.

Attributes can serve any function that the user community can agree upon. Consider this start tag:

<NameAlias MatchWith="Ref01" Type="aka">

In addition to the standard name items for a person, this record includes the subelement **NameAlias**. And this element contains two attributes, each with information assigned for this particular element. The first attribute is linking information to allow a search and retrieval program to associate the alias with the correctly named person. The attribute is **MatchWith**, and the value of the attribute is the same as for the attribute ID of the legitimate **<Name>**. In addition, the court describes this second name's Type (the attribute) as **"aka"** (the attribute's value).

Notice next the element block for **<Address>**. The start tag is **<Address Type="Business">**. It is temping to read that element's tag as "Address Type," but that is wrong. The element type is **Address**. **Type** is an attribute of **Address**. Here it serves to refine **Address**, to describe what type of address the court is using. **Business** is the value of the attribute.

In that same XML court record there is furthermore an element block describing payment information (for court-imposed fines):

```
<PaymentInformation>
    <Credit>
        <Number Qualifier="Credit Card" Format="#### #### #### ####">
            1234 5678 9012 3456
        </Number>
        <Expiration><Date>20011101</Date></Expiration>
    </Credit>
</PaymentInformation>
```

The element **\<Number\>** incorporates first the qualification that the method of the court's extending credit will be via a credit card. Furthermore, the data (1234 5678 9012 3456) is enhanced with some information for a computer program that must automatically read the credit card. The value of the attribute **Format** is actually a format template. The template **"#### #### #### ####"** says that there are four clusters of four digits each, each cluster separated by a single space.

Another record of the same document includes the addressee's phone number:

```
<Telephone Type="Office">
    <Number Qualifier="Telephone" Format="(###) ###-###">
        (505) 476-6900
    </Number>
</Telephone>
```

This is similar to the earlier example. The **Type** attribute describes this entire \<block **(505) 476-6900** as a business telephone. Furthermore the actual content data is enhanced with two attributes. The first is a qualifier, describing unambiguously that the number is a telephone. And once again there is formatting information to assist the external software.

Summary of Element Syntax

Most of the examples we have studied demonstrate how an author, editor, or XML robot must express XML data. But there are certain details left up to the designer of the document type. The following general rules summarize some essential syntax for XML elements and their attributes:

1. An element consists of a start tag, followed by its own content (which may include subelements), followed by an end tag.

2. A start tag consists of a left pointy bracket, followed by an agreed-upon name for the type of element, followed by a right pointy bracket.

3. An end tag matches its corresponding start tag, except for a forward slash immediately after the left bracket.

4. An attribute consists of an opening quotation mark, then the name of the attribute, followed immediately by an equal sign, followed by the value assigned to the attribute, followed by an end quote.

5. The entire attribute goes inside the start tag, separated from the element name by a space.

The items in the list are general syntax rules for XML. But XML does not specify the element types or their names. Nor does XML dictate how the elements are arranged—which are primary and which are subelements, contained within other elements.

Those are the responsibility of the XML architect for the organization or trading community.

ADVANTAGES OF ELEMENTS AND ATTRIBUTES .....

Elements, which now and then include attributes, enable electronic content to expose to a greater degree what we saw in Chapter 6. Because of the uniformity and consistency of XML, a properly marked-up document can communicate much about itself to another XML-aware computer. It can accomplish that communication even across the one-dimensional boundary we discussed in an earlier chapter. Although the receiving computer can see only one character at a time and only one tag at a time, it is able to reconstruct the original tree structure of the content as it originally existed. This sort of automatic deconstruction-transmission-reconstruction had never been possible with traditional methodologies.

FIVE WAYS ELEMENTS AND ATTRIBUTES ADD VALUE TO INFORMATION.....................................

Self-exposing content-as-data through elements and attributes makes several identifiable IT benefits possible if not already real:

1. *Reduced handling costs.* Computers—equipped only with XML-enabled software—can process information intelligently on their own. The role of expensive human data handlers is now drastically reduced.

2. *Low-cost personalization.* Because a computer, as an XML processor, can view individual elements with greater precision, it can potentially re-profile the same content to different audiences. The same base content can therefore service many consumers or readerships at virtually no extra cost.

3. *Reduced data conversion costs.* The tree structure that is native to XML is the traditional database type *hierarchical*. Because XML content is therefore already cast as a standard database type, the expense of migrating XML to databases is drastically cut. It is certainly far less costly than typical conversions.

4. *Increased granularity at reduced cost.* Because elements, by definition, can maintain high granularity in XML content, the information that those elements bear is more readily available than is the case with blobs of pro-

prietary word processing files. The cost of retrieving those granular items of information is therefore drastically reduced.

5. *Reduced cost of content management.* Attributes can expose knowledge of any variety that the designer chooses. That includes knowledge about such things as access, security levels, permissions, revision dates, and all of the other items that comprise a content management system. Prudent information design can reduce the cost and run-up time for implementing a content management (CM) system.

SUMMARY ....

Elements and attributes, the essentials of XML markup, are the formal mechanisms that lend intelligence to content. As formally defined XML mechanisms, they apply to all types of content. Our examples of elements for formally exposing content from Elizabethan drama, purchase orders, and court documents illustrate how general XML really is. Attributes, as part of elements, serve to extend the knowledge value of content. Usually, they expose knowledge *about* a particular element (metadata). But they also may express enterprise-specific business rules that apply to the content.

8 Getting Personal—Attributes

In this chapter...

They Said It...

Getting to know you,
Getting to know all about you.

Oscar Hammerstein II: The King and I

Markup adds knowledge to content, as we have seen. By properly inserting element tags within a document or commercial record, we enabled that content to expose its smarts about its own *structure*. Just seeing the tree structure of a news piece, electronic invoice, or policy manual allows a computer to infer all that it needs to know in order to reconstruct, reuse, and even repurpose that content faithfully. But with attributes, markup can expose a much deeper meaning within the content. True, markup with attributes constitutes a greater initial cost, but the benefits are obvious and immediate. Attributes are an important means of personalizing and clarifying content, targeting content to a particular audience or preprocessing content to fit the user. They also support content in conforming to the business rules of the organization. Attributes are the mechanism supporting the most frequently heard claims for XML: smarter searches, secured data delivery, personalized publication, easy extensibility. Attributes therefore constitute a highly-visible value proposition for XML.

TWO FACES OF ATTRIBUTES ....

In Chapter 7 we saw how attributes can allow content to store and then expose a greater depth of knowledge about content than is possible with elements alone. Some brief examples demonstrated that the attributes of an element can extend and refine the knowledge store of the element considerably:

- Type of payment and layout information of a credit card

- References to closely related documents

- Aliases for persons named

- Type of property at a given address (business or residence)

The mechanics (i.e., syntax) of attributes are simple enough to master in short order. We will offer a sufficient walkthrough in this chapter to provide familiarity. But there is far more to attributes than the syntax required for authoring and editing. It is possible to use attributes to add any kind of knowledge whatsoever to an element. But there are certain applications for attributes that provide immediate benefits to an organization:

1. *Profiling the consumer.* Attributes can customize access to the content so that the content conforms (profiles itself) to the customer, client, or consumer with greater precision, in a more personalized manner.
2. *Profiling the business.* Attributes can customize the behavior of the content so that it conforms to the business rules of the organization.

Some brief examples will demonstrate these two important benefits of attributes.

Attributes: Personalizing Data

We are quite familiar with the Web page that sounds more intimate from the start: "Hi there, Ron! Based on what you've ordered from us before, we think you'll really like this newly released three-disk CD set featuring authentic folk music from Galicia." Profiling a user for a customized Web greeting is an obvious example of personalization. This sort of customer-product match-up is the result of knowledge stored in the purchase history database plus descriptors stored in the product information itself:

```
<Recording media="CD" numberDisks="3">
    <Publisher>Iberian Folklore Society</Publisher>
    <Description type="ethnic">Authentic folk music
        from Galicia</Description>
    <Contents language="Gallego-Portugues">
        <Track Number="1" Instruments="gaita">Canciones de
            Navidad</Track>
          :
          :
    </Contents>
</Recording>
```

In this example, the seller (and the smart Web server) reached into metadata borne by attributes in order to profile the customer. Certain items of knowledge *about* the release is important for this promotion: that it is an ethnic title, its number of disks, the language of the pieces, and instruments featured on each track. Without this rich detail, the only nonattribute information that would help is that it comes from an organization specializing in Iberian music.

Attributes: Implementing Business Rules

Business rules represent a very active arena of database management. The business rules accompanying data most often are access control rules, expressing and enforcing who gets to see what. In actual practice, most out-of-the-box access schemes fall far short of what is required. One reason is that it is very difficult to identify all legitimate users of a database beforehand and with precision. This is all the more complicated by the multiple roles that a single person might fill in an organization. A teller and the teller's manager can and must have access to customer banking records. The level of activity allowed would probably be different for each. That in itself constitutes an important part of an access policy. But the manager may on occasion function as an internal auditor (not a recommended business practice). As an auditor her access privileges would be restricted to read-only. Only a system that implements a role-based access management policy could support such a practice.

XML Access Control Language (XACL) is part of XACL Authoring Environment from the IBM Tokyo Research Laboratory. The language allows an organization to define an access policy that goes far beyond who gets to see what. It offers the precision to articulate who exactly gets to see what. That is because the XACL-based policy can be applied to a single element, regardless of how granular that element might be.

CASE: BUSINESS RULES FOR INVESTMENT RECORDS

This tiny example illustrates how we might apply XACL to implement the following policy for a particular investor's records:

1. Wade (broker) has read and write privileges within the client's records (element name for the records: **custData**).

2. Cheryl (internal auditor) has read-only privileges within the client's records.

3. Unless otherwise defined, the policy disallows any privileges within the client's records to any other party.

An XACL statement of this policy would appear as follows:

```
<policy>
   <xacl>
      <object href="id(custData)"/>
      <rule id="rule1" >
        <acl>
           <subject>
              <uid>Wade</uid>
           </subject>
         <action name="read" permission="grant"/>
         <action name="write" permission="grant"/>
        </acl>
      </rule>
```

```
    <rule id="rule2" >
       <acl>
          <subject>
             <uid>Cheryl</uid>
          </subject>
        <action name="read" permission="grant"/>
        <action name="write" permission="deny"/>
       </acl>
    </rule>
    <rule id="rule3">
       <acl>
          <subject/>
        <action name="read" permission="deny"/>
        <action name="write" permission="deny"/>
       </acl>
    </rule>
  </xacl>
</policy>
```

ATTRIBUTE MECHANICS (SYNTAX) ....

In the example, there are only eight element types. If we discount **policy** and **xacl** we are left with only six element types for articulating a set of access rules. The actual element content is extremely sparse: only "Wade" and "Cheryl" as the contents of **uid**. All of the remainder of the three policies are expressed solely by attributes. In every case, the attribute enhances, extends, or enriches the meaning of its host element:

- **href** identifies the XML element to which the policy applies (**custData** in this case).

- **id** allows us to assign a name (identifier) to the **rule** (**rule1**, **rule2**, or **rule3**).

- **name** lets us specify the particular action (**read** or **write**).

- **permission** is the means of expressing whether or not that action is granted.

The significant XML restrictions on attributes are as follows (refer to the bolded examples in the example code):

- A space separates an element name from its attribute.

- A space separates one attribute from another attribute.

- An equal sign links an attribute's name with its value.

- No space is allowed between an attribute's name and its value; only an equal sign is allowed.

- The value of an attribute is always enclosed in quotes.

Fortunately for authors and editors of XML content, currently available tools assist in enforcing these requirements.

Attributes are a central piece of the XML specification. In Chapters 11 and 12 we will see how XML accounts for attributes in document type definitions (DTDs) and schemas.

SEVEN BUSINESS ASPECTS OF ATTRIBUTES............

1. *Noninvasive added value at minimal cost.* As we have observed in Web page personalization and access control, attributes play a significant role in adding value to content. They enhance an element of content in virtually any way that the designer may choose. Once they are defined for that element, attributes allow us to add valuable metadata to our content. The benefit of an attribute is that it is separate from the actual content. Therefore we do not perturb the content when we add or modify attributes.

2. *Price of added value.* Whether or not assisted by authoring tools, we expend some extra effort when we provide the values (read, write, grant, deny, for example) that an attribute may require. This is a cost that must be factored into maintaining an XML information resource.

3. *Higher skill set.* Attributes typically require human understanding of the particular application. After all, that is the quality of knowledge that enhances the content. But that human effort comes at a cost, and the skill set for intelligent authoring may be somewhat higher than for simple XML tagging.

4. *Run-time penalty (searching).* Whether an attribute of a particular element should really be an element in its own right is a frequently debated topic among XML designers. This apparently arcane distinction has some business ramifications. The central consideration is that a particular attribute may be or may become a searchable item, something that we may later choose for indexing our content. For example, in a large scholarly collection of folklore recordings, it may become critical to do fast searches based on the native languages of the collection. In our example, `language` was only an attribute. Since an attribute is a less exposed structural item than is an element, it would require much longer search times (i.e., greater run-time cost) to locate recordings based on language.

The same would be true for insurance records, military policies and procedures, or contract files. If we think we might engage in frequent searches on some aspect of our information, we should opt for element rather than attribute. In Chapter 18 we shall see how XML itself is able to transform attributes to elements on the fly using XSLT.

5. *Data storage penalty.* Attributes can add significant storage overhead purely in terms of the extra data that is present. This may seem to be an extraneous point, but consider a database with tens of millions of records — the storage of attributes can add gigabytes to the total disk space required. It is important to account for attributes in a physical architecture and design.

6. *Low-cost extensibility.* We can add attributes quite easily to the definition of an XML language. And in doing so, we do not need to alter the structure of our existing content. This means that we can extend our particular XML language in a very pain-free manner. Of course the "X" of XML promises extensibility that is much more radical than simply adding attributes. But even a few business-specific attribute definitions can dramatically enhance the language's usefulness.

7. *Hype that is true.* The examples in this chapter substantiate some frequently-heard claims for XML: smarter searches, secure data delivery, personalized publication, easy extensibility. Attributes play a key role in all of these and therefore constitute a highly visible value proposition for XML.

SUMMARY ....

Attributes bear information about their host elements. That information may be of any variety: security, personalization, dates, revision levels, external identifiers, aliases, or physical locating information. While much of the hype surrounding XML is unfortunately not well substantiated, a surprisingly large number of popular claims for XML are in fact supported very well by the mechanism of attributes.

9 Well-formed XML

In this chapter...

They Said It...

And as for roses, holy Moses!
They can't be got at living prices!
Myrtle is good enough for us.

Eugene Field: Horace Ode I

Thanks to markup, content becomes data. Because it is data, we can publish the content in a variety of forms and media. And because it is data, we can sort it, search it, retrieve it, exchange it, transform it, and process it in ways not imagined by its creators. Unfortunately the world of transparent portability, platform neutrality, and infinite repurposing is virtually unattainable. It would be a reality only if all the layers of exchange infrastructure were uniform. The barriers consist of the variety of hardware, software, transmission schemes, and business practices that exist within even a single industry. Only parts of the information universe have completed their retooling to be able to work effectively with XML. Content-as-data must move beyond the walls of its home-base enterprise. But in order for your trading partners or any other external groups to use your marked-up data, you must all consent to read from the same page. For XML that means to agree on how your shared data will be structured. Where such an agreement is already in place, much of the dream is within reach. But if everyone can at least safely anticipate the content's structure, then it is sufficient for the XML content-as-data to be well-formed. In other words, well-formed XML content is content whose structure has reached consensus between two or more parties. The concept of well-formedness is a breakthrough concept for XML. Well-formedness is likely to drive the majority of actual XML applications.

SELF-EXPOSING MIXED CONTENT? ....

Applying markup is not simply an interesting academic exercise. Besides making content visible, it also makes it extremely portable. How could any barrier possibly exist that would prevent structured, marked-up plain text from moving freely?

In Chapter 5 we compared the movement and transformation of XML data to human speech. The signal is encoded, transmitted, then decoded. And the entire process is reliable thanks to the center-stage prominence of the schema. The schema works with both the encoder and the decoder engines to make certain that nothing gets lost in the transfer. The schema, as we said, is like the internal set of language rules guaranteeing no loss or distortion. In a schema-dominated world (Chapter 5) XML appeared to fit the analogy quite nicely. Once the manufacturer and wholesaler agree on the same schema, reliable exchange can then begin. It is at this point that we say the XML is well-formed.

But what happens if the wholesalers cannot or will not agree to support the same schema as that of the manufacturer? Or in the worst case, what happens if *every* wholesaler works with different schemas, none of them identical with the manufacturer's version?

Something has to give. Either someone must exert some superhuman managerial clout to force each player to comply with a single schema or we must take a hard look at what realistic schema-based exchange really is.

Let's look at historical perspective for a moment. From the 1960s through the 1980s, organizations that exchanged data did so via magnetic tapes or through data connections. They had to agree on the position and purpose of *every character* in the data stream. It was information exchange on the highest order of rigidity. XML removes some of the barriers by conceptualizing data through markup. Now organizations need only agree on the names and purposes of the fields of data they exchange. No longer must they agree upon the tiniest details such as column positioning, and the order of appearance of fields and records. XML may be a flintlock rifle, but data exchange in decades past was arrows and spears.

The situation of incompatible schemas in the workplace is the rule rather than the exception. Consider again our marked-up version of the three samples of the news stories from Chapter 2. Here is the version as released by the supplier:

```
<?xml version = '1.0'?>
<archive>
   <article>
      <domain>International</domain>
      <headline>Fiery Mir plunges into South Pacific</headline>
      <capsule>Russian spacecraft breaks into pieces after
      re-entry</capsule>
      <by-line></by-line>
      <affiliation>Associated Press</affiliation>
      <origin>KOROLYOV, Russia</origin>
      <date>23-Mar-01</date>
      <lead>The Mir space station returned...</lead >
      <href>http://www.ap.org</href>
   </article>
   <article>
      <domain>National</domain>
      <headline>Fed cuts rate; stocks fall</headline>
      <capsule>Central Bank targets economy not Wall Street</capsule>
      <by-line>Peter G. Gosselin</by-line>
      <affiliation>Los Angeles Times</affiliation>
      <origin>WASHINGTON</origin>
      <date>20-Mar-01</date>
      <lead>The Federal Reserve...</lead >
```

```
      <href>http://www.latimes.com</href>
   </article>
   <article>
      <domain>Local</domain>
      <headline>Cocaine smuggler faces life in prison</headline>
      <capsule>Colombian found guilty of seven federal charges</capsule>
      <by-line>Kevin Blocker</by-line>
      <affiliation>Spokesman-Review</affiliation>
      <origin>SPOKANE</origin>
      <date>21-Mar-01</date>
      <lead>A federal jury found...</lead >
      <href>http://www.spokesmanreview.com</href>
   </article>
</archive>
```

This time, only the tags are bolded, just to help us concentrate on the markup. We developed a naming scheme for these tags that is highly self-explanatory. Consequently we seem to have a strategy for content that is self-exposing. If I simply look at our little archive, I can recognize immediately which items are dates, which are bylines, and so on. And the same goes for my special-purpose, news-gathering computer program, the one that our company uses for extracting news items and creating digests that we syndicate to a large number of customers.

So far so good. We humans can read it and deduce the functions of each item. And so can our computer. But what if our company decides to syndicate not only the finished digest but also the raw marked-up text to those customers who are XML-savvy? Now it gets somewhat sticky. What will *their* computers and software do with our XML archives? If their business is to merge our news feed with those from other news gathering and abstracting services, then they and their computers will have some challenging work to do.

Another supplier might have chosen some different framework (schema) for defining the XML structure. Instead of calling each major piece an article, it may refer to these snippets as "head." And instead of "origin" it may use the more common "dateline." And their feed will probably not include the lead paragraph as part of their "head." This describes content that is valid for us but not for the customer. Our customer—the one who must receive and process XML input from a number of news gatherers—is faced with some major overhead. Our marked-up content is indeed humanly readable. And in that regard it is self-explanatory. It exposes journalism-specific content well. But our XML content can be far short of "self-exposing" when it reaches someone else's computer. If the single-schema approach is not practical, then how can XML even survive?

LOWERING ONE BAR ....

As we just said, something has to give. The designers of XML faced the political real-
ities of information exchange and devised a graceful and systematic approach to exchange without schemas. Rather than to insist on universal consistency among an
entire vertical industry community, the specification allows for lowering the bar without compromising the technology. XML allows a community to relax the requirement
for unanimous acceptance of a schema, the mechanism that makes XML content valid. In place of that, the specification allows for content that is well-formed. Instead of
a verbose and highly tailored schema for validation, there is but a single short list of
five criteria for qualifying XML content to be well-formed. We shall look at that list
and a sample XML document shortly.

In discussing this possible solution, we have raised classical management issues surrounding open information exchange. Open exchange in general and XML in particular forces the entire community of information stakeholders to reach agreement on
some key technical and policy issues:

- How much XML preprocessing and transforming effort should we have to
  fund in order to make our alliance work?
- To what degree of detail must we conform: uniform names and spelling of
  tagged items? Consistent order of their occurrence?
- Who's in charge of policing all this?
- What organizational mechanism shall we use for keeping our XML alliance working?

This blend of technical and managerial issues is precisely what open systems is all
about. The moment we begin to think about easy exchange of XML information—
with trading partners, suppliers, customers, other computers—we must accept the demands that open information requires.

Thanks to XML an alliance for information exchange between trading partners or
publications subscribers is possible. But XML technology cannot achieve wide success on its own. It requires that all members of the community agree on certain rules
for that exchange. And fortunately XML—as a specification, not in itself a technology—provides a significant jump start to this process.

NOT JUST "GOOD ENOUGH" BUT PRETTY GOOD...

The W3C work group represented real players of industry. So they proposed well-
formedness, a tier of acceptability for XML content that is practical and adequate for

the majority of smaller-quantity content. As we saw in Chapter 1, one of the primary motivators for XML is that it must not make outrageous demands on the organization that adopts it:

- *It shall be easy to write programs which process XML documents.*

- *XML shall be straightforwardly usable over the Internet.*

Easy-to-write processing programs and straightforward Internet usability. How does XML make this possible? That is, what in the XML specification makes it possible? The specification defines a somewhat relaxed level of conformance for XML content. It uses the term "well-formed" to refer to that content. This is a curious term for two reasons:

1. This informal term appears within the formal specification alongside other terminology that is much more precise and legalistic.

2. The adjective "well-formed" has naturally spawned the noun well-formedness, awkward at best.

"GOOD ENOUGH" XML...

Well-formed XML content is not simply pretty good data but is content that meets a defined standard of acceptability for conducting business. In the specification, the criteria for well-formed XML is somewhat indirectly stated. There is no single, simple list in the formal XML specification. But we may summarize and paraphrase the list of well-formedness requirements:

1. There must be a start- and an end-tag for every element. Use "/>" for an empty element.

2. There must be a single root element. (The tree must have only a single root.)

3. Elements must be properly "nested." (Both the start- and end-tag of a subelement must lie within the start- and end-tags of its parent element.)

4. Case (upper- and lower-) is significant. (The spelling of element and attribute names must be totally consistent, including their *case*.)

5. Attribute values must be enclosed in quotes. In Chapter 8 we noted that every attribute's value is enclosed in quotation marks.

Table 9-1shows examples from the Michigan Code of Law. It summarizes the requirements for well-formed XML even more succinctly:

Table 9.1   *Summary of XML well-formedness*

Requirement	Example(s)
Start- and end-tag for every element, including empty elements	`<popularname>Lemon Law</popularname>` `<styleclause stylephrase="thepeople"/>`
Single root element	`<mcl>` `:` `</mcl>`
Elements properly "nested"	Right: `<history>` `<historydata>` `:` `</historydata>` `</history>`
	Wrong: `<history>` `<historydata>` `</history>` `</historydata>`
Consistent spelling, including case	Right: `<popularname>Lemon Law</popularname>`
	Wrong: `<Popularname>Lemon Law</popularName>`
Attribute values in quotes	`<section.mcl docID="mcl-257-1401">`

CASE: REPOSITORY FOR STATE LAWS ....

The following XML passages are excerpts from the State of Michigan Code of Law. This example is from Michigan's version of a Lemon Law, supplying relief to purchasers of new vehicles that are hopelessly defective. The first portion is mainly header information, metainformation, information about the actual legal code that follows:

```xml
<mcl>
  <mclchapter dmid.mcl="0000000000000000" docID="mcl-chap257">
    <mclchapterhead>
        <mclchapternumber>257</mclchapternumber>
        <mclchaptertitle> MOTOR VEHICLES</mclchaptertitle>
    </mclchapterhead>
    <statute statutetype="act" docID="mcl-Act-87-of-1986">
        <statuteeditorshead source="compilercreated">
         NEW MOTOR VEHICLE WARRANTIES </statuteeditorshead>
        <statuteorigin actorigintype="regular">Act 87 of 1986
        </statuteorigin>
        <statutelongtitle>AN ACT regarding warranties on new motor
         vehicles; to require certain repairs to new motor vehicles;
         to provide remedies for the failure to repair such vehicles;
         and to prescribe duties for certain state agencies.
        </statutelongtitle>
        <editorsnotes>
           <history>
              <historydata>1986, Act 87, Eff. June 25, 1986
              </historydata>
              <historydata> Am. 1998, Act 486, Imd. Eff. Jan. 4, 1999
              </historydata>
           </history>
           <popularname>Lemon Law</popularname>
        </editorsnotes>
        <styleclause stylephrase="thepeople"/>
        <sections>
           <section.mcl docID="mcl-257-1401">
              <excerptinfo>
                 <statuteeditorshead>NEW MOTOR VEHICLE WARRANTIES
                  (EXCERPT)</statuteeditorshead>
                 <statuteorigin>Act 87 of 1986</statuteorigin>
              </excerptinfo>
              <sectref mclnum="257.1401" sectionlabel="1"
               mclchap="257" mclsect="1401"> 257.1401</sectref>
              <catchline>Definitions.</catchline>
              <section-body>
                 <section-number>Sec. 1.</section-number>

                   :
```

Later in the same document, a section defines the purchaser's actual legal remedies:

```xml
<sectref mclnum="257.1403" sectionlabel="3" mclchap="257"
   mclsect="1403"> 257.1403</sectref>
<catchline>Continued existence of defect or condition; replacement of
   motor vehicle or refund; allowance for use; reimbursement for towing
   costs and costs for rental vehicle; determination of ordinary and
   personal use; consent to replacement of security interest;
   presumption; performing repairs after expiration of warranty;
   extension of time for repair services.
</catchline>
```

```
<section-body>
   <section-number>Sec. 3.</section-number>
   <paragraph>
      <paragraph-number>(1)</paragraph-number>
      <p>If a defect or condition that was reported to the manufacturer
         or new motor vehicle dealer pursuant to section 2 continues to
         exist and the new motor vehicle has been subjected to a
         reasonable number of repairs as determined under subsection
         (5), the manufacturer shall within 30 days, do either of the
         following as applicable:</p>
   <paragraph>
```

A typical customer of this XML document may be a consumer watchdog office that simply uses the XML data to access, retrieve, and post the actual remedies. Unlike a legal firm (or the legal counsel for the consumer group), the consumer group will have little interest in any of its origination and locator information. In these excerpts much of that is expressed by the attributes and their values (highlighted). Furthermore the consumer group is not concerned about any possible styling information (e.g., the **styleclause** element in this sample). In cases like this there is a very modest need for a comprehensive understanding of the entire structure of the document. A human reader or a very simple ad hoc script-driven computer program can easily scan the documents for such tags as **\<popularname\>** and **\<catchline\>**. Because the requirements for this kind of application are not so demanding, it is entirely fitting to relax the requirements on the content itself. If a document conforms to the five XML criteria listed above and is well-formed, the customer is well served. (In point of actual fact, this document is also **valid**, achieving the higher standard for XML conformity that we shall cover in Chapter 10.)

WHERE'S THE CATCH?......................................

By downgrading our demands to well-formed, we have eliminated the formalism of the encoding and decoding processes that we highlighted in Chapter 5. The "grammar" in those processes serves as the key to translation and interpretation. By removing that player we have shifted the entire burden of interpretation onto the receiving processor. Without the "key," the XML processor's anticipation of the elements' structure is only a guess. Without the key as its map, it must rely on insider knowledge about the application it is supporting. In other words, the processor must be "wired" to be a purchase order machine or a legal document machine or profiled to whatever other type of content it is expected to process. Lowering the bar for exchanging information raises the demand for intelligent inference on the processor's part. The primary issue here is where to put the intelligence: in the data, or in the systems that produce and process it.

In actual practice, the less formal strategy of "grammar-less" XML transfer is not as risky as it might seem. When the application is straightforward and tightly constrained, and when the processor is closely enough profiled to the application then well-formed data is quite adequate.

Well-formed XML in the Workplace

The popular vision promoted by many XML advocates is grandiose: seamless exchange of XML data, infinite reuse of XML documents, on-the-fly conversion of XML content, bolt-and-play systems integration, and total freedom from proprietary methods of storage, management, and retrieval. In most of today's actual practice, our level of exploiting XML is less ambitious. A responsible manager does not typically embark on large initiatives in large steps. Using well-formed XML to solve a narrowly defined problem is a more frequent sensible first step.

SEVEN REASONS WHY WELL-FORMEDNESS MAKES GOOD BUSINESS SENSE ....

Well-formed does not mean mediocre, second-best, transitory, quick-fix or the like. Well-formed data is the core of a sensible business strategy.

1. *Leveraged investment in legacy content.* It is not imperative to convert an entire data base in order to engage in XML-based publication, commerce, or information exchange. Off-the-shelf database tools allow for on-the-fly conversion of your data to and from well-formed XML. Your original data remains untouched and intact, requiring no initial outlay for a large conversion.

2. *Lower-cost conversions.* Where a large-scale conversion is required, the cost for creating XML data that is well-formed is less costly than fully validating the data against a schema. (We shall investigate the technologies of schemas and validation in the next three chapters.)

3. *Shorter time to proof of concept.* Data exchange that is based on well-formedness allows an organization to implement a convincing application in a very short time. For example, a financial consulting firm could easily design an XML-based system to aggregate clients' investment records of a variety of types. With only a minimal number of element types, it would be straightforward to build a small collection of well-formed XML records for instantly determining a client's net worth. The mix of assets in equities, annuities, insurance policies, real estate, open

contracts, and bank accounts can be uniformly described by a very modest well-formed set of XML elements.

4. *Modest human resources investment.* There is no denying that even an XML initiative can be complex and costly, requiring rare skills sets. A small, well-focused project based on well-formed XML content may be possible to launch with minimal training. That may be as modest as a half-day seminar or a few hours on the job with a self-paced book and interactive CD.

5. *Minimum front loading for tools and environment.* The price of admission to a modest XML project is minimal. For an initiative centered on well-formed XML data, most of the activity will be to create and edit records. The cost of a powerful XML editing tool, one that checks for each record being well-formed, is very modest (less than $200). The footprint for the tool is near-zero: some space on a hard disk.

6. *Minimal paradigm-shift impact.* Most new technologies bring with them some radical paradigm shifts: new frames of reference, new and arcane terminology, new workflow, new skills sets. For a project centered on well-formed content, the players only need to master six terms: **tag** (start and end), **root element**, **nesting**, **case** (upper- and lower-), **attribute**, and **attribute value**.

7. *Maximum benefits for minimal investment.* Enforcing well-formedness in XML content is a modest effort. Yet even a well-formed corpus of XML content shares in most of the benefits of XML described in this book.

SUMMARY ....

Well-formed data allows an enterprise or group of trading partners to begin useful work quickly and at minimal cost. This is because the requirements for XML well-formedness is minimal, numbering only five. The value of this lowered barrier of entry is that every factor of cost is likewise reduced: faster prototyping, simpler tools and environment, minimal training, and liberal enjoyment of the benefits of XML at large.

10 Why a Type Definition?

In this chapter...

They Said It...

The beautiful has but one type, the ugly has a thousand.

Victor Hugo

Large-scale information exchange eventually requires more than well-formed content. It demands mechanisms that can describe complex business content with the precision that a computer can understand. Every newcomer to XML soon realizes that for industrial-strength exchange there is something very significant about a DTD. He or she then discovers that XML Schema is a mechanism akin to a DTD and in fact may replace the DTD altogether. To confuse the matter, "schema" seems also to refer both to DTDs and to this other mechanism, the one called schema. It is important therefore to clarify these terms to make discussion and decision making easier. It is also important to have an executive-level perception of the role of schemas prior to confronting syntactic details of DTDs and XML Schema. We have highlighted elements and their attributes as star performers in XML. The element is the basic logical unit of content. And we have seen that how they are *structured* is as significant to XML as what they *are*. In fact, the structure of XML content is the compelling value proposition for business. Furthermore, the structure of an XML document typically matches the particular industry or business function that it supports. It is therefore essential to understand how XML expresses and supports *structure* with DTDs and XML Schema.

NEED FOR STRUCTURE DEFINITION IN LARGE SYSTEMS

We have insisted from the outset that doing XML is not a closet experience. XML is for moving and exchanging content. That would be impossible were it not for some easy way to describe the content. The examples in the previous chapter demonstrated that a sharable repertoire of element types, agreed upon by everyone in the community, goes a long way toward making that description and exchange possible. For simpler applications, it is entirely adequate for an instance of XML content to be well-formed. The agreed-upon repertoire of element types must adhere to a modest set of requirements. For well-formed content there is no mechanism that defines how the elements fit together. And there need not be as long as the trading partners continue their handshake agreement not to alter the structure of their information.

But for more complex content and for data exchange among a large number of partners or members of a network, a handshake agreement is not enough. To guarantee reliable exchange, the community must have the grammar that we discussed in Chapter 2. This is the component that accompanies the content itself. It is the other indispensable requirement for easily sharable XML. Failing that, every member of a trading community would need to create and modify unique software for every variant of every type of XML-based transaction. For publishing content throughout an enterprise, each variant of every type of document would likewise require specialized software to support it. This is the activity that enterprises exchanging data were doing prior to XML, and it is this activity that XML seeks to minimize.

But free-flowing XML has other consumers besides computers and their software. XML is to be read by humans as well. If there did not exist some separate mechanism for XML professionals to create, edit, and manage the structure of their XML content, XML would have no serious role in the IT world.

DOCUMENT TYPE: WORKING DEFINITION ....

Terminology matters. If this discussion seems a bit obvious, and if you are convinced that you've got it, then by all means go directly to Chapter 11 and the discussion of DTDs. The reason for this chapter is that XML advocates as well as naysayers typically fail to make this minimal technical concept clear to IT decision makers. This has consequently resulted in some serious strategic blunders. XML does not require you to be a flaming bigot over nitpicking terminology. But there is a bare minimum of terms and concepts that are essential. Document type is one of those. The *document type* is the cornerstone concept of XML. XML tools, business practices, content exchange, content management, document reusability, and even some highly publicized IT political controversies revolve around document types[1].

There are two motivating factors in a working definition of *document type*:

   1. A family of documents all share the same repertoire of element types.

   2. A single set of rules dictates how we must arrange those element types.

This should sound familiar. In the previous chapter we surveyed elements and how they are structured. Starting with the Chapter 11 we shall pick up the technical term

---

[1] *Note: we use the term document here and throughout much of this book because it is a technical term. We have inherited it from markup technologies legacy, and it is woven into several parts of the XML specification. So when we say document we are not necessarily referring to a letter, manual, or book. We may in fact be discussing e-commerce business records, audio segments, video clips, XML data records, or even data packets flying between components of computer software.*

document type in two contexts, document type definition, and document type declaration. Furthermore we shall see how most of the current XML consortia activity among industry players revolves around document types. In Chapter 12 we shall see how XML Schemas define document types in a way that makes XML even an easier sell to an IT organization.

Type Test #1: Same Repertoire of Element Types

Consider the following two electronic memos (not necessarily e-mail), examples of XML markup.

Short, informal memo between administrative assistants:

```
<memo>
   <date>15 November 2002</date>
   <sender>Juanita Ripley</sender>
   <recipient>Shawna Hertzvold</recipient>
   <mailStop>E2S-117</mailStop>
   <subject>Friday's food list</subject>
   <message>
      <greeting>Hi Shawna!</greeting>
      <msgBody>Here are the pizza orders for the group design/lunch
               meeting on Friday:
                  1. Anchovies, Mushrooms, Onions
                  2. Extra cheese, Canadian Bacon, Pineapple
                  3. Sausage, Green Peppers, Ground Beef
      </msgBody>
   </message>
</memo>
```

Longer, somewhat more formal memo as summary of a long testing report:

```
<memo>
   <date>10 November 2002</date>
   <sender>Adrian Hennessey</sender>
   <recipient>Quality Assurance Group</recipient>

   <subject>Results of media testing</subject>
   <message>
      <msgBody>First, the executive summary (details in the complete
         document, segments keyed to the original item numbers in Rich's
         initial list):

         1. On Friday we estimated two working days' time to fix
         everything. Allowing a day's overrun would see a Windows CD in
         your hands Thursday morning.
         2. There are NO errors within the applets or within the
         programmers' JavaScript. Therefore no need to call them in.
         3. All errors/incompatibilities are within the HTML.  To fix the
         "missing VCR buttons" problem we're modifying their HTML.
```

```
        4. No need to investigate the possible role of the Java Runtime.
        (I had raised this with Rich on Friday.)
        5. We spent a very intensive weekend (1) isolating the offending
        segments and (2) working up a procedure to fix everything.
        6. The pre-testing we're doing on the chapter 15 Applet Lab
        Problem sets is highly parallel to yours: Windows 98 and NT 4.0
        (SP6).
        7. We got ALMOST the same failures as you did. As I feared, three
        did NOT crash here as they did there. We'll flog those further.
        8. Netscape is doing its best to render the pop-up answers as
        opaque, and it's unfortunately beyond programmers' control to
        make both browsers display the margin consistently.
        9. The only case where you MIGHT want to contact the programmers:
        15:2,3 come up already launched and running. We THINK that's out
        of our control. In our opinion, best to leave it alone.

        We should know by noon Monday (3:00 your time) whether our
        delivery estimate is still good, now that we've gotten everything
        ferreted out.
      </msgBody>
    </message>
</memo>
```

Question: Are these two pieces of XML content of the same type?

Intuitively, it appears that they are . . . maybe. They are both memos. They look some-what alike, although we cannot tell exactly how they will look on screen or in print form. They use the same tag names. (The examples are formatted only for readabili-ty's sake.) On the other hand, our intuition might tell us that they are not alike, because of the clear difference in their length, the differences in grammatical style and usage, and some discrepancies in tag usage.

To determine whether or not they really are of the same XML type, we must ignore in-tuition and apply our two simple tests. With criterion #1 we ask, Does this pair of XML documents share the same repertoire of element types? The obvious answer is that they do not. Juanita's memo includes a physical mail stop element and greeting el-ement, while Adrian's does not. So it appears that that ends the test: they are different XML types.

But the situation is a bit more subtle. The pivotal question is: *Could* there be a physi-cal mail stop element and a greeting element in the second memo? Of course there *could* be a mail stop on the memo. Adrian Ripley is a vice president, so he should be able to write anything he pleases. But not in the XML world. As we hinted in Chapter 2, XML sets limitations on the creation of content so that the receiver can readily an-ticipate and reconstruct that content. And this is just such a case. It happens that both Juanita Ripley and Adrian Hennessey are using the same XML tool for exchanging memos. So the question, slightly reworded, is: Does Mr. Hennessey's XML authoring tool *allow* him to include a mail stop and greeting in his memo? The truth is that we don't know. Our guess is that it does. If it does, then these two memos pass Test #1 after all. They share the same set of XML element types. And it doesn't matter whether all of those types appear in this or that particular instance[2] of the family of XML content we call memo.

If all of the above makes sense, then we should now be asking: What is there within the authoring tool that allows or prevents a writer from using this or that element type? This is precisely the focus of our discussion of DTDs in Chapter 11 and XML schemas in Chapter 12.

This trivial exercise has demonstrated that for a controlled exchange of information we need more than stand-alone well-formed documents. Both of these documents are well-formed. But without some additional knowledge about underlying rules—what we *may* include, what we *must* include—we cannot determine whether they are even of the same type. The exercise would definitely not be trivial in the case of electronic shipping manifests in which an Item Number or Item Description occasionally came up missing.

Type Test #2: Single Set of Rules Determining Arrangement of Elements

Assuming that we assign a Pass to the memos for test #1, let us now apply criterion #2: Do the two memos share the same structure? (That is another way of asking whether a single set of rules determines their arrangement.) We must do a paper-and-pencil exercise to answer this question. Specifically, we must draw the structural tree for each of the memos (see Figures 10.1 and 10.2).

---

[2]*The term "instance" has gotten bad press, or at least funny press, in such surroundings as the Dilbert comic strip. Instance comes from the object-oriented programming world and is arguably more geekish than is proper for this book. But it is necessary to use, because we must frequently distinguish between a family or class of things and a particular member (instance) of the class.*

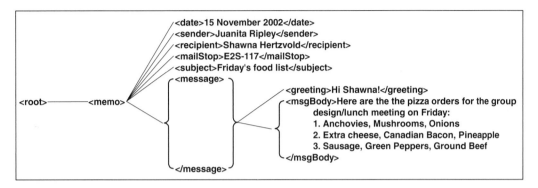

Figure 10.1 Structural tree for short memo

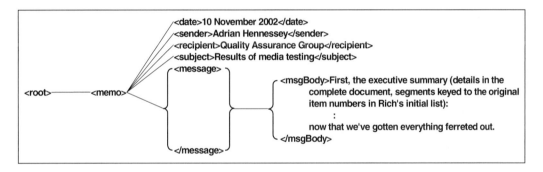

Figure 10.2 Structural tree for long memo

If we assume that the same set of elements is available to both writers, then the tree graphs for the two memos convince us that the same rules are behind both instances. Therefore we conclude that these memos are of the same type.

SOMETHING'S "UNDER THE HOOD" ....

In this brief walkthrough, testing the sameness or difference of document types, we applied paper-and-pencil techniques to reach our verdict. But it should be clear that simple drawings and observation are not enough. Something else must be at work in the XML authoring process—XML mechanisms, XML tools, and additional mechanisms for describing and enforcing XML document types. And something additional must definitely be at work in order for a receiving computer to reconstruct an XML document and to do it right. The silent mechanism is the schema for the document type, a computer-readable statement describing (1) the element types available for the document type and (2) how exactly we may create and a computer may reconstruct a document with those elements.

With nothing more than a single example, we have demonstrated that the schema has to express more than simply a list of element types and more than a static description of how elements fit together. As we explain, it must describe which elements are mandatory and which are optional. Furthermore, it must specify all of the details regarding attributes—everything that we saw in Chapter 8. But, as we shall see in Chapter 11, a DTD can express even more than that. And in Chapter 12, we find that XML schemas take expressivity to the max.

A TALKING DOCUMENT TYPE..............................

IT publications are full of discussions of how (or whether) XML-based e-commerce can replace electronic data interchange (EDI). But before we attempt to take on that large question, let us role-play the computers belonging to a pair of e-commerce business partners.

One is the manufacturer of cordless (infrared transmitting) keyboards. The other partner is a computer manufacturer. These partners have agreed to conduct their business using XML-based supply chain processing. As part of their agreement they have defined a document type for each of the necessary steps of the process. We shall focus on just the electronic shipping manifest.

The paper version that the two partners formerly used looked approximately like Figure 10.3.

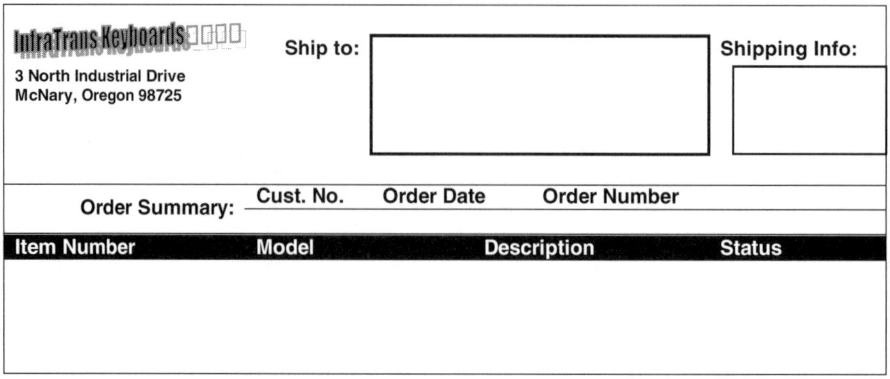
InfraTrans Keyboards

3 North Industrial Drive
McNary, Oregon 98725

Ship to:

Shipping Info:

Order Summary: Cust. No. Order Date Order Number

Item Number	Model	Description	Status

Figure 10.3 *A paper document type*

The manifest deals only with the order as a shipped entity. It contains no pricing information. A minimal (blank) XML manifest record is as follows:

```
<manifest>
   <supplier>
      <suppName>InfraTrans Keyboards</suppName>
      <suppStreet>3 North Industrial Drive</suppStreet>
      <suppCity>McNary, Oregon 98725</suppCity>
   </supplier>
   <ShipTo>
      <ShipToName/>
      <ShipToStreet/>
      <ShipToCity/>
   </ShipTo>
   <ShipInfo></ShipInfo>
   <OrderSum>
      <CustNum/>
      <OrderDate/>
      <OrderNum/>
      <ItemList>
      <Item>
         <ItemNum></ItemNum>
         <Model></Model>
         <Description></Description>
         <Status></Status>
      </Item>
      </ItemList>
   </OrderSum>
</manifest>
```

We shall use plain English to describe the electronic form that replaces the printed manifest. Just to keep things simple, we are basing our "talkthrough" on the two criteria spelled out at the start of the chapter:

1. A comprehensive list of the element types we plan to use.

2. A description of the tree structure of how the element types relate to one another.

Here is our first draft of an XML type description for a shipping manifest, a concise paraphrase of the statements about element types, their arrangement, the number of their occurrences, and their order of appearance.

- A manifest (the root element) consists of a supplier, followed by ShipTo information, shipping information, and a summary of the order.

- The supplier information consists of the supplier's name, street address, and city.

- The ShipTo information likewise consists of the customer's name, street, and city.

- The order summary consists of the customer number, the date of the order, and list of the items shipped.

- The item list contains **any number of items (but at least one).**

- Each listed item contains the item number, the model, its description, and **possible** inventory status information.

Most of the description is a verbose description of a tree, similar to the trees in Figures 10.1 and 10.2. But the two bolded phrases are significant:

1. Inventory status is optional. There is nothing in a simple tree diagram of an XML instance to express that.

2. The tree-like XML indented listing cannot express the important rule that while everything else in the record may appear only once, there may be many items on the manifest.

3. The underlying rules further specify that there must be at least one item in the item list.

This prose narrative, plus the numbered list of rules, is a hint of the information that must be borne by a schema.

But Wait. There's More!

In the memo example, we left two important questions unanswered. First, How does XML allow or disallow a certain element? Recall that there was no **\<MailStop\>** element in Adrian's memo, while there was one in Juanita's. So was this element simply *omitted* from Juanita's memo instance? Or did XML *disallow* that element for Juanita's memo? In other words, did Juanita simply exercise an option or did XML enforce a schema's specification?

The second question is: Where we find (or a computer finds) a certain number of occurrences of some element in an XML document or record, who or what determines that number? If a single purchase order includes 20 items, is that because the buyer Allyson McMillan simply stopped with 20, even though she could have added more? Or did XML somehow prevent Allyson from exceeding 20 items on a single purchase order? In other words, did Allyson simply *choose* to stop with 20 items or did the XML document type for the purchase order *disallow* her adding more?

This kind of subtlety tells us that before we can set to serious work with XML, we need additional items of apparatus, considerably more than what a loose prose description can supply. As we draft our exchange contract, we'll first need to add language to describe (1) whether a particular element must be present and (2) the *number* of those elements that we'll require or allow.

But there's an even more fundamental requirement that a description of a document type must include. For some news syndicates, a summary block appears at the start of the piece. For others it appears at the end or within a sidebar. In other words, an XML description of a news service's document type would have to include a statement about the *order* of its elements. And this is true for all XML content. It will certainly require something more rigorous than plain English in order for a computer to understand it.

Self-describing Structure ... Really?

With the criteria for well-formed documents clearly spelled out, the XML Specification allows for an XML instance to exist without the accompaniment of any formal type definition. The earliest XML enthusiasts recognized this immediately as being part of the obvious "easies" of XML-As-Easy. And from some of the early hype we might have believed that mere XML tagging could do it all. Just by looking at a tagged document we could learn the meaning of its elements. And so could a computer, or so we may have assumed. From the previous chapter, we understand that properly tagged elements alone go a long way in describing elements. But the claim about self-describing XML *without a definition of type* falls apart in the face of serious e-commerce and e-publishing. Only a type definition working together with the actual markup can express the four aspects of elements that we have put forth: repertoire, arrangement, order, and number. When that definition is present, it is entirely honest to say that XML structure is self-describing.

But what if there really is no type definition for some XML content? After all, the specification really does allow for that, and it is certainly possible for an XML-aware computer to process "naked" XML content. With nothing more than the markup, as we saw in Chapter 9, it can inventory the element types that it sees in the particular instance, And with proper embedding of tags (e.g., **<para>** within **<chapter>**) it can reconstruct the proper tree structure. So it is somewhat true that markup without a type definition is self-describing and is sufficient for accomplishing useful work, although to a limited degree.

FIVE REASONS WHY SCHEMAS MAKE GOOD BUSINESS SENSE ....

We have yet to examine either the DTD or XML Schema, the two approaches to describing document structure. But even at this survey stage, there are some clearly perceived benefits of being able to express document structure in a precise and condensed fashion:

1. *Reduced training costs.* Because all XML data is tree-structured and therefore very consistent across all document types, the path to mastery is immensely simplified, resulting in lower training costs. Among data professionals there will be only a minimum of nonproductive learning time.

2. *Information as investment.* Thanks to the data structuring power of schemas, every item of content is, or potentially can become, a valuable resource.

3. *Reduced skill requirements.* Because relatively inexpensive computers with moderately priced software can manipulate tree structures easily, they can achieve in XML workflow much of what would otherwise require highly skilled professionals.

4. *Preserved legacy data investment.* XML data is straightforwardly convertible to and from relational database model form. This preserves investment in existing relational databases, while exploiting that data with XML.

5. *Predictable and controllable conversion costs.* A cautious manager will likely seek small initial XML proofs of concept in order to mitigate risk. The well-defined movement between legacy databases and XML removes the need for a premature, traumatic, and costly commitment to XML-only data handling.

SUMMARY ....

We have demonstrated that all of XML content—whether for traditional content like publications and business transactions, for communication between partners and their computers, or for internal computer processes to communicate among themselves—is in the form of a tree. The advantage to this is that we can now make XML exchange and communication happen for any content. We only need to know that content's type of tree.

A schema is an XML mechanism that describes an entire class of content. It spells out such things as the element types allowed, the order and arrangement of those elements, the allowable attributes, and even the allowable values for elements and attributes. There are two mechanisms for describing a document type, the traditional DTD and XML Schema (the W3C recommendation).

11 The Self-Describing XML Tree

In this chapter...

They Said It...

I think that I shall never see
A poem lovely as a tree.

Joyce Kilmer

Woodman, spare that tree!
Touch not a single bough!

George Pope Morris

The first of our essential core technologies, the DTD is a compact and precise mechanism for describing the structure of XML content. It is the first of two structure-defining technologies. The DTD is central to technicians, to computers, and to management. XML authoring and editing software uses the DTD to enforce the structure rules on human creators of content. XML processing software uses the DTD to interpret and reconstruct the XML content it receives.

Industry groups, consortia, and electronic trading partners develop and share DTDs to enable themselves to exchange XML content smoothly and without error. The DTD is the grammar that we've alluded to in the first 10 chapters. The DTD spells out exactly which element types are allowed in our particular XML language. It dictates the order in which they may occur. It specifies how elements will be arranged—which ones will be subelements, i.e., subordinated to other elements. For each element that may take attributes the DTD gives the author or editor the repertoire of attributes available.

The DTD is a backbone technology, enforcing a hierarchical (tree) data structure in all of the content it supports. Creating a DTD to support widely shared and complex information requires skill and care, because a poorly designed or carelessly managed DTD may be (or become) difficult for humans to read and maintain. The payback for a newcomer's mastering a minimum of DTD basics is far-reaching. Understanding even a small part of DTD mechanics will enable one to read any DTD with a high degree of familiarity. This nodding acquaintance with DTDs is essential to the manager and decision maker who must accurately assess the complexity and scale of an XML initiative.

WHY SHOULD I BOTHER WITH DTDS? ....

A DTD is off-putting to the newcomer. A lot of mathlike notation, terminology that belongs more to programmers than to managers, and chat-room topics that might as well be from another planet. This is a bridge chapter, introducing the technology that makes serious XML work. The DTD is a direct descendant of SGML, simplified greatly in order to make for easier reading by humans (including nontechnical managers) and by computer software. As a bridge, it is not among the XML innovations that we feature in the next chapter. There we present a systematic business case for each chapter's featured technology. For the DTD we simply offer you this survival-level tutorial. It should help you to become fluent enough to read a real-life DTD with some degree of understanding. With even a minimal reading knowledge of DTDs, you are much better equipped for XML fact gathering and decision making. Here are six reasons why.

1. *Assessing the complexity of an initiative or project.* The complexity and the cost of an XML project are directly related to the complexity of the XML content itself. There is absolutely no reliable method for you to assess that complexity without understanding the content's structure. This is possible only through the eyes of the DTD.

2. *Understanding the technology behind the politics.* Practically every discussion about every aspect of XML in the workplace will sooner or later touch on the DTD. Sadly, much of the analysis in popular trade literature is ill-informed or misinformed about DTDs. Fortunately you will not need to rely on second-hand knowledge for your understanding of managerial discussions about XML.

3. *Gauging the progress of XML in your industry's space.* The DTD, as we emphasize yet again, is the grammar behind the language. That language will be an XML-based language, built specifically for your industry or profession: news, law, music, finance, banking, manufacturing, utilities, energy, government,.... The rate of adoption of an XML framework within your industry's workspace will depend on the dissemination and implementation of the particular DTD that your industry has developed and begun sharing.

4. *Evaluating XML products.* Nearly every discussion, promotion, advertisement, news release, and Web page that features XML products will say something about that product's being XML-aware, XML-enabled, or XML-native. The key player in that XML spectrum is the DTD. With even a modest knowledge of the DTD, you can be proactive enough to ask the right questions of a vendor and not be captive to his or her pitch.

5. *Using XML tools more effectively.* Most XML desktop authoring tools are user-friendly and are low impact, technologically speaking. That is, the skill sets are supposed to be lower because so much of the technology is hidden. That usually means the user interface hides most of the DTD. In reality, every user (and user's line manager) will be forced to look beyond the smooth front end. This typically means being able to read a DTD.

6. *Observing the fortunes of the DTD itself.* The DTD, as we noted, is a legacy of SGML. XML owes its fast-start success largely to the DTD, a mature technology that was easy to revise and disseminate and that was readily understood and implemented. But the DTD has serious limitations. Some of them have been serious enough to inhibit the wide adoption of XML for real business. The successor technology to DTD is XML Schema. We will later clarify the confusion between **schema**, general mechanism for describing XML structure, and *"XML Schema,"* the specification released by the W3C as a full recommendation on May 2, 2001. This is a critical zone of the XML specification. While we devote all of Chapter 12 to XML Schema, and while we promote its business case and benefits, the transition has only just begun. In order to be a successful XML Schema watcher, you must know the functionality and downside of the DTD in order to observe and predict the rise of XML Schema. This promises to be a contentious area of XML, one that will have a bearing on your organization's rate of acceptance of XML.

First Impression

Here is the DTD that defines the structure for an XML rendition of an engineering bill of materials:

```
<?xml version="1.0" encoding="UTF-8"?>
<!ELEMENT EngBOM (item)>
<!ATTLIST EngBOM
                            aggr.date CDATA #REQUIRED
>
<!ELEMENT item (item.no, item.indent, desc, quantity, rev, haz.note?,
    parent)>
<!ELEMENT item.no (#PCDATA)>
<!ELEMENT item.indent (item.level, item.seq)>
<!ELEMENT desc (#PCDATA)>
<!ELEMENT quantity (#PCDATA)>
<!ATTLIST quantity
                            UOM CDATA #REQUIRED
>
<!ELEMENT rev (#PCDATA)>
<!ATTLIST rev
                            eff.date CDATA #REQUIRED
                            eco.ref CDATA #REQUIRED
>
<!ELEMENT haz.note (#PCDATA)>
<!ELEMENT parent (#PCDATA)>
<!ELEMENT item.level (#PCDATA)>
<!ELEMENT item.seq (#PCDATA)>
```

We have stressed in previous chapters that XML markup should be human readable. But a DTD, when viewed for the first time, does not appear terribly inviting. We are no longer looking at markup. There is no text within tags. In fact, there are no tags at all. Instead each line resembles a mathematical expression or a statement in a computer programming language. A DTD appears to be in a class by itself.

That is exactly the situation. The DTD uses notation that is borrowed from mathematics. It uses the notation to express a tree structure. But the DTD itself is not the tree structure of the actual XML document. Instead it tells an author (or the author's software tool) how to *construct* a tree, specifying at each juncture which elements to use. Conversely it tells the computer how to *deduce* a tree structure from incoming XML and which element types to anticipate. Because it does not use the familiar start- and end-tag notation and syntax, the DTD is peculiar within the XML universe.

Off-putting or not, there are but a few rules required for reading a DTD with some level of confidence. We shall present those shortly.

HOW A DTD WORKS ....

A DTD, the encoding/decoding grammar for XML markup, must supply certain basic information about the particular type of content it supports:

1. The *repertoire* of element types that are allowed to appear.
2. The *order* in which elements are allowed to appear.
3. The *nesting* relationship of elements within elements.
4. The options allowable for each element's *occurrence*.
5. The *attributes* that are allowed for each element.
6. The *type* of data that each element contains.

Here once again is a shipping manifest, rendered as XML. But unlike the sample manifest in Chapter 10, this one is not blank. It describes two shipped items:

```
<manifest>
   <supplier>
      <suppName>InfraTrans Keyboards</suppName>
      <suppStreet>3 North Industrial Drive</suppStreet>
      <suppCity>McNary, Oregon 98725</suppCity>
   </supplier>
   <ShipTo>
      <ShipToName>MicroComp Integrators</ShipToName>
      <ShipToStreet>15 North Willowood Drive Suite 7a</ShipToStreet>
      <ShipToCity>Cle Elum, ID 83811</ShipToCity>
   </ShipTo>
   <ShipInfo>Ground-2nd</ShipInfo>
   <OrderSum>
      <CustNum>0783-105</CustNum>
      <OrderDate>15 November 2002</OrderDate>
      <OrderNum>20021015035</OrderNum>
      <ItemList>
         <Item>
            <ItemQty>15</ItemQty>
            <ItemNum>1736-35</ItemNum>
            <Model>ECK-R</Model>
            <Description>Ruggedized Extended Character
              Keypad</Description>
         </Item>
         <Item>
            <ItemQty>130</ItemQty>
            <ItemNum>2873-05</ItemNum>
            <Model>HHB</Model>
            <Description>Cable Adapter</Description>
            <Status>Back-ordered</Status>
         </Item>
      </ItemList>
   </OrderSum>
</manifest>
```

(Since our essential mechanics treatment of DTDs concentrates on elements, we have highlighted the tags containing the element names.) This particular manifest is but one instance of thousands that are all of the same document type. Here is the DTD that defines this type:

```
<!ELEMENT manifest (supplier, ShipTo, ShipInfo, OrderSum)>

<!ELEMENT supplier (suppName, suppStreet, suppCity)>
<!ELEMENT suppName (#PCDATA)>
<!ELEMENT suppStreet (#PCDATA)>
<!ELEMENT suppCity (#PCDATA)>

<!ELEMENT ShipTo (ShipToName, ShipToStreet, ShipToCity)>
<!ELEMENT ShipToName (#PCDATA)>
<!ELEMENT ShipToStreet (#PCDATA)>
<!ELEMENT ShipToCity (#PCDATA)>
<!ELEMENT ShipInfo (#PCDATA)>
<!ELEMENT OrderSum (CustNum, OrderDate, OrderNum, ItemList)>
<!ELEMENT CustNum (#PCDATA)>
<!ELEMENT OrderDate (#PCDATA)>
<!ELEMENT OrderNum (#PCDATA)>
<!ELEMENT ItemList (Item+)>
<!ELEMENT Item (ItemQty, ItemNum, Model, Description, Status?)>
<!ELEMENT ItemQty (#PCDATA)>
<!ELEMENT ItemNum (#PCDATA)>
<!ELEMENT Model (#PCDATA)>
<!ELEMENT Description (#PCDATA)>
<!ELEMENT Status (#PCDATA)>
```

Defining the repertoire of elements. The DTD calls out each element that is available for use in this document type with a **declaration**. Each declaration begins with **<!ELEMENT.** The shipper's XML-enabled manifest creation tool knows that these items and only these items can make up the XML manifest.

Defining the order of elements. The entire set of elements describing the supplier in our instance of the manifest follows:

```
<suppName>InfraTrans Keyboards</suppName>
<suppStreet>3 North Industrial Drive</suppStreet>
<suppCity>McNary, Oregon 98725</suppCity>
```

The order of **supplier** elements appears in the actual manifest as name, street, city. The DTD enforces that order:

```
<!ELEMENT supplier (suppName, suppStreet, suppCity)>
```

Defining the nesting relationship of elements within elements. In the manifest all of the specific supplier information resides *within* **supplier**:

```
<supplier>
  <suppName>InfraTrans Keyboards</suppName>
  <suppStreet>3 North Industrial Drive</suppStreet>
  <suppCity>McNary, Oregon 98725</suppCity>
</supplier>
```

Here is how the DTD expresses that element/subelement relationship:

```
<!ELEMENT supplier (suppName, suppStreet, suppCity)>
```

Defining the options for an element's occurrence. In our particular manifest there are two items. The rule is that there can be more than one, but there must be at least one. Here is how the DTD describes that rule:

```
<!ELEMENT ItemList (Item+)>
```

Once again there is an element (**ItemList**) that contains a subelement (**Item**). And by using the single symbol "**+**" the DTD expresses the entire set of rules about **Item**'s occurrence.

Similarly, the information on status is optional. So the first item has no shipping information. The rule is that shipping status is optional and that there can be only one **Status** element per item. The DTD expresses that rule as follows:

```
<!ELEMENT Item (ItemQty, ItemNum, Model, Description, Status?)>
```

The symbol "?" with **Status** means optional and no more than one.

Defining the attributes of an element. In Chapter 8 we looked at an access control policy expressed with XACL. An **action** element is part of each access rule. Here is one such action:

```
<action name="write" permission="grant"/>
```

This element has two attributes, as we saw in Chapter 8. Note that it does not have any content per se, just attributes. We call that type of element empty. Here is how the DTD for XACL defines the behavior of this element:

```
<!ELEMENT action EMPTY>
<!ATTLIST action
   name (read | write) #REQUIRED
       permission (deny | grant) #REQUIRED
```

The DTD's description of these attributes identifies the allowable values for each attribute. It also specifies that it is mandatory to provide values for both of the attributes.

Defining the type of data allowed. For every one of the elements in our example the type of content allowed is simply text, called parsed character data or **#PCDATA**:

```
<!ELEMENT suppName (#PCDATA)>
```

The ability to express data typing is severely limited in a DTD. This single limitation has in fact been a primary inhibitor for XML to achieve a serious foothold in the workplace. Fortunately for XML Schema, the recently developed method for describing XML structure overcomes this limitation completely. We will see how XML Schema not only accounts for different types of data but can even define the specific numeric upper and lower bounds that are allowable for the value of an attribute, for example.

ASSESSING THE DTD..

Until May 2, 2001, the DTD was the only official means of defining and validating XML content. (On that date XML Schema was released as a full W3C specification.) Validation is the base requirement for guaranteeing the integrity of content exchange. Computers that process serious XML content typically do so by first decoding that content according to the strict grammar expressed by the content's DTD.

But DTDs are for humans as well. Nearly every industry work group now developing an XML language is conducting its business with the DTD as the means of initial dialog. When a new language is finally released, the actual publication is typically in the form of a DTD.

But there are certain downsides to the DTD. It is severely limited in handling datatypes, as we have seen. That one limitation alone arguably has been the biggest deterrent to XML's wider acceptance to date. But there are other drawbacks to the DTD as well. The syntax (composition rules) for a DTD are totally separate from the mainstream of XML. This may be a deterrent to humans who are newcomers to XML. It is admittedly a chore to learn the mechanics of XML syntax. But once learned, that knowledge applies over the entire XML landscape to all of the XML standards and to every instance of XML content on the planet. Almost, that is. Ironically the DTD, the core technology for valid XML content, is a syntax island in the vast sea of XML.

An alternate syntax is not difficult for humans to master, as we hope to have demonstrated in this chapter. But for XML software developers, the DTD represents enough of a separate paradigm that they would rather leave it alone, to be used solely by freely available parsers and not read by human eyes. An XML Schema, on the other hand, because it is 100 percent XML, can participate fully in an XML application, functioning alongside the data it supports and available for processing in the same way that data itself is processed.

SUMMARY ....

The DTD was a mature technology already in place at the launch of XML's development. And as such, the DTD is not purely XML, but a somewhat more cryptic animal. It offers precisely the power required to enforce structure through the entire encoding–transmission–decoding process that we described in Chapter 5. And it continues to provide humans with a concise way to describe structure to one another, something that is crucial as industry groups continue to develop specific XML languages. In spite of well-known limitations—particularly its inability to support datatypes to the level that data specialists require—the DTD is an ideal method for describing and interpreting trees (hierarchical data). It is mathematically precise (and concise) in exposing and controlling every aspect of elements' behaviors: which may occur, in what order they must appear, how their parent-child relationships are organized, how many of them may or must occur, and which attributes are allowed or required. As the XML community moves over to XML Schemas, it is certain that DTDs will continue to be the most common method of describing XML structure for years to come.

12 XML Schemas

In this chapter...

They Said It...

I like a thing simple, but it must be simple through complication. Everything must come into your scheme, otherwise you cannot achieve real simplicity.

Gertrude Stein

XML schemas are the result of a centerpiece technology for structured electronic content. They allow for seamless information exchange across barriers. They have lowered the barrier for tool providers to enter the XML marketplace. Like XML itself, schemas present a consistent look and feel to human readers, regardless of the industry or application. As the description mechanism for XML document types, schemas offer a rich vocabulary for highly specific type definitions. In turn, most important of all from an management standpoint, schemas for routine tasks represent a minimal learning curve. Most of these benefits of schemas exist because a schema for describing an XML document type is *itself* an out-of-the-box XML document. We give attention in this chapter to the mechanics (i.e., the syntax) of schemas, including some essential terminology. In doing so we are learning the set of schema's own element types. Schemas provide us with a third approach to describing XML content, in addition to plain English and the formal DTD. The full formal W3C specification of XML Schemas is challenging to master. But the majority of real work that XML schemas support will use only a small part of its advanced options.

WHY SHOULD I BOTHER?....................................

Guaranteed portability. Schemas determine whether or not a piece of content is valid. If it is valid it is sure to be portable, regardless of the consumer's processor or particular application. Some limited exchange of XML content is possible without the on-board support of schemas, but that only works in a tightly constrained environment and with an application of limited complexity. If you even sense the need for making your XML content truly transportable, then you need the expressive ability of XML schemas. Even if your application seems very modest, you should first create the schema for your XML content before you generate actual XML.

Greater processor friendliness. But didn't we already cover the DTD in Chapter 11? And isn't a DTD a perfectly good way to describe a document type? And aren't there a large number of XML authoring and editing tools that come with built-in DTD engines (parsers and markup enforcers)? Yes, and yes. But the first problem with the DTD is its own way of expressing itself. In Chapter 11 we walked through some

DTDs with little difficulty, scarcely noting that we were mastering a special little side dish of rules for reading the **content model** of a DTD. In the following excerpt from a DTD for court filing documents, the content model (highlighted) is straightforward:

```
<!ELEMENT Legal (CourtFiling)>
<!ELEMENT CourtFiling (Filing+ | Confirmation+ | Query | Response)>
```

Interpretation: The element **Legal** consists of a single **CourtFiling** element. A **CourtFiling** element consists of one of the following: one or more **Filing**s, one or more **Confirmation**s, a **Query**, or a **Response**.

Or consider the content model (again highlighted) from this fragment from the DTD that underlies the book you are now reading:

```
<!ELEMENT chap.sect (sect.title,(para+,(ord.list | unord.list)*)+) >
```

Interpretation: The element **chap.sect** consists of a **sect.title**, followed by a group of one of more of the following: one or more **para**s, followed perhaps by either one or more (numbered) **ord.list**s or **unord.list**s.

The rules for reading a content model are just a minor speed bump in a human reader's learning process. Without even being conscious of it, we were mastering another language, and we mastered it rather easily. But for a software application that must be XML-compliant, it requires a separate effort to develop a robust DTD content model interpreter or even to implant one that is freely available.

Preferred medium of collaboration. When industries and professional consortia seek to collaborate via shared definitions of XML documents or records, they do that most frequently with schemas. XML specialists devote much time and effort in helping your trade group or professional society toward a shared suite of XML content types. An outcome of that effort is the suite of XML schemas describing those content types.

Profitable content reuse. You are inevitably going to want to *repurpose* your XML content. For example, certain segments of a utilities company work order constitute a record of particular interest to the accounting department and the inventory office. XML schemas greatly enhance the process of customizing and sharing that data. XML schemas express in an unambiguous manner how the derived content is to be structured.

Framework for human discourse. You may not like the politics of open systems collaboration. You may intend to exchange XML content with only a single trading partner or with only one other division in your company. Nevertheless you still need a human vocabulary and framework for discussing that exchange. Sharing content has typically meant that players must invent their own terminology and approaches. XML Schemas as a specification come ready-made as a framework for just that purpose.

Straightforward mechanism for extensibility. You may be most intrigued by XML because of its claim to be extensible. But extensibility is far more than simply expanding the tag set. The visible part of markup—pointy-bracket tags, occasional encoding characters, plain text—is only the result of underlying mechanisms, including the schema. You may, for example, need to extend your XML vocabulary for personnel records because of a new federal workplace requirement. For you and your XML specialist, that process begins with the underlying XML schemas for the records. Only after that is done will users see revised tag sets (if they ever see tags at all).

Robust database technology. Schemas are a cornerstone concept in database technology. If your work in IT entails traditional databases or if you are seeking to incorporate XML in your database planning, your database specialists will find XML schemas to be a familiar and useful mechanism.

Precision of datatypes. If you have already launched an XML strategy in earnest, you are highly conscious of how XML must fully support your content. You expect that XML will convey and express all of the nuances of your data. This is what *datatypes*, the core concept of database technologies, is all about. But the DTD, is very deficient in its ability to express datatypes. And so one of the main inhibitors of XML's gaining a convincing foothold in the data workplace has been this weakness of the DTD. But with schemas the story is different. The schema recommendation has been a content-as-data specification from the start, incorporating a rich repertoire of datatypes. XML schemas, unlike DTDs, allow you to describe your data with the same level of precision that is possible with database technologies.

HOW DOES IT WORK?......................................

At first glance:

Schemas are on center stage. If you have followed the rise of XML for e-commerce, e-publishing or data exchange of any variety, then you have no doubt seen the word *schema*. It sounds trendy. It denotes something a cut above "dialect." And judging by its frequency in articles and tutorials, it appears to be central to the whole XML movement.

Schema would appear to be more important than markup itself, judging by the frequency with which it appears in technical industry news and the attention it is getting among various industry groups. The discussion in news stories and in online chat room threads even becomes emotional at times. This is because schemas will determine companies' entire methods of organizing, viewing, and transporting content.

XML Schema appears difficult. It would also appear that learning XML Schema—the "real" specification from the W3C—could become a career in itself. The full recommendation consists of three long sections, posted as separate downloadable files. And the entire first file is nothing but the Primer, consisting of 66 pages.

But there is something even more obvious about XML Schema. Its syntax simply makes it *look* long-winded and difficult. Here is the DTD for online book reviews:

```
<!-- Document Type Definition (DTD) for a block of book reviews,
updated in real time and appearing on a bookseller's Web page -->

<!ELEMENT reviews     (review+)
<!ELEMENT review      ((bibl.info,(author+), description))      >
<!ELEMENT bibl.info   (#PCDATA)                                 >
<!ELEMENT author      (#PCDATA)
<!ELEMENT description(#PCDATA)
```

Now consider the description for the same document type, as rendered by an XML schema:

```
<schema
  xmlns='http://www.w3.org/2000/10/XMLSchema'
  targetNamespace='http://www.w3.org/namespace/'
  xmlns:EssentialGuide='http://www.w3.org/namespace/'>

 <element name='reviews'>
  <complexType>
   <sequence>
    <element ref='EssentialGuide:review' maxOccurs='unbounded'/>
   </sequence>
  </complexType>
 </element>

 <element name='review'>
  <complexType>
   <sequence>
    <element ref='EssentialGuide:bibl.info'/>
    <sequence>
     <element ref='EssentialGuide:author' maxOccurs='unbounded'/>
    </sequence>
    <element ref='EssentialGuide:description'/>
   </sequence>
  </complexType>
 </element>
```

```
<element name='bibl.info' type='string'>
</element>

<element name='author' type='string'>
</element>

<element name='description' type='string'>
</element>
</schema>
```

Five lines in the DTD compared to 29 lines in the schema. By the numbers alone, XML Schema *appears* to be complicating the world of XML rather than simplifying it.

Function of a schema

A schema, like the DTD that we saw earlier, is more than just a guideline creating XML content. It dictates for a unit of XML content precisely which elements may occur and in what order. The recipient of that heavy-handed guidance may be a human author or editor of a section of an operating manual for a network shareable printer. Or a schema may guide a robotic XML record generator that is composing a receiver record to acknowledge a shipment of wheel bearings.

On the receiving end, any number of schema-savvy XML tools will rely on the schema to interpret and process the content intelligently. Specifically, a parser will read and interpret the XML text (a single, one-dimensional string, remember?). For an XML structure of any consequence, the parser must rely on the structural knowledge expressed by the schema.

Another common role for a schema is to help transform XML data. A generic off-the-shelf XML transformation tool—possibly free for the download—can do its work on XML data of an infinite variety of types. For that it relies on the schema.

Minicase: Policy Manual Management

EZ-Payables Inc. (Figure 12.1) is an outsourcing service company that handles the entire payables function for large companies. EZ-Payables employs 620 people, including clerical, technical, supervisory, and management employees. After the company had reached a head count of 300, the Human Resources department found itself unable to keep abreast of everything required to keep the employees' *Policies and Procedures* manual current. The various job descriptions and company policies had become too unwieldy to be supported by the department. In addition, some wrongful termination legal actions had made it clear that the document is in fact far more than a set of guidelines. The courts have even referred to their loose-leaf notebook as a legally binding contract. EZ-Payables Inc. decided to distribute and assign specific duties to various offices in the company. Human Resources still deals with traditional day-to-day guidelines and with publishing the manual. But managers in other departments now function as stewards of the actual content for the various sections of the document.

The reassignment of duties for managing the manual has served to stabilize and clarify policies in the company. But by parceling out these duties, it soon became clear that responsibilities themselves can change, some very frequently. Just this week the Board of Directors decided that the company's mission statement is best left in charge of the CEO. Last month, because of federally related contract work, the company found itself required to regulate the use of certain computing facilities, including Internet access. Therefore the company has decided to add an Internet usage section to the manual, to be maintained by the director of information technology. The manual has become a *dynamic document*, and so has the management of the document. Figure 12.1 represents EZ-Payables Inc.'s shared management of their policy manual, just prior to the changes they plan to make.

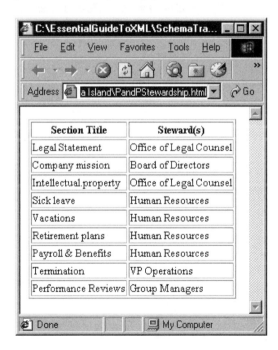

Figure 12.1 A plan for shared management of policies

It might seem unreasonable to spend serious resources on a small data object represented by a ten-row, two-column table (see Figure 12.1). But this particular data object has the potential to ease the publication burden and to guarantee the integrity of sensitive legal language. The underlying rows and columns of data serve as an access control list, a traffic monitor, and access cop, for the stewards who are now contributors. In fact, the IT database people view this little piece of data as just another access control list, a normal database component for all of the company's secured records. When an authorized writer in the legal office opens the electronic document, she can see (i.e., read) any section. But she is authorized to modify (i.e., write to) only those sections for which Office of Legal Counsel is the steward. And this internal monitor also serves the employees directly. When they request to view the manual, they can opt for only a certain section, and within that section they can retrieve to a very detailed level, printing only a page or two if they wish. As might be expected, the manual is soon to appear on the company's intranet, an internal Web site. We will see the first release of the online version in upcoming chapter.

XML has played a leading role in this migration from the policy manual as loose-leaf binder to its mature rendition as an intranet-based electronic document. The content itself is now stored totally and managed as XML text, as are the supporting data structures, including the access table. As a simple data structure, the access table is a good place to start for viewing an XML schema description.

Anatomy of a Schema

Here is the XML content underlying the table above:

```
<?xml version = "1.0"?>

  <!-- PolicyManual.xml -->

<!-- For each "policy,"
     "section" is the title of the policy, and
     "steward" is the business unit responsible for maintaining the
-->

<policies>

     <policy>
          <section>Legal Statement</section>
          <steward>Office of Legal Counsel</steward>
     </policy>

     <policy>
          <section>Company mission</section>
          <steward>Board of Directors</steward>
     </policy>
```

```
<policy>
        <section>Intellectual.property</section>
        <steward>Office of Legal Counsel</steward>
</policy>

<policy>
        <section>Sick leave</section>
        <steward>Human Resources</steward>
</policy>

<policy>
        <section>Vacations</section>
        <steward>Human Resources</steward>
</policy>

<policy>
        <section>Retirement plans</section>
        <steward>Human Resources</steward>
</policy>

<policy>
        <section>Payroll &amp; Benefits</section>
        <steward>Human Resources</steward>
</policy>

<policy>
        <section>Termination</section>
        <steward>VP Operations</steward>
</policy>

<policy>
        <section>Performance Reviews</section>
        <steward>Group Managers</steward>
</policy>
```

```
</policies>
```

Describing the elements of the manual in English is straightforward. In the description we refer to the highlighted items.

- We call the entire table **policies** because it describes the entire document it supports.
- Within **policies** is a series of **policy** sections. There would, of course, always be at least one of these sections, and there is no limit to the number of **policy** sections.

- Within each **policy** section, there are two components: the **section** name and the **steward**, the office or person designated and authorized to update that section of the manual. For each policy there can only be a single **section** (i.e., a single name), and the company has decided that there will be only a single point of contact (**steward**) for each section.

Internally, everything is stored as plain text, to be exposed to the XML processor. To reinforce what we said earlier, the actual stored text may not even include its human-friendly line breaks and indents. An XML editor will automatically insert line breaks and indents. But with or without those formatting helps, here is exactly how the computer sees the XML file:

```
<?xml version = "1.0"?>_<!-- PolicyManual.xml --><!-- For each "policy,""secti
on" is the title of the policy, and "steward" is the business unit responsible
for maintaining the policy.--><policies><policy><section>Legal Statement</sect
ion><steward>Office of Legal Counsel</steward></policy><policy><section>Compan
y mission</section><steward>Board of Directors</steward></policy><policy><sect
ion>Intellectual.property</section><steward>Office of Legal Counsel</steward><
/policy><policy><section>Sick leave</section><steward>Human Resources</steward
></policy><policy><section>Vacations</section><steward>Human Resources</stewar
d></policy><policy><section>Retirement plans</section><steward>Human Resources
</steward></policy><policy><section>Payroll &amp; Benefits</section><steward>H
uman Resources</steward></policy><policy><section>Termination</section><stewar
d>VP Operations</steward></policy><policy><section>Performance Reviews</sectio
n><steward>Group Managers</steward></policy></policies>
```

But isn't that a very ugly representation? For human eyes yes. But not for an XML processor, a computer program serving as an XML processor. We rely on visual cues like line breaks and indentation for our interpretation of structure. The XML processor relies instead on the schema that defines this document type.

Note that the schema's definition applies to the *type* of document, the family to which a particular document (an instance) belongs. It is not a description of this particular instance (i.e., this one particular manual). For one schema there could be dozens of XML instances. In other words, the schema describes the structure of the data, but it is not the data itself. Remember that we could conceivably consider every HTML-encoded page on the Web to be theoretically an instance of a single schema for the entire HTML universe.

The following is an XML schema that expresses in XML the plain-English description above:

```
<schema
    xmlns='http://www.w3.org/2000/10/XMLSchema'
    targetNamespace='http://www.w3.org/namespace/'
    xmlns:EssentialGuide='http://www.w3.org/namespace/'>

    <element name='policies'>
        <complexType>
            <sequence maxOccurs='unbounded'>
                <element ref='EssentialGuide:policy'/>
            </sequence>
        </complexType>
    </element>

    <element name='policy'>
        <complexType>
            <sequence>
                <element ref='EssentialGuide:section'/>
                <element ref='EssentialGuide:steward'/>
            </sequence>
        </complexType>
    </element>

    <element name='section' type='string'>
    </element>

    <element name='steward' type='string'>
    </element>
</schema>
```

We turn now to an *executive talkthrough* of this small XML schema. As we do, bear in mind that while the document type's structure is rather elementary, the mechanics are representative of every schema you will encounter.

Policy Manual Management: Executive Talkthrough

The most striking characteristic of an XML schema is that it is 100 percent XML. There is no side dish language to learn. For example, instead of using a programming language notation to express element-subelement relationships, the schema shows that very graphically. The indentation in our example clearly expresses the various element-subelement relationships.

In the following sections we take up the major milestones that are part of every schema. Our goal is not intended to explain all of the syntactic (mechanical) detail, which the W3C defines thoroughly in the various specification documents. It is to capture the essentials, as demonstrated in an actual example.

XML NAMESPACES IN AN XML SCHEMA.................

Within the schema the topmost three items are the schema's callout of namespaces.

```
<schema
    xmlns='http://www.w3.org/2000/10/XMLSchema'
    targetNamespace='http://www.w3.org/namespace/'
    xmlns:EssentialGuide='http://www.w3.org/namespace/'>

        <element name='policies'>
                <complexType>
                        <sequence maxOccurs='unbounded'>
                                <element ref='EssentialGuide:policy'/>
                        </sequence>
                </complexType>
        </element>

        <element name='policy'>
                <complexType>
                        <sequence>
                                <element ref='EssentialGuide:section'/>
                                <element ref='EssentialGuide:steward'/>
                        </sequence>
                </complexType>
        </element>

        <element name='section' type='string'>
        </element>

        <element name='steward' type='string'>
        </element>
</schema>
```

We deal with XML namespaces as a stand-alone topic in Chapter 15. In this brief example we see how the XML namespace mechanisms serve to prevent collision among different uses for the same name. Applying XML namespaces is necessary for XML schemas because the schema apparatus itself owns several names. It is possible that an organization would like to use the name **element** or **complex** or **mixed** or even **name** for its content's element types. The approach of earlier generation programming languages was simply that programmers were forbidden to use certain **keywords** because these were co-opted by the language itself. But thanks to the XML specification for namespaces, we are free to select names of our choosing.

The way XML namespaces accomplish all of that is simple and elegant. Note again the opening of the schema.

```
<schema
    xmlns='http://www.w3.org/2000/10/XMLSchema'
    targetNamespace='http://www.w3.org/namespace/'
    xmlns:EssentialGuide='http://www.w3.org/namespace/'>
```

The schema is itself an XML document whose own **root** (topmost) element is
<schema>. This element has three attributes (highlighted):

```
<schema
    xmlns='http://www.w3.org/2000/10/XMLSchema'
    targetNamespace='http://www.w3.org/namespace/'
    xmlns:EssentialGuide='http://www.w3.org/namespace/'>
```

And each of the attributes has a value (highlighted):

```
<schema
        xmlns='http://www.w3.org/2000/10/XMLSchema'
        targetNamespace='http://www.w3.org/namespace/'
        xmlns:EssentialGuide='http://www.w3.org/namespace/'>
```

All three of the attributes contribute to the assignment of namespaces for this
particular schema. The two with **xmlns** accomplish the actual namespace separation.
And they do that through two simple mechanisms.

First, we define a **prefix** for a particular namespace that we can attach to each
occurrence of that name. We do that in the namespace definition by using a colon followed by whatever name we choose:

```
<schema
    xmlns='http://www.w3.org/2000/10/XMLSchema'
    targetNamespace='http://www.w3.org/namespace/'
    xmlns:EssentialGuide='http://www.w3.org/namespace/'>
```

Next, we assign a **universal resource identifier** (URI) as the attribute value of
that namespace definition:

```
<schema
    xmlns='http://www.w3.org/2000/10/XMLSchema'
    targetNamespace='http://www.w3.org/namespace/'
    xmlns:EssentialGuide='http://www.w3.org/namespace/'>
```

That prefix, plus the different URIs, now tells the XML processor that each
name bearing the **EssentialGuide** prefix is ours. It is impossible for XML Schema to infringe on the names **policy**, **section**, or **steward**, when they are
prepended with our prefix. The formal way of putting this is that we have disambigu-
ated each of these names.

```
<schema
   xmlns='http://www.w3.org/2000/10/XMLSchema'
   targetNamespace='http://www.w3.org/namespace/'
   xmlns:EssentialGuide='http://www.w3.org/namespace/'>

      <element name='policies'>
            <complexType>
                  <sequence maxOccurs='unbounded'>
                        <element ref='EssentialGuide:policy'/>
                  </sequence>
            </complexType>
      </element>

      <element name='policy'>
            <complexType>
                  <sequence>
                        <element ref='EssentialGuide:section'/>
                        <element ref='EssentialGuide:steward'/>
                  </sequence>
            </complexType>
      </element>

      <element name='section' type='string'>
      </element>

      <element name='steward' type='string'>
      </element>
</schema>
```

So XML Schema owns the remainder of the element names in this particular
schema: **schema**, **element**, **sequence**, and **complexType**... every element
name that does *not* bear a prefix. And how exactly does the namespaces apparatus accomplish that? Consider again the set of namespace definitions, noting the two
xmlns attributes:

```
xmlns='http://www.w3.org/2000/10/XMLSchema'
targetNamespace='http://www.w3.org/namespace/'
xmlns:EssentialGuide='http://www.w3.org/namespace/'>
```

Recall that the XML specification allows us to attach a colon plus some name of
our choosing that we can use later as a prefix. We did that for the **EssentialGuide**
names. But note that there is no colon and no prefix name for the first name space definition: **xmlns**. This may sound very nitpicking, but there actually *is* a prefix name.
Only it happens to be a null, a nothing. So the "missing" prefix in front of element
complexType and so on is actually a null prefix. And it's a very significant null at

that. It tells us (and the XML processor) that each of those null-prefixed names belong to the XML Schema's namespace defined by this attribute:

```
xmlns='http://www.w3.org/2000/10/XMLSchema'
```

As for the values of each of the attributes in the namespace definitions (the URIs), they do not concern us, nor are their internals important to the computer. (We explain this further in Chapter 15.) They are there only to make the separation clear.

The namespace specification owns the name **targetNamespace**:

```
targetNamespace='http://www.w3.org/namespace/'
```

The role of **targetNamespace** is to communicate with the parser (XML processor) that the total namespace described in this schema is the same as that used by the actual document. So a schema supplies not only the road map of a document's internal structure, but it describes the document's namespace as well. That is useful when a document is part of a collection that must later be aggregated.

HOW THE SCHEMA DESCRIBES STRUCTURE...........

We return now to the structure of the document type. That is, we are focusing on the type of XML documents that this schema describes. Just by looking at the underlying XML notation of the policies content we can deduce its tree structure quite easily. Here is a fragment of the XML file again:

```
<policies>

        <policy>
                <section>Legal Statement</section>
                <steward>Office of Legal Counsel</steward>
        </policy>

        <policy>
                <section>Company mission</section>
                <steward>Board of Directors</steward>
        </policy>

        <policy>
                <section>Intellectual.property</section>
                <steward>Office of Legal Counsel</steward>
        </policy>
```

```
<policy>
        <section>Company mission</section>
        <steward>Board of Directors</steward>
</policy>

<policy>
        <section>Intellectual.property</section>
        <steward>Office of Legal Counsel</steward>
</policy>

<policy>
        <section>Sick leave</section>
        <steward>Human Resources</steward>
</policy>


</policies>
```

We find that **policies**, the topmost element (outermost as we view it) contains a sequence of **policy** elements. And those, in turn, contain two other types: **section** and **steward**. Here again is the schema, this time highlighting the container-contained relationship among the element types:

```
<schema
   xmlns='http://www.w3.org/2000/10/XMLSchema'
   targetNamespace='http://www.w3.org/namespace/'
   xmlns:EssentialGuide='http://www.w3.org/namespace/'>

    <element name='policies'>
        <complexType>
                <sequence maxOccurs='unbounded'>
                        <element ref='EssentialGuide:policy'/>
                </sequence>
        </complexType>
    </element>

    <element name='policy'>
        <complexType>
                <sequence>
                        <element ref='EssentialGuide:section'/>
                        <element ref='EssentialGuide:steward'/>
                </sequence>
        </complexType>
    </element>
```

The first element in the schema describes everything that the parser needs to know about policies. In schema language, **policy** is a **complex** data type. This is because a **policy** contains something other than simple text.

```
<element name='policies'>
        <complexType>
                <sequence maxOccurs='unbounded'>
                        <element ref='EssentialGuide:policy'/>
                </sequence>
        </complexType>
</element>
```

The schema describes **policies** as being a **complexType**. This is because policies can have multiple subelements. The next level within this same block tells the parser exactly what it can expect to find inside a **policy** element:

```
<element name='policies'>
        <complexType>
                <sequence maxOccurs='unbounded'>
                        <element ref='EssentialGuide:policy'/>
                </sequence>
        </complexType>
</element>
```

This embedded block informs the parser to expect to see a sequence of elements, all of type **policy**. With its keyword **maxOccurs** the schema then tells the parser that there is no limit to how many **policy** elements to expect. As for the internal details of the embedded **policy** element, this block simply refers the parser to **policy**'s own description. That block of code is next:

```
<element name='policy'>
        <complexType>
                <sequence>
                        <element ref='EssentialGuide:section'/>
                        <element ref='EssentialGuide:steward'/>
                </sequence>
        </complexType>
</element>
```

This is the block of the schema that focuses on the internals of the **policy** element type. The only difference between this and the higher-order description for **policies** is that this time there is a sequence of two embedded elements, **section** and **steward**. Once again, this block of schema code refers (using **ref** as a pointer) to the descriptions of section and steward.

And that takes us to the end of the line for this document type:

```
<element name='section' type='string'>
</element>

<element name='steward' type='string'>
```

Both **section** and **steward** are **simple** data types, according to XML Schema's definition, because they contain only text and no embedded subelements.

Workplace example of a schema

We emphasized in Chapter 2 that the big thing about XML as a truly new paradigm is that *content is data*. This next case study demonstrates first that XML content really is data. But it also demonstrates that data as defined by an XML schema is much closer to the native variety recognized by database specialists everywhere.

For this somewhat more realistic case of XML at work, we turn now to an application for real-time work orders. This supports job order entry, logging, accounting, and reporting for utilities (water, sewer, roads, gas, and electric). The actual requirements are different for each type of work. There is a wide difference between how it would be used within a metro government's utilities division, a private industrial gas pipeline company, and the internal maintenance office for a multisite office complex. But core work-order concepts can be shared across even that diverse a set of requirements. Furthermore, the content of work orders impacts a variety of offices within each organization: accounting, inventory, purchasing, fleet management, shop scheduling, and regulations compliance.

Designing the supporting content as XML will be a prudent investment. The primary attraction of XML is that a maintenance group can easily inherit the XML data definition and *extend* the definition to suit its own needs. That way, it can continue doing business in its own way while conforming to the particular requirements of other offices and regulatory agencies. Table 12.1 displays data elements that make up the core work-order system.

Table 12.1 A core work-order system

Work Order Item	Item Code	Description	Attributes
Work Order ID	wo.id	Alphanumeric job code	date.issu (date issued)
			date.comp (date completed)
Customer/Cost Center	cust	Customer or cost center to charge	type [internal | external]
			acc.code (accounting code)
Description	desc	Description of job	
Shop Code	shop.id	Home base for the job	
Materials List	mat.list	(as many items as necessarry)	
Description	mat.desc	Pick List description of item needed	
Cost	mat.cost	Purchase or listed cost	
Personnel	pers		
Authorization	pers.auth	Official authorizing work	
Workers	pers.work	Roster of persons assigned	
Remarks	remarks	Free-form comments	

Figure 12.2 illustrates how a typical work order record might appear.

Date of work:
     Work Order issued: 2002-03-19
     Work Completed: 2002-03-19

Customer:
     Accounting Code: 3287001
     Name: Water District 19
     Customer type: internal

Description:
     Repair, resurface Mulkato Dam access road

Shop Location:
     Roads and Bridges

Materials used:
     Description: 20 yards asphalt
     Cost: 1560.00

Personnel:
     Authorization: Chick Grenfeldt
     Work crew:
          Louis Becker
          Tom Schinle
          Kathie Burgess

Additional Information:
     Flooding last Saturday night left a large gully, making road impassable.

Figure 12.2 A typical work order

Here is the actual XML file that produced this report:

```
<?xml version="1.0" encoding="UTF-8"?>

<work.order xmlns="http://www.w3.org/namespace/"
xmlns:xsi="http://www.w3.org/2000/10/XMLSchema-instance"
xsi:schemaLocation="http://www.w3.org/namespace/
C:\EssentialGuideToXML\SchemaTrans\WorkOrderREV.xsd">

    <wo.id date.issu="2002-03-17" date.comp="2002-03-19"/>
    <cust name="Water District 19" type="internal" acc.code="3287001"/>
    <desc>Repair, resurface Mulkato Dam access road</desc>
```

```
    <shop.id>Roads and Bridges</shop.id>
    <mat.list>
        <mat.desc>20 yards asphalt</mat.desc>
        <mat.cost>1560.00</mat.cost>
    </mat.list>
    <pers>
        <pers.auth>Chick Grenfeldt</pers.auth>
        <pers.work>Louis Becker</pers.work>
        <pers.work>Tom Schinle</pers.work>
        <pers.work>Kathie Burgess</pers.work>
    </pers>
</work.order>
```

It is not worthwhile for us to dwell on mastering all of the syntax of this or the other XML files. But it is very useful to note how XML Schema is about to make its own strong case as an enabler of data. As we saw in Table 12.1, two of the items in the document have attributes, data that is attached to an element but is not part of the actual text of the element:

```
    <wo.id date.issu="2002-03-17" date.comp="2002-03-19"/>
    <cust name="Water District 19" type="internal"
        acc.code="3287001"/>
    <desc>Repair, resurface Mulkato Dam access road</desc>
    <shop.id>Roads and Bridges</shop.id>
    <mat.list>
        <mat.desc>20 yards asphalt</mat.desc>
        <mat.cost>1560.00</mat.cost>
    </mat.list>
    <pers>
        <pers.auth>Chick Grenfeldt</pers.auth>
        <pers.work>Louis Becker</pers.work>
        <pers.work>Tom Schinle</pers.work>
        <pers.work>Kathie Burgess</pers.work>
    </pers>
```

The parser and other processing machinery that consumes this record must rely on a definition of data types in order to act appropriately. The more that the DTD can tell the processor about the *type* of data it's dealing with, the more useful the XML data will be. But what does the DTD for the work order family have to say about the datatypes of those attributes? The bolded items define those attributes:

```
<!-- Document Type Defnition work order
        Chapter used: Schema

Note DTD's restriction on datatype for attributes. Compare with
        schema version
-->

<!DOCTYPE  work.order [
```

```
<!--            ELEMENT NAME  CONTENT MODEL                    -->
<!ELEMENT     work.order    (wo.id, cust, desc, shop.id, mat.list,
        pers, remarks?)        >
<!ELEMENT       wo.id       EMPTY                               >
<!ATTLIST       wo.id
                  date.issu        CDATA   #REQUIRED
                  date.comp        CDATA   #REQUIRED            >

<!ELEMENT       cust        EMPTY                               >
<!ATTLIST       cust  name         CDATA   #REQUIRED
                      type         CDATA   #REQUIRED
                      acc.code     NUMBER  #IMPLIED             >
<!ELEMENT       desc        (#PCDATA)                           >
<!ELEMENT       shop.id     (#PCDATA)                           >

<!ELEMENT       mat.list    (mat.desc, mat.cost)*              >
<!ELEMENT       mat.desc    (#PCDATA)                           >
<!ELEMENT       mat.cost    (#PCDATA)                           >
<!ELEMENT       pers        (pers.auth, pers.work+)            >
<!ELEMENT       pers.auth   (#PCDATA)                           >
<!ELEMENT       pers.work   (#PCDATA)                           >
<!ELEMENT       remarks     (#PCDATA)                           >

]>
```

Two of the attributes (**date.issu** and **date.comp**) are dates. The accounting code (**acc.code**) is numeric. And with the cost of materials (the **mat.cost** element) real money is changing hands. Unfortunately the DTD's limitations confine it to expressing very little about the datatypes of attributes and even less about elements. The accounting code is numeric, but there is no detail here about the precise type of the data. The cost of materials appears simply as **#PCDATA** again without further detail.

Little wonder that XML has sometimes struggled to become credible with the data-centric community. With so much critical datatype information lacking or not possible in the DTD, programmers have had resolve the ambiguities. They have had to surround an XML data application with custom computer code to capture, deduce, and create the intelligence outside the realm of XML.

But schema has remedied that entirely. Let us look at the XML schema representation of the DTD for work orders. Never mind the long-windedness of the schema. As we've already seen, that's just their nature. So without dwelling on detail, note the highlighted items:

```
<schema targetNamespace="http://www.w3.org/namespace/"
xmlns:EssentialGuide="http://www.w3.org/namespace/"
xmlns="http://www.w3.org/2000/10/XMLSchema">
    <element name="work.order">
        <complexType>
            <sequence>
                <element ref="EssentialGuide:wo.id"/>
                <element ref="EssentialGuide:cust"/>
                <element ref="EssentialGuide:desc"/>
                <element ref="EssentialGuide:shop.id"/>
                <element ref="EssentialGuide:mat.list"/>
                <element ref="EssentialGuide:pers"/>
                <element ref="EssentialGuide:remarks"
                    minOccurs="0"/>
            </sequence>
        </complexType>
    </element>
    <element name="wo.id">
        <complexType>
            <attribute name="date.issu" type="date"
                use="required"/>
            <attribute name="date.comp" type="date"
                use="required"/>
        </complexType>
    </element>
    <element name="cust">
        <complexType>
            <attribute name="name" type="string"
                use="required"/>
            <attribute name="type" type="string" use="required"/>
            <attribute name="acc.code" type="nonNegativeInteger"
                use="optional"/>
        </complexType>
    </element>
    <element name="desc" type="string"/>
    <element name="shop.id" type="string"/>
    <element name="mat.list">
        <complexType>
            <sequence>
                <element ref="EssentialGuide:mat.desc"/>
                <element ref="EssentialGuide:mat.cost"/>
            </sequence>
        </complexType>
    </element>
    <element name="mat.desc" type="string"/>
    <element name="mat.cost" type="float"/>
    <element name="pers">
        <complexType>
            <sequence>
                <element ref="EssentialGuide:pers.auth"/>
```

```
            <element ref="EssentialGuide:pers.work"
                   maxOccurs="unbounded"/>
          </sequence>
        </complexType>
    </element>
    <element name="pers.auth" type="string"/>
    <element name="pers.work" type="string"/>
    <element name="remarks" type="string"/>
</schema>
```

If we compare the highlighted items with their counterparts in the DTD, we begin to sense why XML Schema is such a big deal. The schema for the content becomes a powerful enhancer of the content, adding dramatically to its usefulness. While we claimed earlier that XML content is data, schema allows us to make the claim in earnest.

THE BEAUTY OF NAMESPACES ....

Like many newcomers to XML, you may have remained unconvinced that the namespace apparatus described earlier—the lines of esoteric definitions with their URIs—is really all that beneficial. Or even if it is, then it probably wouldn't benefit a small, simple XML project. As it happens, even something as straightforward and modest as our work-order system benefits immediately and directly from namespaces. Consider again the definition of the **cust** element. We designed the element's structure such that all of its semantic payload is in its two attributes:

```
        <complexType>
            <sequence>
                <element ref="EssentialGuide:wo.id"/>
                <element ref="EssentialGuide:cust"/>
                <element ref="EssentialGuide:desc"/>
                <element ref="EssentialGuide:shop.id"/>
                <element ref="EssentialGuide:mat.list"/>
                <element ref="EssentialGuide:pers"/>
                <element ref="EssentialGuide:remarks" minOccurs="0"/>
            </sequence>
        </complexType>
    </element>
    <element name="wo.id">
        <complexType>
            <attribute name="date.issu" type="date" use="required"/>
            <attribute name="date.comp" type="date" use="required"/>
        </complexType>
    </element>
```

```
<element name="cust">
    <complexType>
        <attribute name="name" type="string" use="required"/>
        <attribute name="type" type="string" use="required"/>
        <attribute name="acc.code" type="nonNegativeInteger"
            use="optional"/>
    </complexType>
</element>
```

Namespaces is an XML strategy for helping us avoid collisions between our data and that of our trading partners or internal collaborators. But sometimes it can help us to avoid collisions with XML itself. The words **name** and **type** are built in to the XML Schema specification. For a human reader and data handler that's only a minor nuisance. But for a computer the confusion between *our* use of the terms and Schema's use of the terms could be catastrophic. In this example, the ambiguities regarding the nature of the date and dollar amount fields in the DTD are well described by the Schema.

In this fragment, we declare the ownership of the attribute's element by a prefix: **EssentialGuide:cust**. That ownership extends to the actual element definition **<element name="cust">**. And much to our relief and to the computer's satisfaction, the next two lines also inherit that ownership by EssentialGuide:

```
<attribute name="name" type="string" use="required"/>
<attribute name="type" type="string" use="required"/>
```

That is, our names **name** and **type** (the ones in quotes) share the namespace protection given to **cust**. So the computer knows whether the owner of **name** and **type** is EssentialGuide or the underlying schema-compliant engine.

SCHEMA-AWARE TOOLS ....

XML Schema, we say once again, is itself an XML application. That is, Schema itself is a single XML document type, defined in turn by its own schema. The payoff from this for the XML workplace is that XML schema-aware tools and products are more straightforward to develop. That means that we can expect to see a convincing variety of schema-enabled editors, document managers, conversion utilities, and styling tools. One such tool is XMLSpy. In Figure 12.3 the main screen depicts the structure of our work-order schema, with the first element (**wo.id**) highlighted. In the lower screen we can view or edit the datatype of our two date-related attributes (**date.issu** and **date.comp**). They are both currently set to **date**.

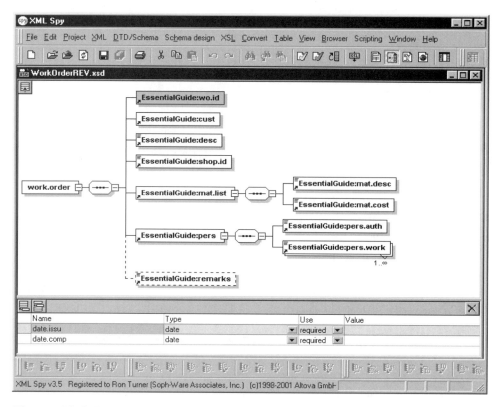

Figure 12.3 The work-order schema structure

The W3C (http://www.w3.org/XML/Schema), lists 11 commercial and open source tools for validating schemas. Most of these are freely available for downloading. These products can perform a variety of tasks: translations (DTD to Schema), navigation within a schema, editing a schema, and even tutoring a schema novice on repairs to an invalid schema, for example. That list (excluding the description of each product) follows:

- XSV, an Open Source XML Schema Validator, with web-form access from University of Edinburgh/W3C (beta) (update Jul 06 2001)

- XSU, an Open Source upgrade transform from the 20001024 to the 20010330 version; free web-form access, from University of Edinburgh/ W3C (beta)

- Microsoft XML Parser (MSXML) 4.0 B2 supports XML Schema validation and type discovery with both DOM and SAX. It is available free from the MSDN XML site, exact location.
- xerces-j 1.4.1 released lmartin@ca.ibm.com (Mon, Jun 25 2001)
- xsbrowser v1.0 released Joerg Rieger Jun 23 2001
- dtd2xs v1.0 released Joerg.Rieger@informatik.med.uni-giessen.de (Tue, Jun 19 2001)
- Xerces-C 1.5.0 is now available Tinny Ng 18 Jun 2001
- Final Release of the new XML Spy 4.0 Suite is now available Altova Sep 10 2001
- Sun's XML Datatypes Library Kohsuke KAWAGUCHI May 04 2001
- IBM XML Schema Quality Checker. Bob Schloss of IBM describes this tool this way:
- Commercial XML Schema (and others) aware streaming validator from TIBCO Extensibility

Schema as under construction

The XML Schema specification is a full W3C recommendation as of May 2, 2001. So it will not materially change over the next several years. But in spite of all the benefits we have spelled out in this chapter, and in spite of the bulk of news, tutorials, and white papers that publicize XML Schema, it is a fledgling technology. This is because of (1) the politics that have swirled around the specification, (2) the difficulty of understanding the released recommendation, and (3) the reluctance of beleaguered managers to invest in yet another unproven technology.

AS THE SPECIFICATION SAYS ....

The W3C XML Schema recommendation is in fact a cluster of three parts: Part 0 "Primer," Part 1 "Structures," and Part 2 "Datatypes." Here are the abstracts for each of those parts:

XML Schema Part 0: Primer

Abstract

XML Schema Part 0: Primer is a non-normative document intended to provide an easily readable description of the XML Schema facilities, and is oriented towards quickly understanding how to create schemas using the XML Schema language. XML Schema Part 1: Structures and XML Schema Part 2: Datatypes provide the complete normative description of the XML Schema language. This primer describes the language features through numerous examples which are complemented by extensive references to the normative texts.

XML Schema Part 1: Structures

Abstract

XML Schema: Structures specifies the XML Schema definition language, which offers facilities for describing the structure and constraining the contents of XML 1.0 documents, including those which exploit the XML Namespace facility. The schema language, which is itself represented in XML 1.0 and uses namespaces, substantially reconstructs and considerably extends the capabilities found in XML 1.0 document type definitions (DTDs). This specification depends on XML Schema Part 2: Datatypes.

XML Schema Part 2: Datatypes

Abstract

XML Schema: Datatypes is part 2 of the specification of the XML Schema language. It defines facilities for defining datatypes to be used in XML Schemas as well as other XML specifications. The datatype language, which is itself represented in XML 1.0, provides a superset of the capabilities found in XML 1.0 document type definitions (DTDs) for specifying datatypes on elements and at

FOUR REASONS WHY XML SCHEMA MAKES GOOD SENSE ....

1. *Decreased front-loaded cost of entry.* Because Schema comes with so many built-in mechanisms for specifying and controlling *datatypes*, there is far less need for custom programming. For example you can specify *precisely* how many items you will allow on a single work order or the maximum number of empty-the-shopping-cart commands that your order-taking web page will allow.

2. *Lower cost of ownership.* The skill level requirement is high for an XML professional who can intelligently build, revise, and maintain a DTD-based XML system. With Schema, that cost is reduced, because the only skills required are (1) the ability to read XML itself and (2) the ability to use a schema editing tool. The task is further simplified because the schema manager needs to be familiar with only a single XML document type, XML Schema itself.

3. *Efficient learning curve.* Exploit all that you know about XML documents in order to read XML schemas. They're only another document type. And every XML schema is only an instance of the very same document type. While there is a grammar (a set of restrictions) for how to

write a DTD, there is an extremely wide variation of style and complexity from one DTD to the next.

4. *Lower cost of integration with legacy databases.* Schema incorporates much more granular, database-like definition (and therefore control) of XML content. Now, for example, you can specify *precisely* how many items you will allow on a single work order or the maximum number of times your order-taking web page will allow the customer to abandon her shopping cart and still remain logged in. This results in reduced costs for custom programming to filter and preprocess XML data as it moves in and out of your databases.

XML SCHEMA: SUMMARY......................................

W3C's XML Schema, released as a formal recommendation on May 2, 2001, is an ambitious and complex piece of the XML family. XML Schema is itself an XML language, an application of XML. That means that it has its own set of allowable elements and tags, its own structure, and its own datatypes. This collection of XML rules constitutes the syntax side of Schema. It is therefore a straightforward task to study Schema in the same way that we study any other XML language.

13 Entities

In this chapter...

They Said It...

Entia non sunt multiplicanda
"Don't proliferate entities" (Occam's Razor)
William of Occam

Everything we have said about the content of XML has had to do with its *logical* structure. True, XML represents a new paradigm of data handling. But it is data nonetheless and we must handle it physically. The methods we use for physically storing, managing, and retrieving XML data are somewhat the same as for any other physical content. The value that XML adds to physical management is that its formal specification makes it easier for logical management across boundaries of disparate platforms, heterogeneous operating systems, and multivendor databases. The XML mechanism we use for physically manipulating data is the **entity**. While the details of entities can be complicated, the concept is simple and compelling.

THE INDISPENSABLE LAYER: WHY?......................

Structured content is physical as well as logical. The mechanisms of tagging and structural type definitions (DTDs, schemas) make it possible for you to convey your content's logical structure to any parser on anyone's XML system. That in itself recommends XML as a breakthrough technology. But conveying structure is not enough to accomplish productive information handling. In order for e-publishing and e-commerce to exploit XML data for serious use, XML data must behave as data.

XML must work with my legacy data. Most of the readers of this book already have a costly investment in stored data which is managed by a licensed database product, proprietary, or home grown application. Most likely you do not have the luxury of building a pure XML database from scratch. And you probably cannot fund a massive reconversion of legacy data to XML. The most likely scenario is that XML will somehow need to interface with an existing database. So whatever you decide to accomplish for your data with XML, your XML system must integrate with off-the-shelf data products.

Compound XML content requires a separate management layer. Apart from a large legacy data store, you will almost certainly create, manage, and exchange large numbers of XML data packages. These may be e-mail messages, transaction records, images, and Web pages. Most often, your content will be of the **compound** variety: mixed fragments of text, images, encrypted data, and system information. Handling compound content requires a separate layer of activity. This layer is not concerned with the internal logical structure of the content. It is concerned with locating and aggregating physical pieces.

Repurposing XML data requires XML entities. You have very likely heard that XML is about repurposing, reusing fragments as part of many items of content. Using XML entities is the most straightforward approach for fragment reuse.

XML entities support collaboration. The most typical workflow scenario for creating content is that several people and perhaps some computers will collaborate. And these creators and editors may not be in the same room or even the same hemisphere. The physical layer of this information activity must monitor and broker the activity of distributed, collaborative content creation.

The XML **general entity** is the mechanism that supports this critical physical layer of the information sandwich.

HOW DOES IT WORK?......................................

At first glance:

Element and entity, both three-syllable words and both starting with "e",—are confusing to me. And the definitions I've heard so far make it difficult to distinguish between them.

If XML entities are about stored content, then how is an XML approach to storage any better than what I've already got with my licensed database product?

The new version of my database product promises to be XML-aware. Doesn't that mean that I can ignore entities and just let the database handle my XML?

So if XML entities are about physical objects and their storage, I presume that entities are the way to incorporate non-XML data (video, audio, graphics) into XML content. I certainly hope so, because I've seen nothing so far in the logical markup mechanism that accounts for non-XML data.

I've browsed through several introductory books on XML, and each one seems to have a unique way of discussing how entities are used. Are they an essential part of the specification or not? If they are, then where exactly do they fit my organization's workflow?

What are Entities? (Executive Overview)

The concept of entities is simple enough. They represent the layer of the information sandwich that deals with actual physical data. The types of entities and their definitions assume that you are as concerned about the *management* of content as you are about expressing its *structure* and *appearance*. The only slightly unfortunate aspect of the definition is that entity begins with e and has three syllables, the same as element. Because of that and the somewhat subtle distinction between logical structure and physical storage, newcomers to XML often fail to appreciate the starring role of entities. The following sections should help to make the distinction convincingly clear. Being clear about entities will help you see exactly what's behind the claim that XML content is portable and reusable. Without the participation of entities, those claims would simply not be true. A simple example will demonstrate that.

Managing physical data is a well understood and appreciated part of IT. Off-the-shelf content management tools allow us to index it, store it, protect it, search it, retrieve it, aggregate and reassemble its pieces, and present it in whatever way the customer or end user desires. The problem with every such product and tool is that the particular units of storage and the methods for handling the data are often proprietary. Therefore once a fragment of your data is hosted by a particular content management system, you are virtually locked in to that vendor's product if you want to keep working with that data fragment.

XML entities are a vendor-neutral method for creating, identifying, and storing physical pieces of content. As entities, your physical data exposes itself in a consistent manner to any XML system. As physical data fragments, however long or short, you can use virtually any content management product and still not be captive to a vendor.

But why the additional overhead of entities? Why not simply treat elements as manageable units and store the content as elements? The simple answer is that you (or your e-commerce servers) create elements to be consumed by parsers. And the parser's job is to recognize logical structure and to reconstitute the original record or page. But when the consumer is a content management system, then you expect management of actual physical data. XML entities allow for precisely this kind of physical management.

But is it not possible to forget entities and simply store and manage elements directly? Yes. Many XML-aware content management systems do in fact allow for direct manipulation of XML logical elements as physical units of storage. So is it really all that detrimental to ignore the distinction between logical and physical? Perhaps not for a very modest XML system. But for a serious XML initiative that hopes for a long and productive life cycle, entities have an essential role.

What Is an Entity (Close-up Discussion)?

Warning: This chapter is not a complete and balanced presentation of XML entities. Nor do we even seek to explain fully the syntactic details within the examples. There are in fact five varieties of entities in XML, each with a legitimate role for systems design and development. Our goal is simply to highlight the most obvious value and benefits that XML general entities offer. We have chosen to highlight **external parsed general entities** in the following example. Another is known as **parameter entities**, which are for authoring and maintaining DTDs.

In the simplest case, an XML entity is any physical unit of text that bears a name and that can be invoked for inclusion within some XML content. You use the name to reference the text. There are five such entities that are built in to XML that demonstrate this referencing notion well. These are **internal** and are built in to (**declared** by) XML itself. You invoke them by name. An entity's name (**reference**) always begins with **&**. Each of these named entities invokes a single character: **<** (for the < symbol), **&** (for the **&** itself), **>** (the > symbol), **"** (double quote), and **'** (apostrophe or single quote). This little repertoire allows us to avoid using the symbols that would otherwise confuse the parser of our XML content. For example, the following line of text would have "broken" our demo in Chapter 12:

```
<policy>
      <section>Payroll & Benefits</section>
      <steward>Human Resources</steward>
</policy>
```

No matter what we intend for our XML data to accomplish, the front-line consumer of that data is an XML parser. Unfortunately for the XML file containing this fragment, the parser sees the "&" and thinks that the following text is the name of an entity. This is because & is the symbol for the start of an **entity reference**. To prevent the parser from misreading the ampersand, we wrote the fragment as follows:

```
<policy>
      <section>Payroll &amp; Benefits</section>
      <steward>Human Resources</steward>
</policy>
```

By referencing an entity, we mean that we wish to invoke (i.e., pull in) some passage of text. That text will then become part of the content when it is sent to the browser, to the printer, to the wireless device, to the business partner's server, or wherever. In this small example the entity consisted of a single character. We turn now to collaborative authoring, in which the entity could be considerably larger and more complex.

ENTITIES OF DISTRIBUTED CONTENT: ONE-TO-MANY

Figure 13.1 shows how a piece of content may be only a shell consisting of entity references:

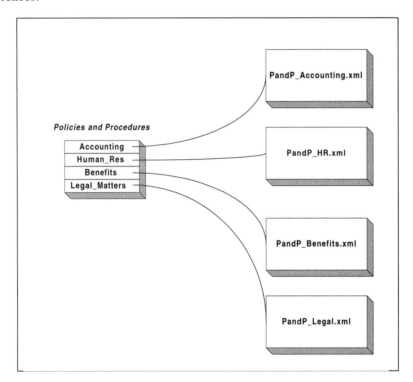

Figure 13.1 *A shell document*

The shell document ("Policies and Procedures") consists only of names of (references to) the actual content (entities). The XML representation of this layout is as straightforward as the picture.

```
<?xml version="1.0"?>
<!DOCTYPE PandPManual [
<!ENTITY Accounting SYSTEM "./chapterSegs/PandP_Accounting.xml" >
<!ENTITY Human_Res SYSTEM "./chapterSegs/PandP_HR.xml" >
<!ENTITY Benefits SYSTEM "./chapterSegs/PandP_Benefits.xml" >
<!ENTITY Legal_Matters SYSTEM "./chapterSegs/PandP_Legal.xml" >

<!ELEMENT PandPManual (Title, Chapter+) >
<!ELEMENT Title (#PCDATA) >
<!ELEMENT Chapter (#PCDATA)>
]>
```

```
<PandPManual>
      <Title>Policies and Procedures</Title>
      <Chapter>&Accounting;</Chapter>
      <Chapter>&Human_Res;</Chapter>
      <Chapter>&Benefits;</Chapter>
      <Chapter>&Legal_Matters;</Chapter>
</PandPManual>
```

We stated at the outset of this chapter that parsers deal with logical structure, leaving physical affairs to a content manager (document management, file management). But while parsers are not the ultimate consumers of physical file information, they rely heavily on entity information in order to do their job. In our walkthrough which follows we are really acting the part of the XML parser.

A validating parser's central mission is to recognize the elements of XML content, and to verify that those elements conform to a DTD. In order to accomplish that for this example, the parser needs to locate the various fragments (the `.xml` files) that make up the content of the manual. Furthermore the parser needs to analyze each of the entities, treating them and the core holding document as if they were all part of a single physical whole.

EXECUTIVE TALKTHROUGH ....

The mechanical aspect (syntax) of markup for an entity is utterly simple in concept:

1. *Declare the entity.* The current document, "Policies and Procedures" in our example, needs to know how to refer to each entity when it invokes it later. The entity may be in some location other than the current document. XML calls such an entity **external**.

2. *Reference the entity.* The shell document now calls up the actual entity. It may be a word, a logo, a paragraph of boilerplate, or a chapter written by someone in a branch office several time zones away.

The actual physical *location* of the file containing an entity may be unknown to the author. But that is not the author's concern. The author needs to know only the *name* of the entity.

So the first markup task is to declare the entities. We do that in this example for each of the stored chapters using an **<!ENTITY>** tag. Within each declaration we provide the name of the stored entity, and directions on how to find it:

```
<!ENTITY Accounting SYSTEM "./chapterSegs/PandP_Accounting.xml" >
<!ENTITY Human_Res SYSTEM "./chapterSegs/PandP_HR.xml" >
<!ENTITY Benefits SYSTEM "./chapterSegs/PandP_Benefits.xml" >
<!ENTITY Legal_Matters SYSTEM "./chapterSegs/PandP_Legal.xml" >
```

This time we have also highlighted the locating information for each entity. For this small demo, the locating information says to the parser "From the directory you're already in (the "**.**" means "start here"), go into the subdirectory called chapter-Segs and look for this file." These are instances of **parsed external general entities**. That means the parser actually uses each of these locating instructions to validate the material inside those remote files as well as the local text "Policies and Procedures." The contents of the file **PandP_Accounting.xml** happen to be simply the character string "Accounting stuff." To repeat, using a direct entity reference like **&Accounting;** is the method for including *parsed* entities in the compound document. For unparsed entities (non-XML data) the approach is different, as we shall see shortly.

The remainder of the document declaration is the DTD, describing the three element types that comprise the logical structure of the publication. The only local text that this markup holds is the title. The rest of the document is entity references. With that the parser is able to traverse the material for the entire document and pronounce all of the content as both **well-formed** and **valid**. The parser is able to do this because all of the content is plain-text XML. We turn next to the common issue of graphical, video, and audio content, which is of course not textual, not XML and therefore cannot be parsed and validated at all. How do we present that content to the parser?

UNPARSED ENTITIES FOR NON-XML DATA.............

An XML parser clearly cannot interpret the internals of an unstructured graphics, video, or audio file. Yet it is important that we be able to include unstructured data along with structured XML text in a compound document. This is a common practice in XML, but the precise approach is not generally agreed upon.

In practice, the most straightforward and common method is to include a single **empty element** in our XML file. Thus if the HR office wished to include a drug policy training video for new employees, it might include the following line in the electronic **PandP_Manual**:

```
<video storage_loc="http://tg118.tech-group.com/training/drug_policy.mov"/>
```

This method (a single-line empty element callout of an unparsed entity) is not the approach in the XML specification. The specification tells us to declare and use an external unparsed entity as follows:

```
[Declaration:]
<!ENTITY drug_film SYSTEM "http://tg118.tech-group.com/training/drug_
     NDATA mov>

<!NOTATION mov SYSTEM "video/mpeg">

<!ELEMENT new_hire_movie EMPTY>
<!ATTRIBUTE new_hire_movie storage_loc ENTITY #REQUIRED>


[Within document:]
<new_hire_movie storage_loc="drug_film"/>
```

The net result of either approach is that the parser knows that this or that non-XML file is part of the content it is analyzing. But it also knows that it cannot penetrate that file in any way. The parser simply completes its task without manipulating the external entities. The scenario of a hands-off parser is in fact the normal case for most serious XML publishing systems.

And what of the browser? While the parser may learn something of the location and type of non-XML data, the parser is only the first-line consumer. Beyond that, it is the responsibility of processing software to do something meaningful with that data. At this time in computing history, there is no guarantee that a browser will do anything meaningful with the code we presented in our example, regardless of how XML-conforming our approach may be. Simply put, we may lack the plug-in to display or play it.

HOW DO YOU CREATE ENTITIES? ....

Entities are physical data. An entity may be native XML data, consisting of valid or well-formed markup. Or it may be an entire non-XML piece of audio or video data. It may, in fact, be a proprietary word processing file, with no XML markup inside at all. Creating entities involves two rather separate tasks: design and production.

Designing for entities requires the author or data specialist to be aware of how the pieces of data will behave. That is, he or she must decide which pieces to treat as physically separate building blocks. In a long and complex publication, for example, it is simply a good design principle to treat the document as an orderly collection of components rather than as a single, cumbersome file. If there is more than one author of the document, then there is no choice. Collaborative authoring demands a component approach. XML was certainly not the prime motivator of collaborative authoring, but XML entities provide the ideal solution for component management. The designer of a long publication will therefore create a document using a component approach with entities, as we saw in our example.

Each author works independently on content that is stored in a separate physical file. When it is time to compile the entire book for review or release, then the editor runs an XML entity management program to collect all of the separate entities into a unified whole. There are several robust and mature publication tools that support collaborative publishing.

But you or your editor or your authors may not be the creators of e-publishing entities. That may in fact be the job of an XML loading program that automatically generates high-volume files for your organization to store, process, and distribute. The loader relies on a formatting spec to know precisely where to segment each piece of the data. The designer has built into the program enough intelligence to name each segment in some way that uniquely identifies it to your internal system. Those named segments are now XML entities. Unless you have licensed a native XML database product, the loader shakes hands with your in-house database, handing over each XML entity to be stored and managed.

But how can you have the best of both worlds, highly portable XML entities and the built-in naming and storage conventions of your database? It is likely that the loader will in fact create a mapping file, a scheme that matches each XML entity with its database form. This enables the document management system to support XML in an intelligent manner.

ENTITIES AS REUSABLE OBJECTS ....

The most frequently touted advantage of XML is that its content is *reusable*, that you only have to write it (or assemble it or compile it) once, and that's that. The same boilerplate will magically be updated in an entire series of electronic manuals. The same new or revised art will immediately appear in the entire suite of the company's Web pages. The same updated earnings figures or tariffs or tax rates will immediately appear in all 38 financial reports that rely on that data. The benefit from each of these advantages is of course the same: dramatically reduced cost of information management.

That claim is entirely true but only if the reusable objects are entities. Figure 13.2 represents two very different online financial records that rely on the prime lending rate.

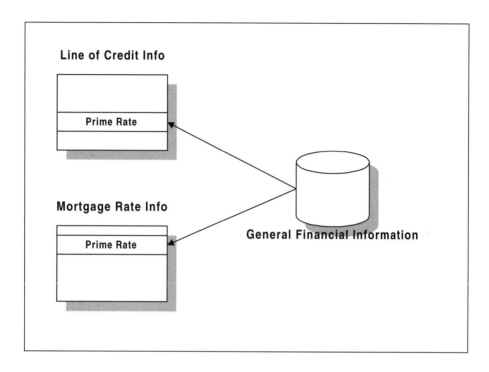

Figure 13.2 *A single entity supplies two applications*

Each of the records must reflect the effects of changes in the prime lending rate in real time. One will report the amount owing on a company's line of credit. The other is an online promotion for home mortgages. As we saw earlier, the rules of XML markup make it a straightforward matter to reference a remote entity (here, the physical access point for the prime lending rate). In this case two XML applications are referencing the same (external) entity. There could just as easily be two hundred or two thousand. That is inconsequential. The monumental issue is that there is only a single entity supplying them all.

IF NO ENTITIES THEN WHAT?...............................

We said earlier that it is possible to store XML elements directly. So for just a moment, let us assume that the XML entity mechanism did not exist. Would it still be possible for multiple XML documents or content to reuse or repurpose (i.e., share) some piece of data? Suppose that a writer spots some logical element

(`<generic.warning>`) in a particular XML safety notice that is necessary to be shared across a chemical producer's entire product line. That element, existing as a subelement in a particular document must somehow be shared by several online advisories in the company's catalog. That is the solution that we demonstrated in Figure 13.2. The shared prime rate data is located physically as an XML entity on only a single storage device and referenced from many documents that need to use it. But this time there is no entity mechanism.

In this entity-challenged environment, it may happen that the `<generic.warning>` element is physically embedded (as an *element*) in a single document. In this case it is largely up to the programmers to implement shared or repurposed elements. The problem is that the original document, the one containing the embedded subelement of interest, is likely stored as a single file. If there were not some special mechanism for keeping `<generic.warning>` visible to the rest of the document set, it would remain locked up in that single document. In order to make it visible and sharable, the programmers or some special tool must allow the user to specify certain elements as sharable or reusable. The system must then be able to flag those items or set them apart in a separate database.

Two observations about this scenario:

- The element-only approach is quite common among XML editing and document management products. And because specialized software is required, the approach almost invariably ties the data and the user to a particular vendor's method of implementing stored elements.

- Whether it is the vendor's element-only solution or something home-grown by the developers in your organization, the solution turns out to be a reinvention of XML entities. And typically, no matter how clever the implementation, it is more complicated than working with XML entities in the first place.

How Does a Document (Content) Management System Work with Entities?

If it's a native XML document management (DM) or Content Management (CM) system, it can recognize formal XML entity declarations. As a native XML system, it will resolve all of the XML-to-physical problems automatically.

More than likely, you do not have the luxury of shopping for the optimum XML content management (CM) system and starting your system design from scratch. So if you would like for your existing CM and/or database system to support XML entities, you must make those entities visible to your system.

No matter what it is called, and no matter what degree of ingenuity you bring to bear, the critical piece of your integration puzzle will be *entity mapping*. Your designers (or programmers or database specialists) will have to build the critical link between entity references and the actual stored files that contain those entities. Mapping an entity means to spell out the association between an entity's location and the references to that location The mapping scheme must be fast, allowing for instant updates to every XML document and record that contains entity references. And it must be smart, aware of every such document or record that reference a particular entity that has just been updated.

Why Not Just Files?

The end-of-chapter list of benefits will help articulate a value proposition for entities. But a data management policy for XML is more than an exercise in check-list features. It must articulate carefully the role of XML entities, if there is to be such a strategy. To plan for an entity-based approach will dictate a certain agenda for vendor selection, integration, conversions, workflow, and training. So the do-entities-or-not issue is more central than most.

The place of entities in the XML landscape is to provide a standardized method of dividing, distributing, and reaggregating physical pieces of XML content. As with files, you can name entities. As with files, you can assign protection and access codes to entities. As with files, you can add metadata (descriptions of the data) to entities. Then how is an entity any different from an ordinary file? And why bother with this part of XML if it only adds new terminology and standards baggage to our work?

There are several attractive advantages and benefits in using entities for the design of XML content. We offer that list at the end of this chapter. But the most immediate and compelling benefits to your content are longevity and portability, benefits that are built in to the very definition of entity. Each section of the employees' manual, because it is a physically separate XML entity, is readily accessible to its authors. The publisher of the manual can issue a revision of the entire manual with near-zero editorial effort, because the manual is entity-savvy. Entities are separate physical clusters of elements. And that guarantees a maximized life cycle for the document.

Entities are built in to the XML specification, as we have seen. Defined as physical segments of XML content, they are the primary access point for managing the content. We have stressed that XML, using elements and DTDs, makes the logical structure immediately understandable across the enterprise and beyond. The same is true for entities. All of the entity-related markup that you insert in your content can be easily transported elsewhere. This kind of easily transportable content management is simply not possible with traditional file management alone.

AS THE SPECIFICATION SAYS... ....

XML 1.0, section 4. Physical Structures

[Definition:] An XML document may consist of one or many storage units. These are called entities; they all have content and are all (except for the document entity, see below, and the external DTD subset) identified by name. Each XML document has one entity called the document entity, which serves as the starting point for the XML processor and may contain the whole document.

Entities may be either parsed or unparsed. [Definition:] A parsed entity's contents are referred to as its replacement text; this text is considered an integral part of the document.

[Definition:] An unparsed entity is a resource whose contents may or may not be text, and if text, may not be XML. Each unparsed entity has an associated notation, identified by name. Beyond a requirement that an XML processor make the identifiers for the entity and notation available to the application, XML places no constraints on the contents of unparsed entities.

Parsed entities are invoked by name using entity references; unparsed entities by name, given in the value of **ENTITY** or **ENTITIES** attributes.

[Definition:] General entities are entities for use within the document content. In this specification, general entities are sometimes referred to with the unqualified term *entity* when this leads to no ambiguity. [Definition:] Parameter entities are parsed entities for use within the DTD. These two types of entities use different forms of reference and are recognized in different contexts. Furthermore, they occupy different namespaces; a parameter entity and a general entity with the same name are two distinct entities.

EIGHT REASONS WHY ENTITIES MAKE GOOD BUSINESS SENSE ....

Many of the frequently-heard benefits of XML are actually the benefits provided by XML entities. And since entities are most closely associated with files and databases, the benefits of entities are clear. They can be more easily perceived and articulated.

1. *Maintain-once-publish-everywhere.* An item of content can forever remain as a small, easily maintainable chunk of data. For frequently changing data objects like stock averages, commodity prices, weather conditions, and cargo tariffs, there is no practical alternative to the entity approach. The cost of manually and separately updating all 50-100 Web pages, online documents, and printer's masters would be prohibitive. But even for less volatile information like regulations boilerplate, it is easy to demonstrate the savings from maintaining only a single master electronic

copy as a remote entity. For publications, this approach results in near-zero-cost maintenance for widely shared items.

2. *Reduced cost for content management integration.* An off-the-shelf entity-aware content management system can add all of access control and versioning smarts that you wish to the chunks of your content.

3. *Longer life cycle and greater ROI in information investment.* With proper foresight and layered XML information design, your entity-based content will never break, even though the chunks reside on far-flung databases or computers and the physical locations of those chunks may change over time.

4. *Low-cost metadata for efficient searches.* Entities are physical storage items, allowing for metadata of your choosing. Adding even minimal metadata to your XML content will make your search and retrieval of XML data both smart and fast.

5. *Minimized skill sets for data management.* XML entities are strictly physical and similar to familiar data paradigms. The skill sets required for technicians to manage them does not require knowledge of the entire set of XML technologies.

6. *Reduced migration costs.* Because a truly entity-based system avoids proprietary methods of segmenting and referencing data, you can more easily port your XML system to a new platform.

7. *Lowered cost of entry for syndicated information.* For the same reasons, you can syndicate your entire content set, including the distributed chunks of XML data, to any native XML system.

8. *Lowered cost of entry for dynamic personalization.* By including a minimal entity management program with your content, you can distribute your content for just-in-time (JIT) profiling and personalization on the user's desktop. If your online content (e.g., catalogs, parts lists, learning material) is stored as XML entities, you can likewise customize and personalize that content at a reasonable cost. This is all the more true if you elect to license an online portal or e-commerce product that directly supports XML markup and entities.

SUMMARY ....

The topic of entities per se is somewhat confusing, thanks to the existence of five varieties of entities in the XML specification. But there are compelling business arguments for parsed external general entities in particular. XML element markup enables a robust mechanism for managing and porting the *logical structure* of XML information. But XML entities represent the *physical* content management side of structured information. By specifying a framework for defining and referencing physical data, the task of getting XML to perform useful work is greatly eased. The practical problems of dealing with legacy data is straightforward, because XML entities allow for notations of any variety. XML is not just another file system. There are demonstrable benefits in making XML entities the center of a data strategy.

14 XPATH

In this chapter...

They Said It...

...Come early under laws
That can secure for you a path of light
Through gloomiest shade;

William Wordsworth: Sacrament

T he tree structure of XML makes content highly portable across an organization or among business partners. It also greatly simplifies the job of an XML processing engine as it finds its way around an XML document or record. We know that the structure of a valid or well-formed XML document is always a tree. (The specification calls this the "abstract, logical structure of an XML document.") So it should require only a modest effort to write a program to locate the parts of a particular document. But XPath has made it even better. Instead of your paying for unique design and original programming code, XPath offers an out-of-the-box language tailored precisely to navigating the tree structure of XML content. Fortunately a compact repertoire of XPath location directives supports the majority of location requirements. This chapter deals solely with XPath and concentrates on its essentials. With only a limited data sample we will view XPath in action as an efficient and precise locator of data. In actual practice the language works in tandem with other members of the XML specification family: XSLT and XPointer.

WHY DO I NEED YET MORE NOTATION? ....

Once again, XML is much more than neat stuff. We demand that XML content cut costs or increase earnings by reducing the cost of processing data or by presenting previously unavailable high level information that can be used for executive decision making. But beginning with this chapter we furthermore demand processing software that is able to manipulate, move, transform, and add value to that content. It is very straightforward for a programmer in your organization to write that software. The serious problem with that is that you are now encumbered with maintaining unique local utilities for processing your XML. Worse, you probably will not be able to share that software with the others with whom you exchange your XML content. Software is not yet enjoying the near-universal portability that data enjoys with XML.

Practically everything you hope to do with your XML content—manipulate, move, transform, add value—are out-of-the-box processes that come with the XML meal. But most of these XML processes entail XML navigation. The process must find its way around your XML document or record. It would be very painful for you to integrate nonstandard homegrown XML navigation software with each of these XML technologies.

Most of all, you need to understand how XPath works because XPath itself supports two other very important members of the XML family of specifications: Extensible Stylesheet Language Transformations (XSLT) and Extensible Pointers (XPointers).

Finally, because XML navigation is so basic to XML processing, we need a compact, readable, and universally understood language for IT humans (including managers). Learning the essential traveller's vocabulary of tree navigation pays off in being able to explain the behavior of your content.

HOW DOES IT WORK?...

At first glance:

There appears to be a uniformity problem with XPath. For practically every XML mechanism we have looked at so far, we have been able to represent the operation as XML. We can even represent a DTD as a schema, using pure XML. Not so with XPath.

The reason for this apparent anomaly is that XPath is a language in its own right. Unlike the language of XML, XPath really *is* a language, a programming language. Unlike C++ or Java, XPath is not a general-purpose language; it's not for engineering or graphics applications or even general XML applications. Rather its sole purpose is to locate nodes within an XML tree. It can also manipulate XML content to a limited degree, but it is primarily a node navigator.

Navigating a Tree: Sonnet as XML Document

In order to view XPath at work, we turn to a document type that is arguably the most tightly structured (in several languages), the sonnet. Here is Shakespeare's 23rd sonnet, rendered as XML:

```
<sonnet
  author="Shakespeare"
  title="23">
    <quatrain>
        <line>As an unperfect actor on the stage</line>
        <line>Who with his fear is put besides his part</line>
        <line>Or some fierce thing replete with too much rage,</line>
        <line>Whose strength's abundance weakens his own heart;</line
    </quatrain>
    <quatrain>
        <line>So I, for fear of trust, forget to say</line>
        <line>The perfect ceremony of love's rite,</line>
        <line>And in mine own love's strength seem to decay,</line>
        <line>O'ercharg'd with burthen of mine own love's might.</lin
    </quatrain>
    <tercet>
        <line>O, let my looks be then the eloquence</line>
        <line>And dumb presagers of my speaking breast</line>
        <line>Who plead for love, and look for recompense,</line>
    </tercet>
    <tercet>
        <line>More than that tongue that more hath more express'd.</l
        <line>O, learn to read what silent love hath writ!</line>
        <line>To hear with eyes belongs to love's fine wit.</line>
    </tercet>
</sonnet>
```

The sonnet represents a concise and highly restrictive document type. A sonnet consists of two groups of four lines each (two quatrains) followed by two groups of three lines each (two tercets). We are by now well acquainted with XML markup for structured text. We also recognize the embedding mechanism whereby certain elements are subelements of other elements. In this case a line is a subelement of a quatrain and of a tercet. And the quatrain and the tercet are subelements of a sonnet. By modifying slightly the layout of the XML listing, we can more easily visualize this XML document as a tree (see Figure 14.1).

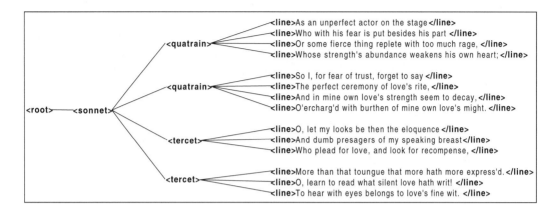

Figure 14.1 An XML document as a tree

The plain-English description of the structure of this XML tree, using XPath terminology, is as follows:

The topmost node of the entire tree is the **root**. (This is true for all XML documents.)

The **root element** of this document is **sonnet**.

The **sonnet element node** has four **child nodes**: two **quatrain** nodes and two **tercet** nodes.

The first quatrain node has four child nodes of type **line**.

The first **line** node contains "As an unperfect actor on the stage" as its **text node**.

Of course, we could have done an exhaustive description of the entire tree. The purpose of this miniwalkthrough is to note (1) the *hierarchical structure* of the tree and (2) the *sequential order* of the nodes. That is, using the language of trees, we identify the tenth line of the sonnet as being the second **line** of the first **tercet** of the **sonnet**. Note that there is a variety of node types in XPath, seven in all. We have drawn attention to three: **root**, **element**, and **text**.

The whole purpose of XPath is to provide a language that expresses locations in a tree-specific manner. And it does so much more tersely than we did. It uses symbols and keywords rather than whole phrases. After a survey of essential XPath, we shall return to Shakespeare's 23rd sonnet to watch XPath in action.

ESSENTIAL SYNTAX..

Word usage note: we use *syntax* in this book to mean mechanical aspects of the language. Syntax is the rule set defining how a developer is to write things. Every language has its syntax. XML's syntax specifies, for example, how tags are to be written and placed. A language's syntax exists in order for programmers to write expressions, commands that allow the language to do useful work. In this chapter we will cover an essential traveler's guide of XPath syntax and expressions.

As a programming language, XPath has inherited some of the syntactic lore that is common knowledge to hands-on users, programmers, and data specialists in the UNIX world. This is not surprising because UNIX is a totally tree-structured universe. Certain terms and symbols are now widely recognized conventions. Here is a list of a few of those conventions. With each we include simply a definition-by-example, not a formal definition:

context node – My current location in the tree. See the shorthand notation, using the period.

document root node – This is the node called **root**. While it may seem like splitting hairs to distinguish between this and the root element, that is the relationship that an XML tool sees. See the single slash shorthand notation.

document root element – In our example this is **sonnet**.

descendant – In our tree, every element below **sonnet** is a descendant of **sonnet**. The second set of four **lines** are descendants of the first **quatrain**, and of **sonnet**.

children – The first-generation descendants of the context node. If the context node is the second tercet, then the children are the last three lines of the sonnet.

parent – The second quatrain is the parent of the second cluster of four lines.

grandchildren – The two quatrains and the two tercets are the grandchildren of the document root node. The entire set of all of the lines of the sonnet are the grandchildren of the sonnet element node.

/ [forward slash] – When it appears alone or at the head of an XPath expression this is shorthand for document root node.

. [single dot] – This is shorthand for context node.

.. [two dots] – This is shorthand for parent node, the level just above the context node. If the current node happens to be the fifth line of the sonnet then the parent would be the second quatrain.

// – This is shorthand for all of the descendants of the context node. If the context node is sonnet, then **//** would select every element below sonnet.

path – The formal description of how to get from the current node to a node somewhere else in the document. The examples which follow will include path expressions.

SELECTING NODES: LOCATION PATHS AND LOCATION STEPS..

We use XPath syntax to construct XPath expressions. There are various types of expressions, but the one that is of greatest interest to us is **location path**. The location path means somewhat the same thing as the precise directory or folder location of a report or memo or spreadsheet on your hard disk. It is a way for you (or your computer) to find your way back to the document, beginning at the top, or the root however you choose to think of the tree. A location path assumes (1) that you are at a given location in the tree and (2) that, from that location, you wish to locate (identify) other elements (or other types of nodes). The first item is the context node. The second item is a location step. More picky detail over terminology, it would seem, but the two-part description is a rather good working definition of location path: an expression specifying that (1) you are here and (2) you want to select a node from there.

The most succinct location path is the very top of the document, identifying the node that includes all others. This is the root location path (Refer to Figure 14.1 to recall the difference.) The authors of the XPath specification borrowed a useful item of shorthand from the UNIX world to identify this single location path: /. By simply using the slash you have placed yourself at the document root node and have identified the entire document, including all of the nodes beneath the root. As a cultural background note, UNIX users, until rather recently, have been forced to be constantly aware of where they are located in UNIX's tree-structured file system. That is why the UNIX port of their shorthand is such a natural.

XPATH MEETS THE BARD....................................

In this brief exhibit we will display a variety of XPath expressions, each defining a location path to select segments of Shakespeare's sonnet 23. There is a transformation engine at work behind the scenes, an XSLT processor that specializes in accessing XML trees. The processing engine uses our XPath expressions, together with XSLT code, to create alternate HTML browser files. We shall experiment with seven different groups of XPath expressions and view the seven renditions of the sonnet that they produce. (Our most sincere apologies to William and to the Modern Language Association for this butchery, albeit for a good cause!). In each case we first display some lines from the XSLT procedure, highlighting the XPath expressions. Then we state in plain English what the XPath notation accomplishes. Next we show the result of applying the procedure. (see Figure 14.2).

XPath Exhibit #1: All lines of each quatrain, all lines of each tercet

```
<xsl:for-each select = "/sonnet/quatrain">

    <xsl:for-each select = "line">
         <xsl:value-of select = "."/><br/>
    </xsl:for-each><br/>
</xsl:for-each>
</p><p><xsl:for-each select = "/sonnet/tercet">

    <xsl:for-each select = "line">
         <xsl:value-of select = "."/><br/>
    </xsl:for-each><br/>
</xsl:for-each>
```

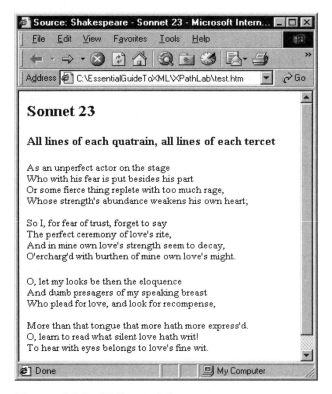

Figure 14.2 *All lines of the sonnet*

The XPath expression **/sonnet/quatrain** instructs XSLT to locate the quatrain elements as the context nodes. Note that the initial **/** is the root node. So we may describe the location path of the quatrain nodes as root–>sonnet–>quatrain. The next selection is for each **line**. With each **line** identified in turn as the context node, the single dot tells the HTML outputting mechanism "Take this line as the value of your next piece of output."

XPath Exhibit #2: All but the final line of each quatrain

```
<xsl:for-each select = "/sonnet/quatrain">

    <xsl:for-each select = "line[position()!=last()]">
        <xsl:value-of select = "."/><br/>
    </xsl:for-each><br/>
</xsl:for-each>
```

The location path is root–>sonnet–>quatrain. But this time with **line[position()!=last()]** we limit the lines to display, disallowing the last line (see Figure 14.3). This XPath expression says "take each line in the quatrain context as long as it does not occupy the last position in the quatrain." (**!=** means not equal to.)

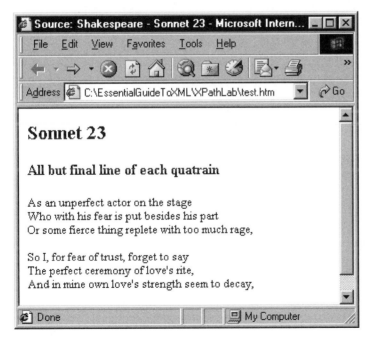

Figure 14.3 *All but some final lines*

Exhibit #3: Last two lines of each tercet

```
<xsl:for-each select = "/sonnet/tercet">
    <xsl:for-each select = "line[position() &gt; 1]">
        <xsl:value-of select = "."/><br/>
</xsl:for-each>
```

The location path for the initial context node is root–>sonnet–>tercet. Then, as it visits each of the lines within each tercet, XPath checks to determine that the line is not in the first position. If a line passes that test, the XSLT engine outputs the line (see Figure 14.4). The single dot (in quotes) identifies that line.

Figure 14.4 The last two lines of the tercet

Exhibit #4: All lines of entire sonnet

```
<xsl:template match="/">
      :
      :
    <xsl:for-each select = ".//line">
        <xsl:value-of select = "."/><br/>
    </xsl:for-each><br/
```

This selection relies almost totally on XPath expressions, and those expressions require only nine characters in all. The initial **/** selection fixes the initial context at the root. The expression **.//line** directs the engine to select all of the root's line element descendants (see Figure 14.5). And the single dot again directs the engine to output repeatedly the current element node, which is the line element.

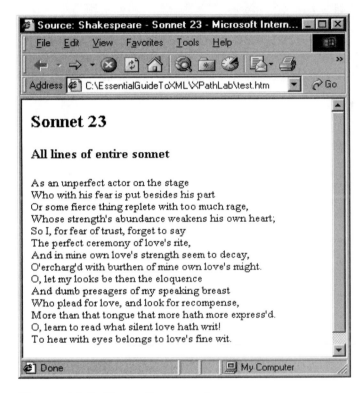

Figure 14.5 The entire sonnet

Exhibit #5: Second line of each quatrain

```
<xsl:for-each select = "/sonnet/quatrain">
    <xsl:for-each select = "line[2]">
        <xsl:value-of select = "."/><br/>
    </xsl:for-each>
```

The expression **/sonnet/quatrain** sets the context as being the series of the two quatrains. Within that context **line[2]** selects the second line of each quatrain (see Figure 14.6).

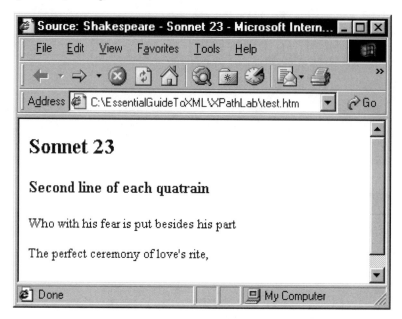

Figure 14.6 Second line of each quatrain

Exhibit #6: All lines of the second quatrain

```
<xsl:for-each select = "/sonnet/quatrain[2]">
    <xsl:for-each select = "line">
        <xsl:value-of select = "."/><br/>
    </xsl:for-each ><br/>
</xsl:for-each>
```

The first XPath expression **/sonnet/quatrain[2]** defines the location path for the context as root–>sonnet–>quatrain #2. The expression **line** locates each of the lines within the second quatrain (see Figure 14.7).

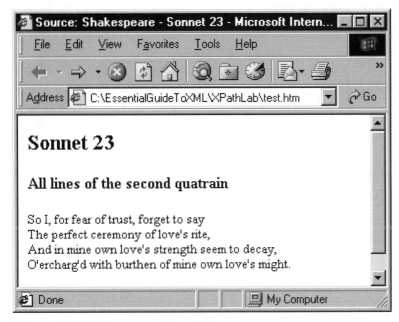

Figure 14.7 The second quatrain

Exhibit #7: All lines of the sonnet, sorted by length

```
<xsl:template match="sonnet">
        :
        :
<xsl:for-each select = ".//line">
    <xsl:sort select = "string-length(.)" order = "ascending"/>
            <xsl:value-of select = "."/><br/>
```

This is an example of XPath's ability as a language to participate in processing data. The program first sets the sonnet element as the context. With the expression **. /
/line** it tells the processor to select all of the descendants of the sonnet node. It hands those nodes over to the XSLT engine, which then sorts the lines

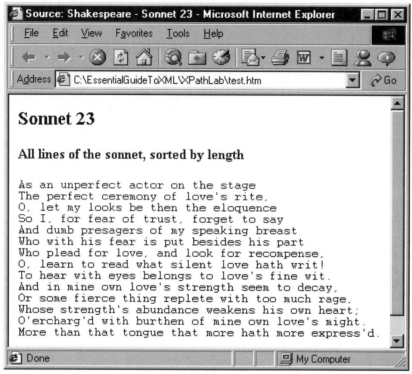

Figure 14.8 Lines sorted by length

AS THE SPECIFICATION SAYS... ....

XML Path Language (XPath)

Version 1.0

W3C Recommendation 16 November 1999

Abstract

XPath is a language for addressing parts of an XML document, designed to be used by both XSLT and XPointer.

1. Introduction

XPath is the result of an effort to provide a common syntax and semantics for functionality shared between XSL Transformations [XSLT] and XPointer [XPointer]. The primary purpose of XPath is to address parts of an XML [XML] document. In support of this primary purpose, it also provides basic facilities for manipulation of strings, numbers, and booleans. XPath uses a compact, non-XML syntax to facilitate use of XPath within URIs and XML attribute values. XPath operates on the abstract, logical structure of an XML document, rather than its surface syntax. XPath gets its name from its use of a path notation as in URLs for navigating through the hierarchical structure of an XML document.

FOUR REASONS WHY XPATH MAKES GOOD BUSINESS SENSE ....

1. *Near-zero programming cost for locating data.* If you are already working with native XML data, then you can readily apply the tools that manipulate the tree structures of XML. Those tools may rely on the document object model (DOM) or the simple API for XML (SAX) or both for their view of the tree. But the benefit for you is that you can remain totally indifferent as to how the tree materializes. You can assume that it has been reconstructed on demand. You simply use XPath to address your content. The various layered products and resources understand that addressing protocol immediately with no ad hoc programming on your part.

2. *Zero-cost maintenance of dynamic data locating mechanisms.* You need invest only once in programming and setup for accessing your XML data. That data may be relatively stable as with insurance contracts, for example. Or it may be highly dynamic, as in the case of high-volume, transient buy-sell orders in a large brokerage. As long as the underlying schemas remain constant, your initial investment in code with XPath location remains intact. This is true no matter how the large and deeply layered the underlying trees may grow, so long as they conform to their schema definitions.

3. *Reduced training and run-up costs for development.* The 80/20 rule applies well to XPath. While XPath is a language in its own right, a developer need master only a small subset of it in order to accomplish most of what your application will demand. And once learned, that subset of the language provides a convenient developer's shorthand. This greatly reduces the overall volume of code that must be written to locate and navigate your tree-resident content.

4. *More efficient use of other XML technologies.* XPath is not a stand-alone technology. It is interwoven with XSLT and XPointer. By mastering XPath initially, developers can more quickly master these other critical technologies. And they can do so in a way that makes their code more compact and more readable.

SUMMARY ....

XPath is a handmaiden member of the XML family, a mature special-purpose language that exists to make other parts of XML (XSLT and XPointer) possible. Because it has a unique (non-XML) syntax, it adds to the skills set requirements for XML developers. But because it is part of the XML specification family, it shares all of the rights and privileges of easily exchangeable XML. The embedded XPath tree manipulation code that you develop or buy for your application is guaranteed to run on any other XML-compliant system as well. The notation of XPath can be off-putting to the newcomer. And its extensive syntax and repertoire of functions represent a potentially high cost of entry. But in actual practice most applications require only a small subset of the language. That subset requires only modest run-up costs.

15 XML Namespaces

In this chapter...

They Said It...

Said the Central "I'm Pacific;
But when riled, I'm quite terrific.
Yet today we shall not quarrel,
Just to show these folks this moral,
How two Engines—in their vision—
Once have met without collision."

Francis Bret Harte: What the Engines Said,
Opening of the Pacific Railroad

As the parser works its way through marked-up content, it encounters *names* from a variety of possible sources. There may be multiple collaborators for the actual content. These may use privately owned tag sets that include the same name for entirely different purposes. And a single XML document may include notation from different XML specifications (e.g., XSLT, XLink, XSD). A specification likewise has built-in naming conventions, including names that are likely the same as those used by an author or another specification. This situation is entirely legal in XML. Otherwise XML would be useless for serious content. The problem is with the parser. Among the names for elements and attributes—numbering perhaps in the thousands for a single item of content—every name must be absolutely unique (**unambiguous**). The purpose of XML namespaces is (1) to allow absolute freedom for creators to name elements as they wish, (2) to allow every type of XML notation that is necessary, and (3) to present the parser with totally unique names across the entire XML instance that it must interpret.

XML FOR SERIOUS WORK ....

For trivial examples of XML content, there is nothing wrong with element names like `name`, `type`, `account`, `quantity`, `date` and the like. An information system designer needs the freedom to devise a schema and repertoire of named tags that fit the application. But it is likely that, over time, the system will need to incorporate somewhat different content, content that uses the same element names as the first but in a different way. For example `type` may refer to an *insurance code* in the billing portion of a patient's record but to *blood* in the clinical record. Furthermore the schema for this application already uses type as an attribute name for describing the document itself. The semantics of the name are clearly different in each context.

This names-in-conflict issue is inevitable when we exchange data. The meaning and layout of **partNumber** for the manufacturer may be quite different for **partNumber** for the OEM customer who uses the part in a particular machine.

We cannot view the collision of same names with different meanings as a *problem* to fix. It is rather a common situation that must be *managed*. There is in fact no practical way to mandate and then enforce naming conventions that will guarantee that collisions would not happen. It is a condition that demands a clean solution. XML namespaces provides that solution.

HOW DOES IT WORK?......................................

At first glance:

I note a lot of 'extra' verbiage in these XML listings, hundreds of repetitions of the same word like **xsd:** and **xlist:**. This makes XML look even more cumbersome and complicated.

The word namespace keeps popping up in every part of the XML standard I look at. It looks like yet another instance of one specification getting seriously commingled with several others.

THE SYNTAX...

Here is the schema for the data supporting a revised version of the Policies and Procedures example, a revision that will be necessary in Chapter 16.

```
<?xml version="1.0" encoding="UTF-8"?>
<xsd:schema xmlns:xsd="http://www.w3.org/2000/10/XMLSchema@
elementFormDefault="qualified">
  <xsd:element name="policies">
    <xsd:complexType>
      <xsd:sequence maxOccurs="unbounded">
        <xsd:element name="policy">
          <xsd:complexType>
            <xsd:sequence>
              <xsd:element name="section" type="xsd:string"/>
              <xsd:element name="steward" type="xsd:string"/>
          </xsd:sequence>
        </xsd:complexType>
      </xsd:element>
    </xsd:sequence>
```

```
    <xsd:attribute
            name="style"
            type="xsd:CDATA"
            use="required"
            value="pretty|plain"/>
    </xsd:complexType>
  </xsd:element>
</xsd:schema>
```

We declare a namespace by setting the name of that namespace equal to a URI. In our example **xsd** is the name of the declared namespace, and **http:// www.w3.org/2000/10/XMLSchema** is the URI. It makes no difference whether or not the URI is a legitimate Web address. The URI is only a means of identifying our prefix. This is called mapping a prefix to a URI. Every occurrence of the **xsd** prefix is a message to the parser that the following name belongs to the XML Schema Definition's namespace. We might, for example, choose to name something element (the element in a portable heater) using our schema. And that would in no way conflict with XML Schema's use of the name. That is because the schema's namespace is *protected* by the prefix and always appears as **xsd:element**.

The Default Namespace

Not every name in XML needs to bear a namespace prefix. And in the example several in fact do not: **policies**, **policy**, **section**, **steward**, and **style**. These nonprefixed names belong to the **default namespace** of this document. All that is needed to declare a default namespace is to omit a namespace name in the declaration. To declare a nonprefixed default namespace explicitly we could have included the following line, omitting the **:** and the name, as in **xmlns="http://www.w3.org/ 202/myDefault"**. With very minimal overhead, the parser is now able to distinguish between names that belong to XLink and XML Schema, and those that we have invented.

Declaring a Namespace

The way we designate explicit, prefix-notation namespace protection is to include a **namespace declaration** with a value for **xmlns**. Note the highlighted attribute in the example; **xmlns:xsd** informs the parser that there is a namespace called **xsd**. The remainder of that line appears to be a full-fledged Web address, but a real Web page does not exist at that location. Instead the HTTP address serves here only as a means of making certain that this namespace is distinguished from others.

Here is a segment of an example that we shall visit in our discussion of XLink in Chapter 20:

```
<DAMFile xlink:type="extended"
        xmlns:xlink="http://www.w3.org/1999/xlink">
```

This is the data file for a Digital Asset Manager, to be supported by XLink. As we shall see, XLink relies heavily on ready-made attributes that we are to embed within our own elements. Once again, an XML namespace declaration defines **xlink** as the name of that namespace. (That name is arbitrary; we could have picked any name we wish.) Here is a fragment of the markup that appears in the data for the asset manager:

```
<!-- Define arcs linking each news piece with its local
     repository location -->
     <inReposAt
            xlink:type="arc"
            xlink:from="UPArch-006"
            xlink:to="CD-Directory"/>
```

Three attribute names in the fragment bear the **xlink** prefix: **type**, **from**, and **to**. It is easy to see why the namespace protection mechanism is critical here. A mobile application for frozen food delivery routing might very likely need these same names, and they would be perfectly legal.

Namespaces for Sanity: the Parser

One further fragment should further convince us that namespace is critical. In the fragment in the previous example, the name **type** is in XLink's namespace, as the prefix notation makes clear. But **type** is also hard at work in the XML schema that supports this document. Here is the segment of that schema that represents the highlighted expression:

```
<xsd:attribute name="xlink:type" use="fixed" value="arc">
```

The value of the name attribute (**type**) is actually part of XLink, not of XML Schema. The semantics of the name are quite different in these two environments. This is an example of how XML uses its own mechanisms to protect against internal collisions among names.

Finally, another instance of **type**, this time as part of the XML Schema namespace. Here the attribute **name** and its value **type** are part of the **xsd** namespace simply because **name** is contained within **xsd:attribute** element.

```
<xsd:attribute name="type" use="fixed" value="resource">
```

This scheme of name protection appears somewhat subtle at first, but it is efficient, as the example demonstrates. Without attempting to explain what these lines of code are doing, we have focused only on the roles of the name **type**. They reside in entirely separate namespaces, each with their own semantics. Fortunately for us human readers, we can practically ignore this entire subtlety, thanks to the power of namespaces. But the parser cannot ignore anything, so the semantic separation provided by namespace is absolutely crucial to the parser.

Namespaces for Sanity: the Human Reader

Some namespace distinctions are much less subtle than what we just noted. Consider this sample manufacturing bill of materials that contains data from a remote supplier's database:

```
<?xml version="1.0"?>
<masterAssembly>
    <part>Part1</part>
    <part>Part2</part>
    <subAssembly
    xmlns="http://www.w3.org/2002/subAssembly">
        <part>Part1</part>
        <part>Part2</part>
    </subAssembly>
    <part>Part3</part>
</masterAssembly>
```

The master bill of materials consists of three parts, whose element names are **<part>**. The namespace for those parts is the default namespace for this high-order parts list. But the indented parts list, the one for the subassembly, comes from a remote supplier. That supplier's parts list is entirely different, although the element names and the elements themselves bear names that are identical to those on the master list. This tiny example is a hint of how to manipulate content from different sources without having to worry about the element naming conventions being in conflict.

AS THE SPECIFICATION SAYS... ....

Abstract of *Namespaces* in XML, World Wide Web Consortium 14-January-1999

XML namespaces provide a simple method for qualifying element and attribute names used in Extensible Markup Language documents by associating them with namespaces identified by URI references.

Names from XML namespaces may appear as qualified names, which contain a single colon, separating the name into a namespace prefix and a local part. The prefix, which is mapped to a URI reference, selects a namespace.

FIVE REASONS WHY XML NAMESPACES MAKES GOOD BUSINESS SENSE ....

Were it not for the XML Namespaces specification, the entire XML superstructure would instantly topple. With Namespaces the various specifications can work together without conflict. But Namespaces is not just for XML's own survival and benefit. It is a vital cost-saving (and possibly revenue-earning) technology for our content.

1. *Fast-path project launch.* We can confidently launch major authoring and data exchange initiatives, even without lengthy and costly run-up efforts to standardize names.

2. *Easier legacy conversions.* There is a near-zero cost for inheriting legacy data, different pieces of which may have conflicting naming conventions (i.e., identical names for different elements).

3. *Easier maintenance.* Written XML, especially for large and complex projects, is much easier to read and therefore less costly to maintain wherever the design has called for explicit prefixing. In other words, the more verbose, the less costly it is to maintain.

4. *Reduced training costs.* Use of namespace prefixing also brings a nice learning-curve benefit to namespaces. Where XML elements are liberally prefixed, it is much easier to master an unfamiliar system.

5. *Zero overhead to schemas.* The use of namespaces does not add any cost to the design and maintenance of DTDs (Data Type Definitions) and schemas. To a DTD or schema a name is a name, whether or not it contains a colon.

SUMMARY ....

Namespaces, in spite of their verbosity and subtleties, offer the best hope for XML's accomplishing large-scale data exchange and serious electronic business. Because it supports elements and every other type of named item within XML itself, namespaces is an XML *supporting* technology. And because it supports names of every variety in our content markup, it is an indispensable *applications* technology.

16 Transforming Your Data with XSLT

In this chapter...

They Said It...

*Observe always that everything is the result of a
change, and get used to thinking that there is
nothing Nature loves so well as to change
existing forms and to make new ones like them.*
Marcus Aurelius: Meditations

XSLT is a programming language that is the ultimate best fit for manipulating XML
content. The often-heard claims about XML for on-the-fly transformations, dynamic
personalization, desktop processing, and content repurposing have a better chance
with XSLT. Because it is a language, it generates much interest among developers.
Because it is native XML, it has a built-in attraction for open systems planners. Because it deals with data, it demands a close evaluation by organizations with data-centric activities and large investments in legacy content. And because its whole reason
for being is to manipulate and transform content, it is bound to impact workflow.
Therefore XSLT immediately raises management issues that require serious thought.
XSLT is a large topic, appearing as a centerpiece technology in XML books, as the
headline topic for numerous online tutorials (some of them interactive), as the mission
of a very busy developers' chat room, and as a banner topic at nearly every XML professional conference. Our method of attack for this substantial technology is to divide
and conquer. This is the first of two chapters dealing with XSLT. In this executive
overview we use examples to pinpoint the central issues for managers, planners, and
decision makers. Then we use executive talkthroughs to understand some basic tasks
that XSLT frequently performs. XSLT's ability to transform XML of every variety has
some compelling benefits.

WHY DO I NEED XSLT? ....

The overarching assumption throughout these two chapters on XSLT is that you are
seriously interested in or are about to buy into the markup paradigm. You have seen
the value proposition of XML content, and so you are convinced that XML makes
sound business sense. But what is probably not so obvious is how to make XML deliver on the promises: reusable data, dynamic transformations, increased personalization, increased capability on the desktop, and whatever other payoffs you are seeking.
The brief list that follows is a view of an XML world *without* XSLT. It should help
you see that without XSLT very little of the promised benefits would be possible. If it
sounds somewhat alarmist and bloated, that is because XSLT is a full-blown, feature-
rich, XML-native language, not just another aspect or feature of XML.

Costly reinvention. It is conceptually liberating to simplify the data world by declaring every object to be a tree. We said exactly that in an earlier chapter. But without a mature and widely disseminated programming language to process that data, we would each have to develop our own software internally. Or we might be prudent and join forces with other industry players in defining an XML processing language, precisely what the W3C has already accomplished with XSLT.

Chaotic workflow. As the longer case studies will demonstrate, doing XML means to create, manage, protect, transform, and deliver content. For electronic content, the challenges of moving data safely through its many milestone events are major, XML or no XML. There is of course no out-of-the-box set of workflow and conversion procedures in XML. Yet the XSLT specification tends to impose order on processes in much the same way that it imposes structure on content. If every organization had to reinvent totally its own procedures for XML-to-XML conversions, the burden would surely be a serious deterrent to XML adoption.

Painful learning curves. Take away a mature W3C specification (i.e., recommendation) and the XML community would thereby lose all of the costly lessons learned in the specification process. These lessons invariably involve technological dead-ends, faulty assumptions, and unrealistic schedules. Without the established standard, there would furthermore be no established bibliography, no mature training courses, and no networked user's groups.

Collateral prerequisites. As we shall see, XSLT embeds not only its own language mechanisms. It directly includes Xpath as well. Some observers have complained bitterly about this mutual (incestuous) cross-reliance among XML specifications, arguing that it works against the openness of XML. The simple truth is that in order to *manipulate* content we first need to *find* it. Before we could process tree-structured data, we would also have to develop an entire methodology for navigating trees.

Crippling isolation. The dominant idea behind XML content-as-data is that the data may (1) go anywhere and (2) be processed anywhere. And that includes far-flung networks of business partners, local desktops, and yet-to-be-developed wireless technologies. Without a consistent method for transforming data on the fly, it would be suicidal for vendors to develop entirely new XML processing technologies for widely differing methods of presentation. Were it not a very straightforward task to "down-translate" virtually any XML content to HTML, we would likely have to (1) hard-wire content to play on the Web and (2) rely heavily on whatever the Web browsers might support.

Programming Tower of Babel. XSLT does for programming languages what XML does for data. Like XML or Java, XSLT is a neutral language. Whereas XML expresses the structure of content, XSLT expresses much of the core operation of transforming XML data. Without XSLT, every application on XML data—certainly all transformations—would be in a scripting language or a programming language. How well that application survives would depend on the fortunes of the various languages and how easy it would be to convert code from one language to another.

HOW DOES IT WORK?......................................

At first glance:

There are some curious anomalies associated with XSLT. Following are some first-impression comments (appearing here in quotes) motivated by various aspects of XSLT. If they sound skeptical, that is because XSLT is a weighty part of XML. Much of your decision about XML may be based on your perception of XSLT, and rightly so. We shall respond to several of these points over these two chapters. So do not regard these observations as this book's final word on XSLT!

"An entire language dedicated to processing XML? I thought that one of the open standards benefits of XML data was its openness to being processed by *any* language." If you are strictly a *user* of products and technologies with XML under the hood—strictly under the hood—then how to process XML data is of little concern to you. However, if data specialists or even authors in your organization ever hope to manipulate XML data on their own, then the issue of language becomes central. If you have ever been part of a programming language decision, you are well aware of the ramifications: training, reference materials, consultants, third-party tools, program conversions, life cycle of the language, and long-term maintenance. And perhaps you are still recovering from having adopted a language that went nowhere. If adopting XML really means also to embrace XSLT, then the entire XML decision is indeed even more weighty than you might have imagined.

"It appears that XSLT is 'double jeopardy' for my IT organization, requiring XPath as well. Every XML book I pick up shows XPath back-to-back with XSLT. Isn't this an open standards conspiracy to force more of XML into my organization?" It is absolutely true that XPath performs a handmaiden role in XSLT. For that reason, we dedicated Chapter 14 to XPath in order to prepare us for XSLT. As an integrated technology, XSLT offers no alternative. No user or vendor can alter XSLT so as to remove XPath. Implement XSLT and you must master XPath as well.

"How exactly did XSLT get to where it is anyway? I still read about Extensible Stylesheet Language (XSL) but what has *styling* got to do with *transformations*?" The history of the XSL specification is complicated. But one obvious outcome is that it resulted in two separate specifications, XSL and XSLT. During the W3C process it became clear that the concerns of page and screen layout are separate from issues of how to transform data, even when the transformation is for the sake of screen, page, or audio layout. Transforming data does not necessarily mean rendering it for a user to view (or hear). That history has left us with a somewhat awkward landscape of terminology. An XSLT program is not really called a program but a **style sheet**. (We will nevertheless violate that distinction shamelessly!) An XSLT file is stored on your computer with an **.xsd** extension. That stands for extensible stylesheet definition. And a particular XSLT style sheet may have nothing at all to do with the layout variety of style. As for extensible, that word in most peoples' minds is now simply a relic that goes with any part of the XML family. On the other hand, it is possible to extend an XSLT stylesheet (program?), just as one can straightforwardly extend an XML schema.

"XSLT had better be a very slick and compelling programming language. We simply can't afford to staff and maintain an XSLT colony just to support a few transformation routines. So XSLT will have to prove itself to us as a robust language." The good news is that XSLT is a bona fide language, incorporating mainstream language design principles. More good news is that it is dedicated to XML content, totally aware and instantly savvy about your XML data. And third, XSLT is XML. That is, every XSLT program is in fact an XML document. That helps to enforce programming standards as never before. Hence there is not a new syntax for your developers to learn.

The bad news is that XSLT indeed is a language, requiring an XML developer to be a programmer. So the classified ads are accurate when they say "XML programmer." The company is probably seeking someone with XSLT skills. The second item of bad news is that XSLT is indeed dedicated to XML. Specifically, it exists solely for converting from one XML type of content to another. XSLT cannot be viewed as general purpose. It is unlikely that XSLT would totally support a general accounting or inventory application, for example. The third downside observation is that every XSLT program is indeed an XML document. That means that the only tools for interpreting and executing XSLT are XML products that are totally XSLT-aware. That narrows the field considerably for XSLT as a programming language. And as we shall observe, XSLT-as-XML also means that the vocabulary for describing XSLT programs is totally entwined with that of XML itself. So XSLT appears to have yet another built-in prerequisite for would-be developers.

"Programming *language*? A programming language has a debugger. Tool vendors offer a friendly integrated development environment (IDE). A mature programming language attracts many authors who generate entire bookstore shelves worth of titles. The list of books on XSLT is currently less than 20 but is growing. A widely accepted language also has certification standard." If an open standard policy is somewhat difficult for data exchange then an open standard for a programming language is much more so. The slight ambivalence we feel about XSLT as a programming language is probably well founded. As we describe how developers use XSLT, you will be able to assess for yourself whether XSLT deserves the respect of serious developers.

"I'm still back at Page One with that promise of humanly readable XML. The XSLT samples I've seen while browsing the bookstores not only look like computer programs, but programs that are even less readable than, say, Java or Visual Basic." True, XSLT for the newcomer may appear daunting. It is verbose. And it incorporates some cryptic use of symbols. (We've already mentioned XPath.) While these chapters do not claim to present enough to make you a developer, we think that the executive talkthroughs and the sheer number of examples will at least make you a little more comfortable with the layout of an XSLT program (or stylesheet or document!).

XSLT IN THE IT WORKPLACE ....

You probably have heard the claim that XML is the enabling technology for the Web. We hope that we have demonstrated that that is certainly true for moving data. But we are about to demonstrate a much more visible role that XML has for the Web: Transforming XML data to HTML. We have waited long for the Web browsers to support raw XML. And in certain limited respects, the browsers do that already. For example, here once again is the .xml file for the policies and procedures document we discussed in Chapter 12:

```
<?xml version="1.0"?>
<!-- PolicyManual.xml -->
<!-- For each "policy,"
      "section" is the title of the policy, and
      "steward" is the business unit responsible for maintaining
       the policy.
-->
<policies style="plain"
    xmlns:xsi="http://www.w3.org/2000/10/XMLSchema-instance"
    xsi:noNamespaceSchemaLocation=
      "C:\EssentialGuideToXML\SchemaTrans\Data Island\PandP.xsd">
      <policy>
            <section>Legal Statement</section>
            <steward>Office of Legal Counsel</steward>
      </policy>
      <policy>
            <section>Company mission</section>
            <steward>Board of Directors</steward>
      </policy>
      <policy>
            <section>Intellectual property</section>
            <steward>Office of Legal Counsel</steward>
      </policy>
```

```
        <policy>
                <section>FARs conformance</section>
                <steward>Controller</steward>
        </policy>
        <policy>
                <section>Sick leave</section>
                <steward>Human Resources</steward>
        </policy>
        <policy>
                <section>Vacations</section>
                <steward>Human Resources</steward>
        </policy>
        <policy>
                <section>Retirement plans</section>
                <steward>Human Resources</steward>
        </policy>
        <policy>
                <section>Payroll &amp; Benefits</section>
                <steward>Human Resources</steward>
        </policy>
        <policy>
                <section>Termination</section>
                <steward>VP Operations</steward>
        </policy>
        <policy>
                <section>Performance Reviews</section>
                <steward>Group Managers</steward>
        </policy>
</policies>
```

Figure 16.1 shows what happens when we simply tell Internet Explorer to **open** the XML file:

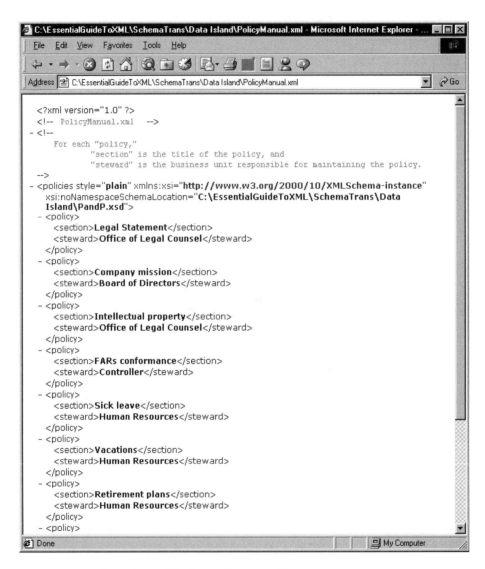

Figure 16.1 Opening a file from Chapter 12

The current version of Internet Explorer does indeed recognize that this is an .xml file. It even renders part of the page in color. But the browser does more. It is a semi-intelligent .xml viewer, offering the user some real interaction with the .xml file. When you click the minus sign beside an element symbol, the browser "rolls up" the element, hiding the element's contents from the viewer (see Figure 16.2).

Figure 16.2 *Clicking the minus sign*

When you click the plus sign beside an element symbol, the browser rolls down the element, opening the element's contents again to the viewer (see Figure 16.3).

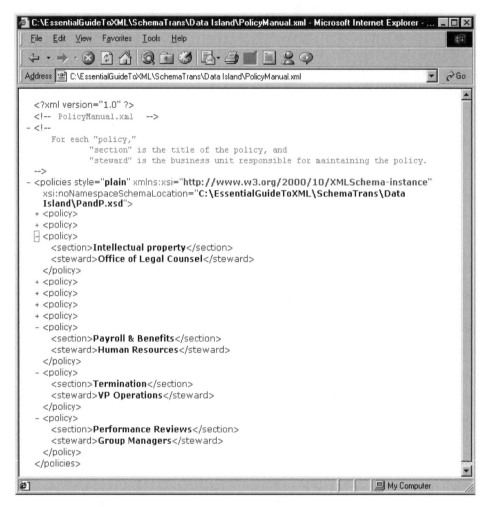

Figure 16.3 Clicking the plus sign

As of right now, this is the best that we can expect to see from browsers when they are given a raw .xml file to display. The embedded XML awareness and intelligence of Internet Explorer translates the XML content on the fly to a form that this browser can then display. The underlying source (what you can see with the browser's View Source option) is the original XML.

The second common way to display XML directly is with the help of Cascading Style Sheets™ (CSS). CSS is a common method for applying alternate styles to HTML for Web display. It works particularly well in the HTML universe because the browser already understands how HTML expects itself to be formatted. Because XML contains no formatting information whatsoever, CSS must shoulder the entire burden if it is to display XML properly. That raises the bar somewhat for the CSS programmer. That in turn creates even more difficulties because of some serious incompatibilities of CSS across its own versions and the platforms on which must run. But CSS is a workable option for displaying XML on desktop browser.

The most practical approach for shipping XML to the browser is first to down translate the XML data to HTML. Some program must receive the XML and then insert all of the HTML tagging that the browser needs in order to recognize it as a native HTML (Web-ready) file. XSLT is a large language meant to perform a broad range of XML-to-XML translations. But the most frequent task of XSLT is to transform XML to HTML. That is the preferred strategy of most Web developers today, one that will continue for as long as HTML is the browser language of choice. And that is the strategy we follow in these two chapters.

MANAGEMENT ISSUES IN WEB DISTRIBUTION ....

XML entails far more than Web pages, as we demonstrate in the "XML At Work" unit at the end of the book. Nevertheless, the Web currently dominates most people's thinking about how to deliver XML. If you have any experience with Web distribution of content, then you may have already heard some "management alarms" go off. The word "browser" appears over a dozen times in the previous section, along with three browser screens as figures. We note what the browser does with our file: How the browser formats it (or not), how we can assist the browser with style sheets, how a certain browser is XML-aware, and how we can expect a browser to behave in the future. The proactive manager of Web-centric strategy must never forget that a browser is a third-party product whose lifecycle and development are totally beyond his or her control. The behavior and capabilities of browsers differ widely from one supplier to another. The browser from a single supplier will behave differently based in its own revision level. The browser from the same supplier will work differently from one platform to another. And the characteristics of the desktop computer will further complicate predictability.

We will spend the next several pages developing a simple but creditable browser-based application, one that we hope is a clear tutorial. And we proceed with little attention to any of these real-world problems. But we do so at our peril. Although Figure 16.6 displays a dazzling Web page as a culmination to the tutorial, we are in for a major unpleasant surprise. If you cannot guess the problem and cannot stand the suspense, you are welcome to jump ahead to the opening of Chapter 17. So while we hope that this chapter enlightens you about XSLT, we encourage you to view the larger picture of this chapter as a cautionary tale.

XML AS DATA ISLANDS ....

One very simple way to process XML data for Web presentation is to import it directly into an HTML table. We do this by inserting raw XML data into an HTML file as a data island. The browsers' capabilities for interpreting XML even in data islands are limited. The following example uses pure HTML code operating on pure XML data. The HTML program uses no filters. And the XML data requires no preprocessing. Since the entire burden in this approach is on the HTML file, you invest in HTML programming skills that include a good knowledge of XML in order to create and maintain the HTML container file. We have simply wrapped some .html code around the .xml file as follows (original unretouched XML file highlighted):

```
<!DOCTYPE HTML PUBLIC "-//W3C//DTD HTML 4.0 Transitional//EN">
<HTML>


<BODY>

<XML ID = "xmlDoc">

  <policies>

      <policy>
            <section>Legal Statement</section>
            <steward>Office of Legal Counsel</steward>
      </policy>

      <policy>
            <section>Company mission</section>
            <steward>Board of Directors</steward>
      </policy>

      <policy>
            <section>Intellectual.property</section>
            <steward>Office of Legal Counsel</steward>
      </policy>

      [cut a few out here]

      <policy>
            <section>Payroll &amp; Benefits</section>
            <steward>Human Resources</steward>
      </policy>

      <policy>
            <section>Termination</section>
            <steward>VP Operations</steward>
      </policy>
```

```
        <policy>
                <section>Performance Reviews</section>
                <steward>Group Managers</steward>
        </policy>

   </policies>

</XML>

<TABLE BORDER = "1" DATASRC = "#xmlDoc">
   <THEAD>
   <TR>
      <TH>Section Title</TH>
      <TH>Steward(s)</TH>
   </TR>
   </THEAD>

   <TR>
      <TD><SPAN DATAFLD = "section"></SPAN></TD>
      <TD><SPAN DATAFLD = "steward"></SPAN></TD>
   </TR>
</TABLE>

</BODY>
</HTML>
```

This is one of the simpler methods of dropping in raw XML data for the browser to process directly. Here the HTML file references the elements **<section>** and **<steward>** to fill in each row of the table. The highlighted portion of that .html file is the original .xml file, literally dropped into the middle. That XML segment is known as a data island. The browser knows enough about native XML to adopt the content on the fly, treating it as though it were a native piece of HTML.

Processing XML files as data islands is straightforward. But in actual practice the approach we've taken would be very inefficient. Every time there is a change to the data (a new policy title and steward, a change in policy name, a change in steward name) someone needs to re-edit the actual .html file. EZ-Payables Inc. has recently contracted with some large federal contracting firms. All of those companies' business is governed by the Federal Acquisition Regulations (FARs), a very large volume of regulatory documents. That means that EZ-Payables must likewise conform to certain sections of the FARs as well. Consequently there is now a new section of the Policies and Procedures manual, tended by a conformance manager, a new hire in HR. That person also collects and disseminates federal and state employment and workplace regulations. Here is the change to the .html file would reflect this change in management (note highlighted revision):

```
<html>
   <body>
      <xml id="xmlDoc">
         <policies>
            <policy>
               <section>Legal Statement</section>
               <steward>Office of Legal Counsel</steward>
            </policy>
            <policy>
               <section>Company mission</section>
               <steward>Board of Directors</steward>
            </policy>
            <policy>
               <section>Intellectual.property</section>
               <steward>Office of Legal Counsel</steward>
            </policy>
            <policy>
               <section>FARs Conformance</section>
               <steward>Human Resources</steward>
            </policy>
            <policy>
               <section>Sick leave</section>
               <steward>Human Resources</steward>
            </policy>
            <policy>
               <section>Vacations</section>
               <steward>Human Resources</steward>
            </policy>
            <policy>
               <section>Retirement plans</section>
               <steward>Human Resources</steward>
            </policy>
            <policy>
               <section>Payroll &amp; Benefits</section>
               <steward>Human Resources</steward>
            </policy>
            <policy>
               <section>Termination</section>
               <steward>VP Operations</steward>
            </policy>
            <policy>
               <section>Performance Reviews</section>
               <steward>Group Managers</steward>
            </policy>
         </policies>
      </xml>
```

```
<table border="1" datasrc="#xmlDoc">
   <thead>
      <tr>
         <th>Section Title</th>
         <th>Steward(s)</th>
      </tr>
   </thead>
   <tr>
      <td><span datafld="section"></span></td>
      <td><span datafld="steward"></span></td>
   </tr>
</table>
   </body>
</html>
```

And the table now looks like Figure 16.4 in the browser.

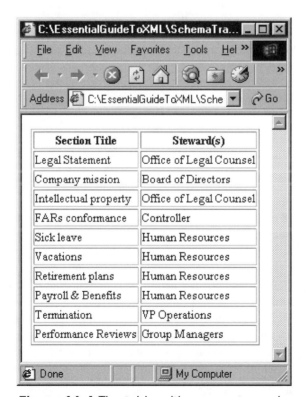

Figure 16.4 The table with a new steward

Modifying .html files directly indeed gets the job done. But for most Web publishing applications, the underlying .html files are complex. Constantly editing them in this manner is a never-ending, error-prone process, requiring the skill of an HTML programmer. From a workflow standpoint it might be far better to separate the .xml file from its host .html file altogether. Here is how we would change the .html file to accomplish that:

```
<html>
   <body>
      <xml id="xmlDoc" src = "PolicyManual.xml">

<!-- Here is where the .xml data used to be. It's now a
     separate file -->

      </xml>
      <table border="1" datasrc="#xmlDoc">
         <thead>
            <tr>
               <th>Section Title</th>
               <th>Steward(s)</th>
            </tr>
         </thead>
         <tr>
            <td><span datafld="section"></span></td>
            <td><span datafld="steward"></span></td>
         </tr>
      </table>
   </body>
</html>
```

Now the .html file remains intact while semiskilled data entry people maintain the .xml file. This example of course is very simplistic, and both the data and the .html file are relatively static. In fact, in order for this solution not to break, the .html file *must* remain intact. We have split the maintenance task to two individuals or groups, one for updating the .xml data and another for modifying and debugging the .html code. But for a lively Web-based financial application, the situation would be far different. The .xml data file could be huge and might be changing every few seconds. This time it is a computer, not humans, that is responsible for supplying the data. Still, our solution would work because the .html file stays intact. The user would invariably see the data in rows of an HTML *table*. For any serious Web publishing application, even for your organization's own internal use, this would be totally unacceptable.

A better solution would be for the server computer, the one supplying the data, also to rewrite the .html code. If the computer is composing .html on the fly, then it could make some intelligent choices of its own, based on what it sees in the data. That is a fairly accurate definition of down translation: Preparing .xml data for presentation on a Web browser. It means to create HTML from XML on the fly.

As undramatic as the table may be, let us first see how the computer might create, totally on its own, an identical .html file for producing the same table that we've been viewing throughout this chapter. This time the difference is that XSLT is the central player. And this time the code that drives it all is a style sheet. As a file the style sheet is stored with an .xsl extension. And this time the code in the file is not HTML at all. Or is it? Look carefully at the following .xsl file, which we are calling an XSLT program:

```
<xsl:stylesheet xmlns:xsl="http://www.w3.org/1999/XSL/Transform" versi
<xsl:output method="html"/>
<!-- Transforms P and P .xml file to a true .html table -->
  <xsl:template match="/">

  <html>

  <body>
    <xml id = "xmlDoc">
      <policies>

        <xsl:for-each select="policies/policy">

        <policy>
          <section><xsl:value-of select="section"/></section>
          <steward><xsl:value-of select="steward"/></steward>
        </policy>

        </xsl:for-each>

      </policies>
    </xml>

  <table border = "1" datasrc = "#xmlDoc">
    <thead>
      <tr>
        <th>Section Title</th>
        <th>Steward(s)</th>
      </tr>
    </thead>
      <tr>
        <td><span datafld = "section"></span></td>
        <td><span datafld = "steward"></span></td>
      </tr>

  </table>

  </body>
  </html>
</xsl:template>
</xsl:stylesheet>
```

Does this example look somewhat familiar? It should. Here is our HTML example again, the one that combines HTML code and XML data all in one file. We've cut out almost all of the XML fragment, just to make the comparison easier:

```
<html>
   <body>
      <xml id="xmlDoc">
         <policies>
            <policy>
               <section>

[stuff cut out here]

               </section>
               <steward>Group Managers</steward>
            </policy>
         </policies>
      </xml>
      <table border="1" datasrc="#xmlDoc">
         <thead>
            <tr>
               <th>Section Title</th>
               <th>Steward(s)</th>
            </tr>
         </thead>
         <tr>
            <td><span datafld="section"></span></td>
            <td><span datafld="steward"></span></td>
         </tr>
      </table>
   </body>
</html>
```

The .xsl code appears to be a a curious mix of XML (our original data), HTML (the code to create a table), plus something new: the XSLT instructions (highlighted). Look once more at the two examples and note their differences.

Before we do our talkthrough for XSLT, it is important to note how an .xsl file works, where it fits in the XML workflow. The fact is that with XSLT we alter the workflow, which in turn affects the skills sets required to manage the process. Figure 16.5 is an overview of the players in the revised workflow.

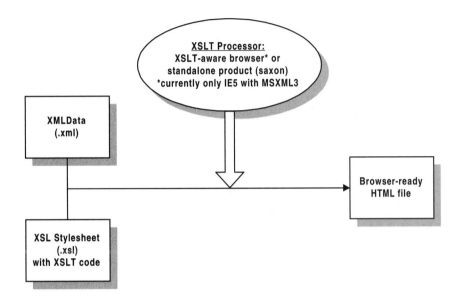

Figure 16.5 An overview of an XSLT process

The new players are the .xsl file and an XSLT-aware processor (freely available Saxon, in this case). To summarize the revised process, without regard to what's happening under the covers, we hand to the style sheet processor an .xml file and its corresponding .xsl style sheet. The processor then generates output on its own. For the example, the processor will create an .html file, ready for the browser.

This HTML code in this example is admittedly very simple and of little interest. But the method of its creation is of extreme interest to anyone seeking to exploit XML for dynamic data updates. The magic is in the XSLT program responsible for reading the XML file and creating the HTML file on the fly.

EXECUTIVE TALKTHROUGH: CREATING AN HTML DATA ISLAND ....

The XSLT program (officially called a style sheet, remember!) is as follows:

```
<xsl:stylesheet xmlns:xsl="http://www.w3.org/1999/XSL/Transform" version="1.0
<xsl:output method="html"/>
<!-- Transforms P and P .xml file to a true .html table -->
  <xsl:template match="/">


  <html>

  <body>
    <xml id = "xmlDoc">
      <policies>

        <xsl:for-each select="policies/policy">

        <policy>
          <section><xsl:value-of select="section"/></section>
          <steward><xsl:value-of select="steward"/></steward>
        </policy>

        </xsl:for-each>

      </policies>
    </xml>


  <table border = "1" datasrc = "#xmlDoc">
    <thead>
      <tr>
        <th>Section Title</th>
        <th>Steward(s)</th>
      </tr>
    </thead>
      <tr>
        <td><span datafld = "section"></span></td>
        <td><span datafld = "steward"></span></td>
      </tr>

  </table>

  </body>
  </html>
</xsl:template>
</xsl:stylesheet>
```

As we urged before, our aim in these talkthroughs is not to clarify all of the syntactic detail of the code. Instead, we focus only on our immediate concern: observing how the XSLT program is both creating an HTML file from scratch and then populating it with XML data for display as an HTML table.

First, some simple observations:

- Most of the lines of this style sheet (.xsd file) look *exactly* like the lines of the .html file we studied earlier. Look again at the highlighted portions of the file. In fact, all of the tags we needed in the .html file appear in the example.

- The .xsl is itself an XML file. This is more profound than you might think. We said earlier that the stylesheet was a curious mixture: XML, HTML, and XSLT. So is this an XML file, or is it a mixture of all three types? Actually, it is both. That is possible because all three—XML, HTML, and XSLT—follow precisely the same rules for being well-formed. So when the XSLT processor views this file, it sees only XML. It looks for properly balanced start and end tags. It checks to see that indented (contained) sub-elements are properly structured. And it makes sure that attributes (like **id**, **select**, **border**, and **datafld** above) are properly punctuated.

- Thanks to namespaces declaration, the processor knows whose elements are whose. But it plays no favorites. That is, it is just as rigorous about the HTML code's being well-formed as it is about the proper structuring of the XSL elements. The processor, as we just said, is indifferent.

- There are two distinct blocks of code in this program: The HTML emitter (highlighted lines) and the XSL processor (not highlighted...yet). This demonstrates another fundamental reason for XSLT's existence. The stylesheet (any .xsl file) need not say anything about whether to output something. If the text is there *as text* the XSLT processor will output the text. The text may be text for filling an HTML table, for paragraphs to be read on a Web page, or for HTML tags. Again, the processor is blind. And this constitutes a huge feature of XSL(T). Because everything is just text, even XML code, a style sheet can create new XML data files, new HTML files, and new XML content of any variety. The business impact of this feature is profound, for two reasons:

1. It is now possible to consider software and computers, not humans, for creating and maintaining HTML files and XML data. And for generating HTML files on the fly, the software may be more accessible than we'd imagine. All of the screens for this chapter were generated by the browser (Internet Explorer 5 with its built-in XML parser) installed on the author's laptop.

2. The skills set for this new paradigm (computers, not humans, tending and creating data) includes the ability to write programs that write data. That is, the skills bar has been raised from Web page technician to XML de-

veloper. And just how much skill is required? Hopefully the examples in these chapters will offer an adequate clue.

The most interesting code (i.e., the part that dynamically loads the XML data) is also the shortest. Only three lines (**elements**) accomplish all of that:

```
<xsl:for-each select="policies/policy">

    <policy>
      <section><xsl:value-of select="section"/></section>
      <steward><xsl:value-of select="steward"/></steward>
    </policy>

</xsl:for-each>
```

We will keep one eye on this little segment of the style sheet as we do an English paraphrase of what it is accomplishing for us (in quotes because this is the XSLT code talking):

- "I am going through the XML file of **<policy>** elements, one **<policy>** element at a time."
- "Every time I come to a **<policy>** I'll write out the tag **<policy>** to the new HTML file I'm creating."
- "I'll then grab the **<section>** element from the original XML file (**Legal Statement**). Using that I'll write out both a tag (**<section>**) and the value of the **<section>** element to the new HTML file, followed by the end tag (**</section**)."
- "Same thing for the **<steward>** element: **start tag, data, end tag**."
- "Write out a **</policy>** end tag and go for the next **<policy>** element in the .xml file."

When the XSLT processor executes just those six lines, it creates the following (now familiar) XML data:

```
<xml id="xmlDoc">
        <policies>
            <policy>
               <section>Legal Statement</section>
               <steward>Office of Legal Counsel</steward>
            </policy>
            <policy>
               <section>Company mission</section>
               <steward>Board of Directors</steward>
            </policy>
            <policy>
               <section>Intellectual.property</section>
               <steward>Office of Legal Counsel</steward>
            </policy>
            <policy>
               <section>FARS Conformance</section>
               <steward>Controller</steward>
            </policy>
            <policy>
               <section>Sick leave</section>
               <steward>Human Resources</steward>
            </policy>
            <policy>
               <section>Vacations</section>
               <steward>Human Resources</steward>
            </policy>
            <policy>
               <section>Retirement plans</section>
               <steward>Human Resources</steward>
            </policy>
            <policy>
               <section>Payroll &amp; Benefits</section>
               <steward>Human Resources</steward>
            </policy>
            <policy>
               <section>Termination</section>
               <steward>VP Operations</steward>
            </policy>
            <policy>
               <section>Performance Reviews</section>
               <steward>Group Managers</steward>
            </policy>
         </policies>
```

So the computer itself has re-created from scratch the following .html file:

```
<html>
   <body>
      <xml id="xmlDoc">
         <policies>
            <policy>
               <section>Legal Statement</section>
               <steward>Office of Legal Counsel</steward>
            </policy>
            <policy>
               <section>Company mission</section>
               <steward>Board of Directors</steward>
            </policy>
            <policy>
               <section>Intellectual.property</section>
               <steward>Office of Legal Counsel</steward>
            </policy>
            <policy>
               <section>FARS Conformance</section>
               <steward>Controller</steward>
            </policy>
            <policy>
               <section>Conformance</section>
               <steward>Human Resources</steward>
            </policy>
            <policy>
               <section>Sick leave</section>
               <steward>Human Resources</steward>
            </policy>
            <policy>
               <section>Vacations</section>
               <steward>Human Resources</steward>
            </policy>
            <policy>
               <section>Retirement plans</section>
               <steward>Human Resources</steward>
            </policy>
            <policy>
               <section>Payroll &amp; Benefits</section>
               <steward>Human Resources</steward>
            </policy>
            <policy>
               <section>Termination</section>
               <steward>VP Operations</steward>
            </policy>
```

```
            <policy>
                <section>Performance Reviews</section>
                <steward>Group Managers</steward>
            </policy>
        </policies>
    </xml>
    <table border="1" datasrc="#xmlDoc">
        <thead>
        <tr>
            <th>Section Title</th>
            <th>Steward(s)</th>
        </tr>
        </thead>
        <tr>
            <td><span datafld="section"></span></td>
            <td><span datafld="steward"></span></td>
        </tr>
    </table>
  </body>
</html>
```

The browser can take this newly created .html file and display it directly because it is just another .html file. The browser doesn't care who or what created it. The output is identical to the screen depicted in Figure 16.4.

So what has XSLT bought us? At this point we have simply proven that XSLT can re-create the example code that we demonstrated earlier. It is indeed able to down translate or wrap XML data in a way that a browser can handle it and that a human can view it in a rather natural setting (a table). But if the computer can use XSLT to generate that HTML code, couldn't it use the same XML data to cast the data in other settings? Indeed it can. That is precisely the beauty of XSLT: to extend in whatever way the format and layout of data, depending on the target audience.

XSLT FOR MORE EXOTIC DATA ISLANDS ....

In this chapter we are restricting ourselves to a computer's life in the slow lane. For XML data islands an XSLT processor (which may be only your browser) simply grabs XML data and drops it somewhere into the text that it will produce. For our purposes we are focusing on HTML code as the output text. (It could just as well be yet another file of pure XML data.) Recall those four magic lines of XSLT code that we imbedded into our previous example, the block of code that loads the XML data:

```
<xml id = "xmlDoc">
   <policies>

      <xsl:for-each select="policies/policy">

         <policy>
            <section><xsl:value-of select="section"/></section>
            <steward><xsl:value-of select="steward"/></steward>
         </policy>

      </xsl:for-each>

   </policies>
</xml>
```

The net result of executing those lines was to cause our stored XML policies data to self-inflate within an HTML file. For our final example we are going to supply a different HTML shell, one with several more lines of HTML code. If you are not familiar with HTML and how it creates special effects, ignore those details altogether.

```
<xsl:stylesheet xmlns:xsl="http://www.w3.org/1999/XSL/
Transform" version="1.0">
<xsl:output method="html"/>
<!-- Transforms P and P .xml file to a true .html table -->
  <xsl:template match="/">


   <html>

    <head>
       <meta http-equiv="Content-Type"
        content="application/xml; charset=utf-8">
       <title>Essential Guide: HTML Down Translation</title>
    </meta>
    </head>
    <body bgcolor="white">
       <p align="right"><img src="corp_pix.jpg"
              width="100" height="99"/><br/><font size="+2">
          <nobr><b>EZrPayables Inc.</b></nobr>
          <nobr><i>We pay</i></nobr>
          </font>
       </p>
       <p align="center"><br/><font size="+3" color="blue">
          <nobr><b>EZrPayables Incorporated: Policies
             Management</b></nobr></font><br/><font size="+2">
          <nobr><b><i>Points of contact for individual
             company policies</i></b></nobr></font></p>
       <p align="left"><font size="+1">
          <nobr><b>Because our company is "growing up" . . .</b></nc
             </font></p>
```

```
   <p><font size="+1">
           We have revamped our Policies and Procedures "manual" so that
               it is now a <EM>multi-volume on-line publication</EM>.
           Each volume is now under the control of various designated
               offices in the company. The list below identifies the
               "steward" for each policy. If you have any specific questions
               about this "new face" of the P &amp; P, feel free to drop
               an e-mail to <a href="http://ezrpayables.mail.hr">
           Human Resources</a>.
           </font></p>
     <hr/>

   <xml id = "xmlDoc">
     <policies>

       <xsl:for-each select="policies/policy">

       <policy>
         <section><xsl:value-of select="section"/></section>
         <steward><xsl:value-of select="steward"/></steward>
       </policy>

       </xsl:for-each>

     </policies>
   </xml>


       <xml id="xmlDoc">
       </xml>

       <table align="left" border="0" cellspacing="0" cellpadding="0"
               width="100%" datasrc="#xmlDoc">
        <thead>
          <tr align="center" valign="middle">
            <th><BIG>Policy</BIG></th>
            <th><BIG>Point of Contact</BIG></th>
          </tr>
        </thead>
          <tr align="left">
             <td><span datafld="section"></span></td>
             <td><span datafld="steward"></span></td>
          </tr>
       </table>

   </body>
</html>
</xsl:template>
</xsl:stylesheet>
```

All of the highlighted matter in the example is pure HTML code, the commodity that web designers produce day in and day out. It is of little concern to us because the XSLT processor is simply going to regurgitate this when it creates the HTML file. As for the nonhighlighted passages, these are the familiar lines that we have seen repeatedly. Our focus again is on the block of XSLT code that the processor uses to read the XML file and explode the data into the final HTML file.

When we run the processor, telling it to associate our XML data file with this style sheet (.xsl file), the result is an HTML file containing our fully exploded data:

```
<html>
   <head>
      <meta http-equiv="Content-Type"
       content="text/html; charset=utf-8">

      <meta http-equiv="Content-Type"
       content="application/xml; charset=utf-8">
         <title>Essential Guide: HTML Down Translation
         </title>

   </head>
   <body bgcolor="white">
      <p align="right"><img src="corp_pix.jpg" width="100" height="99"
            <font size="+2">
            <nobr><b>EZrPayables Inc.</b></nobr>
            <nobr><i>We pay</i></nobr></font></p>
      <p align="center"><br><font size="+3" color="blue">
            <nobr><b>EZrPayables Incorporated: Policies
               Management</b></nobr></font><br><font size="+2">
            <nobr><b><i>Points of contact for individual
               company policies</i></b></nobr></font></p>
      <p align="left"><font size="+1">
            <nobr><b>Because our company is "growing
               up" . . .</b></nobr></font></p>
      <p><font size="+1">
            We have revamped our Policies and Procedures
              "manual" so that it is now
            a <EM>multi-volume on-line publication</EM>.
            Each volume is now under the control of various
              designated offices in the
            company. The list below identifies the "steward"
              for each policy.
            If you have any specific questions about this
              "new face" of the P &amp; P, feel free to drop an e-mai
              <a href="http://ezrpayables.mail.hr">
              Human Resources</a>.
            </font></p>
      <hr>
```

```
<xml id="xmlDoc">
   <policies>
      <policy>
         <section>Legal Statement</section>
         <steward>Office of Legal Counsel</steward>
      </policy>
      <policy>
         <section>Company mission</section>
         <steward>Board of Directors</steward>
      </policy>
      <policy>
         <section>Intellectual.property</section>
         <steward>Office of Legal Counsel</steward>
      </policy>
      <policy>
         <section>FARS Conformance</section>
         <steward>Controller</steward>
      </policy>
      <policy>
         <section>Sick leave</section>
         <steward>Human Resources</steward>
      </policy>
      <policy>
         <section>Vacations</section>
         <steward>Human Resources</steward>
      </policy>
      <policy>
         <section>Retirement plans</section>
         <steward>Human Resources</steward>
      </policy>
      <policy>
         <section>Payroll &amp; Benefits</section>
         <steward>Human Resources</steward>
      </policy>
      <policy>
         <section>Termination</section>
         <steward>VP Operations</steward>
      </policy>
      <policy>
         <section>Performance Reviews</section>
         <steward>Group Managers</steward>
      </policy>
   </policies>
</xml>
```

```
<xml id="xmlDoc"></xml>
<table ALIGN="left" border="0" cellspacing="0" cellpadding="0"
 width="100%" datasrc="#xmlDoc">
   <thead>
      <tr ALIGN="center" valign="middle">
         <th><BIG>Policy</BIG></th>
         <th><BIG>Point of Contact</BIG></th>
      </tr>
   </thead>
   <tr align="left">
      <td><span datafld="section"></span></td>
      <td><span datafld="steward"></span></td>
   </tr>
</table>
  </body>
</html>
```

Once again, note that the XSLT lines in the style sheet instructed the processor to generate all of the highlighted code from the previous example. Because XSLT has simply emitted a larger volume of HTML, there is not much additional intelligence in this version over the simple table version. But the difference in the final output is indeed striking (see Figure 16.6).

The much-improved page in Figure 16.6 includes a graphic, a live link (to the company mailbox), a variety of fonts, and center-justified captions for the table. This is all produced by the enhanced HTML code stored within the style sheet. But the purpose of this exercise was not to see how much we could dress up a Web page. HTML in the hands of a good designer has no limits. The point is that we can store that HTML in a stylesheet, ready to wrap itself around underlying XML data, thanks to the power of XSLT.

ISLAND HOPPING WITH XSLT...............................

So far we have seen XSLT at work in only a limited way, importing and styling output in two very different formats. In a sense that is *dynamic*. It demonstrates that by applying a different style sheet to the same data, we can achieve radically different results. An advanced facet of the dynamic concept would be to make that process *data driven*. That is, we would like to customize the output, based solely on real-time data received by the XSLT processor. This is the spirit of web page **personalization**, a concept that is central to effective electronic commerce and publishing.

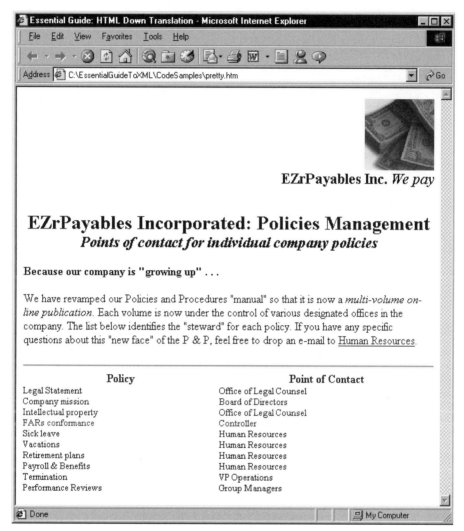

Figure 16.6 A page enhanced by XSLT's power

The easiest way to make our application data driven is to allow for the XML data to store just one more item, some expression that would tell the XSLT processor how to proceed. We add to the structure of the schema the single attribute **style** for **<policies>**, the topmost element. Then in the XML data itself, we insert a value of either **pretty** or **plain** as follows:

```
<?xml version = "1.0"?>

<!-- PolicyManual.xml -->

<!-- For each "policy,"
        "section" is the title of the policy, and
        "steward" is the business unit responsible for
         maintaining the policy.
-->

<policies style="pretty">

        <policy>
                <section>Legal Statement</section>
                <steward>Office of Legal Counsel</steward>
        </policy>
```

In the style sheet we add a bit of XSLT decision code that inspects the value of the attribute and selects the appropriate block in its own file for building the HTML. Here is the segment that shows the XSLT **if** statement:

```
<xsl:stylesheet xmlns:xsl="http://www.w3.org/1999/XSL/
Transform" version="1.0">
<xsl:output method="html"/>
<!-- Transforms P and P .xml file to a true .html table -->
<!-- Selects block of styling code based on attribute of
 "policies": plain or pretty -->
  <xsl:template match="/">

  <html>

  <xsl:if test="policies/@style='pretty'">

   <head>
```

As we saw earlier, every time XSLT refers to some data object, it uses XPath's tree-aware syntax to get there. Here the program first sets the current pointer to the topmost node of the entire XML data file. Because of that the **xsl:if** test knows that **<policies>** is in its direct path. Specifically the code directs the test to the attribute **style** of the element **policies**.

With the style sheet's ability now to switch from one output format to another, we are assured that it may remain totally intact. We also know that the data change required for the switch is quite incidental. Since data is only the value of an attribute and not an element, we can truthfully say that the XML data almost never gets touched.

AS THE SPECIFICATION SAYS ....

XSL Transformations (XSLT)Version 1.1

W3C Working Draft 12 December 2000

Same as Version 1.0

W3C Recommendation 19 November 1999

This specification defines the syntax and semantics of XSLT, which is a language for transforming XML documents into other XML documents.

XSLT is designed for use as part of XSL, which is a style sheet language for XML. In addition to XSLT, XSL includes an XML vocabulary for specifying formatting. XSL specifies the styling of an XML document by using XSLT to describe how the document is transformed into another XML document that uses the formatting vocabulary.

XSLT is also designed to be used independently of XSL. However, XSLT is not intended as a completely general-purpose XML transformation language. Rather it is designed primarily for the kinds of transformations that are needed when XSLT is used as part of XSL.

FIVE REASONS WHY EVEN ELEMENTARY XSLT TRANSFORMATIONS MAKE SENSE ....

1. *Reduced cost for content maintenance.* Just as XML in general separates the logical structure of content from its final appearance or layout, XSLT preserves the separation of original XML files from the final transformed versions of those files. This means that with XSLT a single XML file can remain totally intact and untouched while XSLT code transforms the data to as many forms as necessary. The expense in programming XSLT is only one-time, not an ongoing cost for constant content revisions. This is particularly significant for Web content that is constantly changing.

2. *Minimal software investment.* The options among programming languages for data conversions are wide-open. This is costly in the long run because of the risk of language proliferation in the development center. By making XSLT the language of choice for XML conversions, the development strategy—including training, tools, methodology, and workflow—is stable and stays focused.

3. *Minimal time-to-market.* XSLT is a transformation language. So for all of its size and maturity, it is a language with limited scope. This means that once a developer masters the most frequently required elements of the

language, the steps to completing an application are very short and very few.

4. *Minimal development tools.* XSLT is XML. This means that a developer can use the same XML editor for checking the well-formedness of an .xsl file as for any other XML content. In the same manner, there exist freely downloadable tools for working with XSLT files.

5. *Minimal ramp-up costs for content exchange.* Chances are that both you and your partnering organization will need to perform transformations on the same content. The same XSLT program can easily serve as a template for each partner, resulting in further reduction of development costs.

SUMMARY ....

XSLT is useful, even for something as straightforward as data islands: dropping XML content directly into HTML for Web pages. With XSLT in the process, the developer can opt for just-in-time processing or for background (batch) loading, all under direct program control. Because XSLT really *is* pure XML, it appears to the parser and processor simply as more XML content. Data islands in HTML represents only one application in which XSLT literally manufactures computer programs on the fly (HTML in our examples). The collateral effects of this XSLT feature are impressive: workflow simplification, overall reduction of skills sets, easier maintenance of data and programs, total compatibility with open systems products, and increased leverage of investment in content.

17 XSLT for Adaptive Content

In this chapter...

They Said It...

Full fathom five thy father lies,
Of his bones are coral made;
Those are pearls that were his eyes;
Nothing of him that doth fade,
But doth suffer a sea-change
Into something rich and strange.

William Shakespeare: The Tempest

There are painters who transform the sun into a
yellow spot, but there are others who, thanks to
their art and intelligence, transform a yellow
spot into the sun

Pablo Picasso

Nothing is easy . . . straightforward maybe, but never easy. Even with valid XML content, totally conforming to an accepted schema, there are hurdles to clear before it can accomplish real work. In a perfect world, management policies, IT infrastructures, workflow, business practices, vendors' products, and stored content would all uniformly adhere to portable open standards. In spite of the Holy Grail of open information exchange, the real world demands that we make all of the above work together, whether or not everything is totally in place. XML markup for content is a huge start. XSLT offers a giant leap forward for putting things together, content of every variety. When off-the-shelf products won't or can't conform, XSLT may be a likely piece of a solution. When legacy data or disparate data design prevent departments or customers or business partners from easily exchanging their data, XSLT is very likely to be a heavy player. When high-level management restrictions preclude some obvious technical solution, XSLT may offer an acceptable fast-track alternative.

UNLOCK MY SYSTEM...PLEASE! ....

There is no end to the ways that products, platforms, and practices can prevent your content from easy exchange. Here are a few representative cases:

Captivity by incompatible browsers. A Web-based publication system has worked perfectly at the home office for months. But it fails completely within the newly acquired subsidiary, although the entire company adheres religiously to open standards and XML. The problem? The other company has all along disallowed the use of an XML-compatible browser. The reasons have to do with contracting terms with customers. Everyone has heroically supported the XML initiative, and the content is guaranteed pure. But the content is being held hostage by browser incompatibilities.

Captivity by incompatible data. A high-level company decision mandated an XML-pure strategy for all of its divisions. Not surprisingly, some division-level data design (schema) decisions occurred in isolation. The deadline for launching a major information portal is only weeks away. But the minor schema differences between the XML records across the various divisions threaten to halt the initiative entirely. The content is totally valid. But the content is being held hostage by almost-but-not-quite compatible XML schemas that were developed in isolation.

Captivity by design differences. A county's Information Services (IS) department plans to help launch a mobile work management system, designed and prototyped by the Fleet Services office. IS management wisely directed Fleet Services not to reinvent its databases but to adopt the design and methodology of the central IS department. The problem is that some of Fleet Services' XML management, display, and presentation tools require a simpler XML schema for the same data. Specifically, some of the central office's data items are stored as *attributes*, while Fleet Services needs to store these same data items as *elements*. Fleet Services and the IS center must constantly exchange work order information, so this discrepancy is serious. In addition, Fleet Management is adding new technologies: wireless data delivery and global positioning systems (GPS) to support its mobile initiative. So GPS requires them to extend the uniform work order schema to include GPS data. Everyone is totally XML-compliant. The changes in schema required by Fleet Services are totally in line with XML best practices. And central IS is proper to insist on uniformity. But for the moment the mobile work order system is being held captive to non-uniform XML schemas.

HOW DOES IT WORK?......................................

At first glance:

Each of the following quotes are typical workplace reactions to XSLT. They are a blend of management and technical concerns. We will address each of these items indirectly through the examples, and we will revisit this list explicitly in the summary.

"In one way, resolving incompatibilities among XML data is a no-brainer. I've heard that among the transformations that XSLT can accomplish is the transformation of *schemas*. But real-life *schemas*, unlike plain XML *content*, are notoriously difficult to read. We can see how a little XSLT coding can convert marked up content. But if we have to invest in the skills set for altering schemas...forget it!"

"There's a smell of complexity about this that scares me. Whatever is involved in solving incompatibility problems, it is bound to require more than simply dropping occasional XSLT statements into some existing files. We went the XML route because we viewed it as a strategy for programmerless information management. I now see some very large and (to me) incomprehensible books on XSLT. It surely looks like programming to me! We finally finished a long and bloody effort in converting some critical data to XML. I don't think that I can go back now to my management for yet more funding for XML conversions."

"I have watched the traffic in the XSLT developers' Internet chat list (as only a casual manager-observer) for three weeks now, and some of the threads I'm seeing there convince me that our organization may be getting into something beyond our capacity. For example, I've read pieces by experienced programmers in prestigious companies who've burned up *days* trying to make an XSLT program work. If XSLT is really a language, and if it's the preferred way of manipulating XML schemas and content, I'm apprehensive."

"I've been a programmer myself, so I'm not easily put off by cryptic notation. But the commingling of XPath notation, part of nearly every line of XSLT programs, tells me that the developer's job may now be doubly complicated."

"I *am* a programmer, and I am very familiar with XML. And it's not what I see about XSLT that worries me, it's what I *don't* see. I don't see a large, well-publicized library of XSLT freeware. I don't see more than a handful of books on XSLT. And the general XML titles, with their little book list and purchase order examples, don't come near to addressing the complexity we deal with in our organization. I don't see a variety of XSLT tools, though I know that several products have them inside. And I especially don't see XSLT debugging tools."

BROWSER WARS HIT DATA ISLAND BEACHES........

So we thought that by last chapter's end, we had successfully closed out the data islands project: working HTML, attractive screens, easily controlled output options, customizable workflow, minimal XSLT programming effort, and nearly zero-level maintenance of the XML data itself. What could be wrong with such a beautiful scene? The small problem is that for many millions of Internet users, not a single one of the examples in that chapter will work! That is because for every one of the examples we assumed the browser to handle our XML data island code in a certain way. The reality is that only Internet Explorer can do it our way. Under Netscape (the version most widely installed as of the date of this publication), none of the table data will appear on the screen.

Before we turn to solving the sudden death of our dazzling examples, we need to do a post mortem.

The manager asks, "Who's at fault, Microsoft or Netscape?" Neither is to blame. The proper response is that we were at fault to embed the following highlighted code in our HTML files:

```
<XML ID = "xmlDoc">

  <policies>

      <policy>
            <section>Legal Statement</section>
            <steward>Office of Legal Counsel</steward>
      </policy>

      </policy>
[records deleted for brevity=s sake]
      <policy>
            <section>Performance Reviews</section>
            <steward>Group Managers</steward>
      </policy>

  </policies>

</XML>

<TABLE BORDER = "1" DATASRC = "#xmlDoc">
   <THEAD>
   <TR>
     <TH>Section Title</TH>
     <TH>Steward(s)</TH>
   </TR>
   </THEAD>
```

The ability to populate an HTML table with XML data using only that minimal code was a convenient and time-saving strategy. And that's precisely the problem. We adopted without further question a vendor's convenient add-on feature and made a *strategic* design decision based on that feature.

The development line manager asks, "What should we have done differently?" The answer is the same as for practically all such open standards issues: follow the standard. The simple facts are (1) that Netscape Navigator and Microsoft Internet Explorer adhere faithfully to the HTML standard and (2) that we should do likewise.

The programmer asks, "How can we fix it?" The answer is following the HTML standard means that in our HTML programming we should leave nothing to be done without our explicit knowledge. All we had to do was point to the data with **DATASRC = "#xmlDoc"** and Internet Explorer magically handled the population of the data cells in our table. It is true that the daemon inside followed the HTML standard in loading the table. For our revision we will assume no such daemon.

The operations manager asks, "Couldn't we just have everyone replace their current browser if it doesn't work?" The first answer is the same as we said earlier: Netscape *does* work; it is totally HTML-compliant. The second answer is that many of the world's Web players doing serious commerce, publishing, data exchange, and software development are contractually bound to use the browsers they already have.

The development lead asks, "Doesn't this affect how we define the flow of data?" It surely does. Throughout Chapter 16 we assumed that the browser could handle XML data import on the fly and process it on its own. We have learned that we cannot assume that.

The following section will present the ultimate portability revision for our example application. We reserved this exercise for this chapter for three reasons:

1. It demonstrates how to follow an explicit standard (HTML) explicitly (no assumptions).

2. It demonstrates the powerful ability of XSLT to transform XML to access and manipulate data.

3. It demonstrates that XSLT can create XML notation of any variety. Here we will alter the table-populating block of code in our HTML file.

Peace Returns to the Data Island

For the moment, let us assume no XSLT, no transformations of any kind, no magic whatsoever. If we wish to hand our file to the browser, *any* browser, and expect it to work without fail, here is what the now-familiar table code must look like:

```
<table align="left" border="0" cellspacing="0"
 cellpadding="0"
   width="100%">
   <thead>
      <tr align="center" valign="middle">
         <th><BIG>Policy</BIG></th>
         <th><BIG>Point of Contact</BIG></th>
      </tr>
   </thead>
   <tr align="left">
      <td>Legal Statement</td>
      <td>Office of Legal Counsel</td>
   </tr>
```

```
     <tr align="left">
       <td>Company mission</td>
       <td>Board of Directors</td>
     </tr>
     <tr align="left">
       <td>Intellectual.property</td>
       <td>Office of Legal Counsel</td>
     </tr>
     <tr align="left">
       <td>Sick leave</td>
       <td>Human Resources</td>
     </tr>
     <tr align="left">
       <td>Vacations</td>
       <td>Human Resources</td>
     </tr>
     <tr align="left">
       <td>Retirement plans</td>
       <td>Human Resources</td>
     </tr>
     <tr align="left">
       <td>Payroll &amp; Benefits</td>
       <td>Human Resources</td>
     </tr>
     <tr align="left">
       <td>Termination</td>
       <td>VP Operations</td>
     </tr>
     <tr align="left">
       <td>Performance Reviews</td>
       <td>Group Managers</td>
     </tr>
</table>
```

When *any* HTML-compliant browser sees this fully-populated table, it knows precisely what to do. Note that there are no longer any **<xml>** tags, nor is there any longer a pointer in the table block (**DATASRC = "#xmlDoc"**). Everything is explicit and preprocessed. Nothing is left to chance.

But to answer the manager's question about workflow, the picture is now (literally) changed. Earlier we depicted the progress of XML data-to-browser display as shown in Figure 17.1.

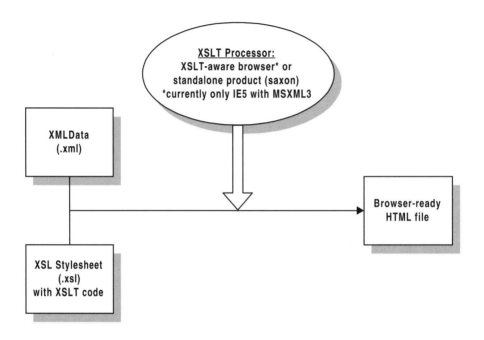

Figure 17.1 *XML data-to-browser display*

With our newly acquired paranoia, we revise that picture to reflect that in Figure 17.2.

Instead of trusting the browser to execute the XSLT code in the stylesheet file, we now explicitly call in the XSLT processor to apply those rules prior to display time.

That change in workflow might suggest that we no longer have a system that we can call dynamic. All of the data will have been canned long before the user sees it in the table. But that is only partly true. It is true that the table will be fully populated before the browser software sees it. But background need not mean batch or off-hours. It is very likely that the designers of a system to support lively XML data (i.e., content that may be updated every second or so) will place the XSLT processing in the last step just prior to delivery. The decision about when to put the processor to work is left totally to the designer.

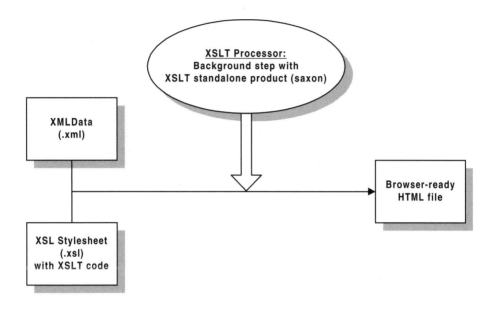

Figure 17.2 *The rules applied before display time*

The only minor detail now is to view the segment of the XSLT style sheet that rescues our code from the browser bondage we inflicted on it in the last chapter.

Here is the revised **<table>** segment from inside the stylesheet:

```
<table align="left" border="0" cellspacing="0"
 cellpadding="0" width="100%">
   <thead>
     <tr  align="center" valign="middle">
       <th><BIG>Policy</BIG></th>
      <th><BIG>Point of Contact</BIG></th>
     </tr>
   </thead>
<xsl:for-each select="/policies/policy">
  <tr align="left">
    <td><xsl:value-of select="./section"/></td>
    <td><xsl:value-of select="./steward"/></td>
  </tr>
</xsl:for-each>

</table>
```

We are about to walk through the simple structure of the P and P XML data file in the same way that the XSLT processor does: a tree. The processor uses XPath notation to do this. To XPath, as we emphasized earlier, all the world is a tree. We will call out each of the junctures at which XPath helps us navigate. First, a treelike rendition of the content (see Figure 17.3).

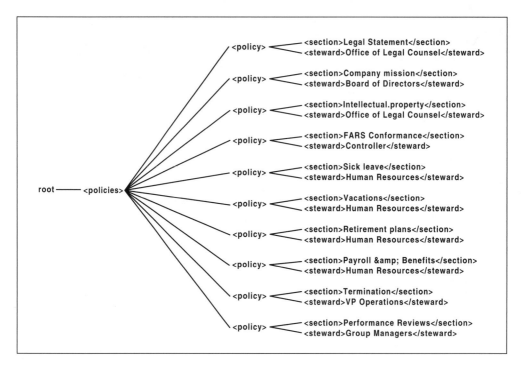

Figure 17.3 *A treelike rendition of P and P content*

At the very start of the style sheet appears the instruction that assigns the current value of our location in the data tree of **PolicyManual.xml**:

```
<xsl:template match="/">
```

That topmost XSLT instruction parks the locator at the very top of the Policy-Manual data tree. XSLT uses that information later in the **<table>** code when it navigates through the tree to fill in each of the table data (**<td>**) cells.

The **.** is a very significant piece of the XPath notation. It always says Start where you are. In this case we are at the root of the tree, thanks to the **<xsl:template match="/">** statement.

The next XSLT statement uses that location information to move the pointer down into the tree: **<xsl:for-each select="/policies/policy">**. We are now located at the first **<policy>** element in the tree. The **for-each** will take us to each of the **<policy>** elements in turn.

Now parked at the element **<policy>**, the XSLT instruction **<xsl:value-of select="./section"/>** says from where you are in the tree right now (**.**) go downward to a child element called **<section>**. Now take whatever is between the **<section>** tags and write that out to the file you're creating. The XSLT program does exactly that, creating an HTML line that reads **<td>Legal Statement</td>**. Convince yourself of this by looking at (1) the tree diagram (for **Legal Statement** inside its **<section>** tags and (2) the fully inflated HTML code for the table. The XSLT code is creating and populating the table one HTML line at a time.

The next XSLT statement **<td><xsl:value-of select="./steward"/></td>** is doing for each of the **<steward>** data exactly what it did for the **<section>** data.

When the processor finishes its styling of the Policy Management database, we have the HTML code for a Web page that will play on any browser. And all of this thanks to less than half a dozen XSLT statements. There is nothing new to show here because the screens are identical to those we included in Chapter 16. The only difference is that the application, taken as a whole, now plays on any browser. Our simplistic, nonstandard, short-cut approach to data islands became a casualty to the browser wars. In order to salvage our application we used XSLT to populate the HTML tables directly with XML data. This little demonstration is an indication that XSLT potentially can port the same content to a wide variety of new applications.

We turn next to a case in which XSLT is more aggressive in transforming content. The XSLT code (with its built-in XPath notation) will already be totally familiar to you.

XSLT FOR SCHEMA TRANSLATION ....

Ask any IT manager what she recalls most vividly about a major systems migration or integration project and she will probably mention the pain of dealing with **legacy data**. Seldom is it cost-effective for an organization to revamp its data to accommodate some new technology. So the pain of conversions, filtering, and endless hand work turned out to be the surprising part of the project, an unplanned-for ordeal (read cost overruns) that seemed to never end.

Similarly, offer an IT manager the latest and greatest data management technology and his or her first question will be "What are you going to do to my *data*?"

You may be part of a large, established organization with content that is relatively stable. Or you may work with very lively content that changes many times per second. In either environment *data is king*. Whatever problem you may hope to solve with XML, any solution is doomed to failure if it does not include a proactive strategy for preserving the organization's investment in its data. In this chapter's next case, we find an organization that has planned as proactively as possible for a comprehensive XML-based information system. The problems that have arisen between the central IS and one of the satellite data centers were the fault of no one. The only culprit is the unmanageable advance of technology. This case illustrates how XML preserves a data investment not only because of XML as a data markup notation but because of the various XML technologies we have covered in this book.

Background: A county government's Central IS department has long struggled with data incompatibility problems. Every such government must deal with a nightmarish variety of data repositories, each with incompatible or nonexistent format standards. Seven years ago, the department decided to adopt SGML as an exchange notation for a first step at easing the information gridlock. As management saw the key specifications of the XML standard appear, they revised their plan, perceiving that XML would be much more straightforward. The major initiative (and toughest upselling job) was to convert some of their core databases to XML. Those conversions are nearing completion. The next tier of effort is to export the core XML schemas to all of the satellite offices that exchange data with Central Services: Accounting and Payroll, Public Health, Assessor, Superior Court, County Examiner, Criminal Records, Engineering (including Roads and Utilities), Libraries, Treasurer, and several others. There is no funding for all of these satellite data custodians to convert their data to XML, unless the longevity of those data might justify it.

Fleet Services supports many of these departments by providing vehicles, heavy equipment, and personnel (including skilled operators). They are physically based in three different locations: Roads and Bridges, Maintenance Shop, and Transportation Pool. Fleet Services is part of the Engineering Department but accepts work orders to perform jobs for practically any entity (customer) within the organization. This interdepartmental approach is of course quite standard for service groups. But it demands an efficient accounting and charge-back system. That is why Central Services placed the work order within its group of Core Data. They have completed the formal definition (DTD and now schema) for the work order. Central Services has purchased and integrated several specialized software packages for originating work orders and for processing closed out work. Fleet Services has worked with Central Information Services to test a few hundred mock-up work order records, and the beta workflow test, based solely on the test suite provided by Central Information Services, was successful.

Problem: Fleet Services has no full-time programmers. They, like most other departments, also cannot expect serious programming help from Central Services. They have been fortunate to recruit summer interns from a local university for some of the more pressing tasks. An on-going data headache has been to create and maintain a small database for locating county properties: bridges, utilities (poles, pump houses, and substations), buildings, and other stationary items that they must support. This is important for their work order system, because the charge back accounting must properly designate townships, land tracts, and any other tax-related entities.

The advent of reasonably priced on-board geographical positioning systems (GPS) was an easy up-sell for Fleet Services. Using geographic coordinates is a uniform and accurate method for locating anything. It is also a cost-saving method for specifying county properties for which GPS coordinates are already stored. Fleet Services has negotiated a bulk purchase of GPS instruments for all service vehicles. As part of the deal, the vendor has provided a wireless system for receiving and sending XML work order information, including the GPS locator data.

The problem now is that Fleet Services' XML data definition (schema) does not *quite* match that of the core work order. Not only does the new schema contain an extra data element (GPS), but the items of information that it shares with the official schema are laid out differently.

WORKFLOW BROKEN: INCOMPATIBLE SCHEMAS ..

Here is a comparison of the two schemas' XML notation for the same work order:

```
<work.order>
    <wo.id date.issu="2002-03-17" date.comp="2002-03-19">2001.03.09</wo.id>
    <cust type="internal" acc.code="3287001">Water District
        19</cust>
    <work.loc>Mulkato Dam access road</work.loc>
    <desc>Repair, resurface Mulkato Dam access road</desc>
    <shop.id>Roads and Bridges</shop.id>
    <mat.list>
        <mat.item>
            <mat.desc>20 yards asphalt</mat.desc>
            <mat.cost>1560.00</mat.cost>
        </mat.item>
        <mat.item>
            <mat.desc>50' x 24" culvert</mat.desc>
            <mat.cost>475.00</mat.cost>
        </mat.item>
    </mat.list>
```

```
    <pers>
        <pers.auth>Chick Grenfeldt</pers.auth>
        <pers.work>Louis Becker</pers.work>
        <pers.work>Tom Schinle</pers.work>
        <pers.work>Kathie Burgess</pers.work>
    </pers>
    <remarks>Flooding last Saturday night left a large gully,
  making road impassable.</remarks>
</work.order>
```

Fleet Services' work order schema defines an XML record that looks like this:

```
<work.order created.by="Core2Fleet XSLT">
        <wo.id>2001.03.09</wo.id>
        <date.start>2002-03-17</date.start>
        <date.close>2002-03-19</date.close>
        <cust.info>
                <cust.name>Water District 19</cust.name>
                <cust.type>internal</cust.type>
                <cust.acct>3287001</cust.acct>
        </cust.info>
        <work.desc>Repair, resurface Mulkato Dam access road
        </work.desc>
        <site.info>
                <site.desc>Mulkato Dam access road</site.desc>
                <site.gps>***** GPS DATA HERE *****</site.gps>
        </site.info>
        <shop.id>Roads and Bridges</shop.id>
        <mat.list>
                <mat.item>
                        <mat.desc>20 yards asphalt</mat.desc>
                        <mat.cost>1560.00</mat.cost>
                </mat.item>
                <mat.item>
                        <mat.desc>50' x 24" culvert</mat.desc>
                        <mat.cost>475.00</mat.cost>
                </mat.item>
        </mat.list>
        <pers>
                <pers.auth>Chick Grenfeldt</pers.auth>
                <pers.work>Louis Becker</pers.work>
                <pers.work>Tom Schinle</pers.work>
                <pers.work>Kathie Burgess</pers.work>
        </pers>
        <remarks>Flooding last Saturday night left a large
  gully, making road impassable.</remarks>
</work.order>
```

The only difference in payload between these two representations is that the Fleet Services schema includes a GPS element and a single attribute in **\<work.or-**

der created.by="Core2Fleet XSLT">. The attribute is **created.by** and its value is **"Core2Fleet XSLT"** All of the remaining data elements in the original schema's record are present in the second. Take a moment to see how the new schema is laid out.

XSLT TRANSFORMS THE SCHEMA ....

The optimum strategy for Fleet Services is a clean room approach: demand nothing from Central Services (no preprocessing, no filtering, no revision to the official work order schema), accept the official work order as-is, convert the Work Order record on the fly for internal use, then convert it back to its original schema form when the job is closed.

Figure 17.4 is the tree-form representation of the original record, as received.

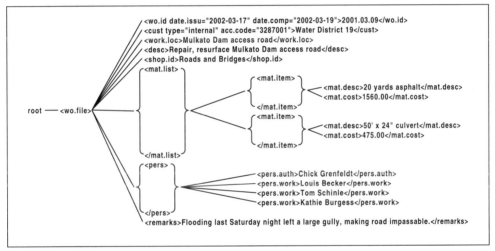

Figure 17.4 The original record in the tree form

There is no difference between this picture and the XML record on which it is based. The only enhancements are the lines, the extra spaces, the curly braces, and the addition of the file's root.

Our solution for Fleet Services is to transform each work order record from this form to an XML record that matches the output shown above. What we will accomplish is to *transform data from one schema's definition to another*. It is important to note that we are not touching the schemas themselves. It is only in this narrow sense that we are doing schema transformation. We need to make this clear, because it would be much more challenging if XSLT data conversion meant that we also had to manipulate the schemas themselves.

The actual style sheet (program) for accomplishing the conversion should be a welcome surprise. It consists of exactly the same processes that we used in our earlier demo (Policy Manual for HTML and the Web). We will create the revised work order record by fetching actual content from the *elements* and *attributes* of the original work order record and writing out new XML tags and element content to produce the new work order record. That's it. And this time there is no browser to complicate matters. Here is the program that does the original-to-revised-schema conversion:

```
<xsl:stylesheet xmlns:xsl="http://www.w3.org/1999/XSL/Transform" version="1.0"
<xsl:output method="html"/>
    <xsl:template match="/">
    <wo.file>
        <xsl:for-each select="wo.file/work.order">
        <work.order>
            <xsl:attribute name="created.by">Core2Fleet XSLT
            </xsl:attribute>
            <wo.id><xsl:value-of select="./wo.id"/></wo.id>
             <date.start><xsl:value-of select="./wo.id/@date.issu"/>
                </date.start>
            <date.close><xsl:value-of select="./wo.id/@date.comp"/>
                </date.close>
            <cust.info>
                <cust.name><xsl:value-of select="./cust"/>
                </cust.name>
                <cust.type><xsl:value-of select="./cust/@type"/></cust.type>
                <cust.acct><xsl:value-of select="./cust/@acc.code"/>
                </cust.acct>
            </cust.info>
            <work.desc><xsl:value-of select="./desc"/>
            </work.desc>
            <site.info>
                <site.desc><xsl:value-of select="./work.loc"/></site.desc>
                <site.gps>***** GPS DATA HERE *****</site.gps>
            </site.info>
            <shop.id><xsl:value-of select="./shop.id"/>
            </shop.id>
            <mat.list>
                <xsl:for-each select="/wo.file/work.order/mat.list/mat.item">
                <mat.item>
                <mat.desc><xsl:value-of select="./mat.desc"/></mat.desc>
                <mat.cost><xsl:value-of select="./mat.cost"/></mat.cost>
                </mat.item>
                </xsl:for-each>
            </mat.list>
```

```
      <pers>
          <pers.auth><xsl:value-of select="./pers/pers.auth"/></pers.aut
          <xsl:for-each select="/wo.file/work.order/pers/pers.work">
          <pers.work><xsl:value-of select="."/></pers.work>
          </xsl:for-each>
      </pers>
      <remarks><xsl:value-of select="./remarks"/></remarks>
  </work.order>
  </xsl:for-each>
</wo.file>
</xsl:template>
</xsl:stylesheet>
```

When our XSLT processor associates this style sheet with the work order record received from Central Services, it generates a new record matching the definition of the new schema. That new record includes the element **`<site.gps>***** GPS DATA HERE *****</site.gps>`**.

A newly created XML record, generated automatically by the XSLT style sheet is shown in Figure 17.5. The GPS coordinates have been filled in.

XSLT RESTORES ORIGINAL STRUCTURE ....

The Central-to-Fleet scenario is very typical of electronic transaction exchange. The host and the partner must exchange content in the same-but-not-exactly-the-same formats. So far we have seen the first half of the transaction. The final step is to complete the round trip for the content. Central Services expects to see the completed and updated work order so that it can properly close out the job and initiate a charge back advice.

The process for XSLT, as you might expect, is but a mirror image of the first transformation. The only difference is in the underlying schemas themselves. Some of the data that Fleet Services stores as *elements* must be returned as *attributes* in the core record. We already saw that difference in the first transformation.

Figure 17.6 is the style sheet that completes the round trip.

We used the term clean room to define this exchange between Central Information Services and Fleet Services. This means that there is no messy human intervention or handwork as data moves back and forth between the central office and its satellite group. This small example demonstrates that XSLT can allow trading partners to exchange their data in the same way. Neither party must seriously alter its way of doing business. No human intervention or human-driven conversions are necessary. Best of all, there may not even need to be any serious conversions of legacy data. The burden is borne totally by XSLT.

```
Converted Work Order                                              _□X

<?xml version="1.0" encoding="UTF-8"?>
<!-- edited with XML Spy v3.5 (http://www.xmlspy.com) by Ron Turner (Soph-Ware Associates) -->
<!DOCTYPE wo.file SYSTEM "C:\EssentialGuideToXML\SchemaTrans\WorkOrder\WorkOrderSPY\
WorkOrder_GPS.dtd">
<wo.file>
  <work.order created.by CentralIT>
    <wo.id>2001.03.09</wo.id>
    <date.start>2002-03-17</date.start>
    <date.close>2002-03-19</date.close>
    <cust.info>
      <cust.name>Water District 19</cust.name>
      <cust.type>internal</cust.type>
      <cust.acct>3287001</cust.acct>
    </cust.info>
    <work.desc>Repair, resurface Mulkato Dam access road</work.desc>
    <site.info>
      <site.desc>Mulkato Dam access road</site.desc>
      <site.gps>117.43.28/47.50.15</site.gps>
    </site.info>
    <shop.id>Roads and Bridges</shop.id>
    <mat.list>
        <mat.item>
          <mat.desc>20 yards asphalt</mat.desc>
          <mat.cost>1560.00</mat.cost>
        </mat.item>
        <mat.item>
          <mat.desc>50' x 24" culvert</mat.desc>
          <mat.cost>475.00</mat.cost>
        </mat.item>
    </mat.list>
    <pers>
      <pers.auth>Chick Grenfeldt</pers.auth>
      <pers.work>Louis Becker</pers.work>
      <pers.work>Tom Schinle</pers.work>
      <pers.work>Kathie Burgess</pers.work>
    </pers>
    <remarks>Flooding last Saturday night left a large gully, making road impassable.</remarks>
  </work.order>
</wo.file>
```

Figure 17.5 An XML record generated automatically by XSLT

```
XSLT Stylesheet to transform XML back to original schema's definition  _ □ X
<xsl:stylesheet xmlns:xsl="http://www.w3.org/1999/XSL/Transform" version="1.0">
<xsl:output method="html"/>
 <xsl:template match="/">
 <wo.file>
  <xsl:for-each select="wo.file/work.order">
  <work.order>
   <wo.id>
    <xsl:attribute name="date.issu"><xsl:value-of select="./date.start"/>
    </xsl:attribute>
    <xsl:attribute name="date.comp"><xsl:value-of select="./date.close"/>
    </xsl:attribute>
    <xsl:value-of select="./wo.id"/>
   </wo.id>
   <cust>
    <xsl:attribute name="type"><xsl:value-of select="./cust.info/cust.type"/>
    </xsl:attribute>
    <xsl:attribute name="acc.code"><xsl:value-of select="./cust.info/cust.acct"/>
    </xsl:attribute>
    <xsl:value-of select="./cust.name"/>
   </cust>
   <work.loc><xsl:value-of select="./site.info/site.desc"/></work.loc>
   <desc><xsl:value-of select="./work.desc"/></desc>
   <shop.id><xsl:value-of select="./shop.id"/></shop.id>
   <mat.list>
    <xsl:for-each select="/wo.file/work.order/mat.list/mat.item">
    <mat.item>
    <mat.desc><xsl:value-of select="./mat.desc"/></mat.desc>
    <mat.cost><xsl:value-of select="./mat.cost"/></mat.cost>
    </mat.item>
    </xsl:for-each>
   </mat.list>
   <pers>
    <pers.auth><xsl:value-of select="./pers/pers.auth"/></pers.auth>
    <xsl:for-each select="/wo.file/work.order/pers/pers.work">
    <pers.work><xsl:value-of select="."/></pers.work>
    </xsl:for-each>
   </pers>
   <remarks><xsl:value-of select="./remarks"/></remarks>
  </work.order>
  </xsl:for-each>
 </wo.file>
</xsl:template>
</xsl:stylesheet>
```

Figure 17.6 *XSLT stylesheet to transform XML back to original schema's definition*

XSLT AND XSL-FO ....

XSLT and XSL-FO (XSL Formatting Objects) are closely related, not simply by their common history but in actual practice. XSLT deals primarily with ordering and reordering of logical structures, as we have demonstrated in this chapter. And in actual practice, the next step in a conversion workflow will likely be to style that restructured content for its precise appearance or layout. That is the task of XSL-FO, the topic of the next chapter.

AS THE SPECIFICATION SAYS... ....

XSL Transformations (XSLT)Version 1.1

W3C Working Draft 12 December 2000

Same as Version 1.0

W3C Recommendation 19 November 1999

This specification defines the syntax and semantics of XSLT, which is a language for transforming XML documents into other XML documents.

XSLT is designed for use as part of XSL, which is a style sheet language for XML. In addition to XSLT, XSL includes an XML vocabulary for specifying formatting. XSL specifies the styling of an XML document by using XSLT to describe how the document is transformed into another XML document that uses the formatting vocabulary.

XSLT is also designed to be used independently of XSL. However, XSLT is not intended as a completely general-purpose XML transformation language. Rather it is designed primarily for the kinds of transformations that are needed when XSLT is used as part of XSL.

FOUR MORE GOOD REASONS WHY XSLT MAKES GOOD SENSE FOR SERIOUS DATA EXCHANGE ......

All of the benefits cited in Chapter 16 still apply. But this chapter has highlighted how XSLT is particularly beneficial to more serious electronic exchange activity.

1. *Near-zero impact on legacy content.* With XSLT it is possible for trading partners to conduct business using disparate data. Ordinarily one party or the other or both would have to convert large quantities of legacy data and systems in order to accomplish this. With XSLT, legacy data can probably remain unconverted.

2. *Minimum-cost real-time conversions.* Once written, XSLT routines can perform conversions as part of the normal workflow across boundaries.

3. *Minimal software investment for large-scale exchange.* Just because some XSLT tools may be free, it does not follow that software comes

without cost. But for XSLT that cost is minimal: no licensing, no compilers (XSLT will be interpreted at run time, not precompiled).

4. *Low-cost conversion piece within information workflow.* In a large system XSLT may function as only a single player in some complex workflow. Because XSLT is XML and because it reads and writes XML directly (including valid HTML), it can readily (and inexpensively) link with other XML and database tools.

SUMMARY ....

XSLT presents a consistent, XML-native method for XML-to-XML conversions. Most frequently that means down translation of XML to HTML. The commonly heard phrase "schema conversion" usually means conversion of XML of one data type to XML of another type, each conforming to its own schema. While XSLT is a programming language, its own narrow focus on XML conversions makes it easier for a developer to learn than a general purpose language. While even an experienced programmer can hit brick walls in developing with XSLT, the largest share of tasks that require XSLT will only demand a small and easily learned part of the language. Even though it is an officially released XML recommendation, XSLT is young. But there is a growing list of XSLT books, a large network of supportive XSLT users, and a growing store of XSLT code that can serve as templates for new programmers. XSLT works hand in hand in the larger sense of conversion: from one structure to another (with XSLT) and from XML data to totally styled output (with XSL-FO).

18 XSL for Format

In this chapter...

They Said It...

To me style is just the outside of content, and content the inside of style, like the outside and the inside of the human body—both go together, they can't be separated.

Jean-Luc Godard, French filmmaker

Content structure is the cornerstone concept of XML content. But the XML specifications are just as diligent in dealing with the content's final presentation. XSL includes XSLT, but that is only the first segment of XML styling. XSLT represents the get-the-content-arranged stage of XML delivery. The other segment of the XSL specification deals with the actual look, feel, and sound of content, how it is finally to be presented. The core technology for accomplishing this is XSL's **formatting objects**. While XSLT conversions are extremely useful for preparing content for the Web as HTML, that step assumes that the browser will handle all the final formatting. But XSL assumes there to be no formatting help downstream. The XSL developer's work is typically to create stylesheets that allow XSL to produce formatting objects or to compose formatting objects directly. Off the shelf products transform formatting objects to finished pages (or wireless files or other media). The XSL specification is now a full recommendation, and is already widely used in the workplace. This includes full support for the format-rich W3C publications themselves. XSL is only one option for presentation, CSS being the other popular approach. Therefore the content manager has the leisure to weigh carefully the benefits and costs of XSL.

NO STYLE, NO CONTENT......................................

For Web-based delivery, a strategic planner can largely ignore the finer details of style. HTML, together with CSS, has amassed a huge body of knowledge for how to accomplish about any look and feel one would want for a page. But for non-Web delivery (printed pages, mostly), we must deal squarely with *all* of the page layout problems that occupy serious print publishing: running heads, self-referencing page references, proper out-placement of marginal matter (footnotes), and tight constraint of column behavior, to mention a few. And these issues are aggravated by scale. Book- and multi-volume length publications are more complex just because of their size. CSS, a mature and official W3C specification, fulfills much of the publishers' needs, both for Web-based and print publication. But it cannot (yet) go the last mile.

XSL, like every other XML construct within the specification family, is structured. Its commands are really element tags. The material that is to occupy the pages are really elements. You use an XML editor to create, modify, and manage XSL style sheets. A true XSL processor guarantees a well-formed XSL style sheet. For XSL, especially publisher-grade XSL, the management of those stylesheets becomes central. Keeping style sheets correct and properly mated to their content is a chore that ought to be managed by a tool, not by a person's memory. Without XSL, the structure-to-structure workflow is broken. There is no guarantee of well-formedness, only reliance on the styler's ability and recall.

Prior to XSL's becoming a full W3C recommendation (October 15, 2001), the XML user community sensed that an important piece of the puzzle was still missing. With the recommendation now official, we offer a demonstration that is one scenario of how XML formatting objects will really work.

HOW DOES IT WORK?......................................

At first glance:

The following comments are typical managerial responses.

This part of the XML specification has been a full recommendation for only a very short time. Why should I invest any resources to master a technology that is immature, and not yet widely supported?

Formatting Objects and XSL-FO Properties?! There go the geeks again! This does not appear to be a friendly part of XML.

Based on its sheer depth and volume, this specification will eventually support major-league publishers in good fashion. But for internal and restricted publications, XSL appears to be overkill.

We'll have not just an XML learning curve but a page layout learning curve as well. Many of the elements for creating XSL formatting objects are tied to the printing industry, which is notorious for its jargon. With what-you-see-is-what-you-get (WYSIWYG) page publishing tools, we were able to skate by a lot of the terminology. We can't do that with XSL.

If the XSL specification has taken this long to evolve, and if in the process, it has actually split into two specifications, then it has probably had enough time to become something *very* complex!

EXECUTIVE ORIENTATION ....

XSL is now a full W3C **recommendation**. It is the direct heir of two very mature styling technologies: cascading stylesheets (CSS) and document style semantics and specification language (DSSSL). In fact, much of the notation of XSL is taken verbatim from CSS. That means that XSL is very likely to become a reliable and widely applied specification as soon as the structured information community feels safe in adopting it. Our strategy in this chapter therefore is to offer a technical heads-up for XSL, more than a passing comment but less than a tutorial. We aim to highlight the important architectural pieces of XSL for the workflow: what sort of tools are required and how XML content migrates through the styling process. In our "Five Reasons Why..." we'll address some of the management concerns expressed earlier.

THE BOOKENDS ....

Moving from XML markup to final page appearance has been up to this point been almost trivial because we have relied on the browser and its native understanding of HTML. But much of the IT world is still a place of tightly formatted print pages. And even if the original media, the production process, and the prototype are all purely electronic, the formatting requirements are generally highly demanding. At the higher end of the spectrum, the delivery of content now includes video, audio, and interactive multimedia. For all of these, the process of moving content toward delivery is multistage, multilayered, and resource-intensive. We begin our survey totally upstream from finished documents and Web pages. Figure 18.1 shows the opening portion of the XML file for the current release of the XSL Recommendation:

Figure 18.1 W3C recommendation for XSL: XML fragment

It is not our intention to become intimate with the internals of the file, only to note that it is a well-formed and valid XML document.

If you have already been to the W3C site to view any of their specifications, you will have had the option of viewing (and optionally, downloading) a document in a format of your choosing: typically HTML, PDF, XML, or a .zip file (containing the HTML and XML versions, including graphic files). Figure 18.2 shows the browser's rendition of the HTML version.

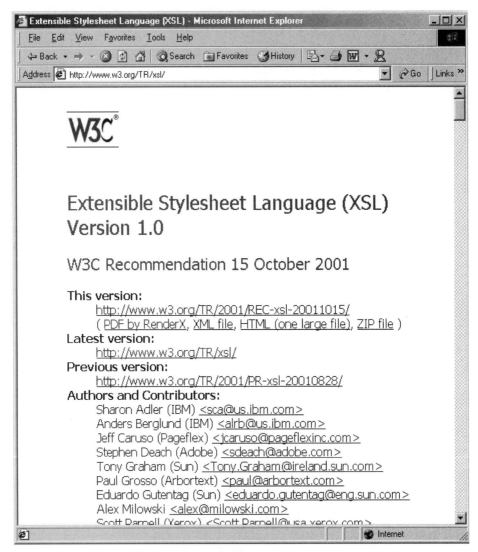

Figure 18.2 A browser's rendition of the W3C XSL recommendation as HTML

From our walkthrough of XSLT conversions, we already have a fair notion of what must happen to XML in order for it to become HTML fit for the browser. Of course, the HTML behind this page (Figure 18.3) is far more complex than the code we generated for our data islands example in Chapter 16.

```
C:\TempDownload\XSL-Rec\xslspec.html                                   _ □ ×
<!DOCTYPE html PUBLIC "-//W3C//DTD HTML 4.0 Transitional//EN">
<html>
<head>
<meta http-equiv="Content-Type" content="text/html;charset=ISO-8859-1">
<title>Extensible Stylesheet Language (XSL)</title>
<style type="text/css">code { font-family: monospace }

        @media print {
                th.propindex { font-size: 8pt }
                td.propindex { font-size: 8pt }
        }
        div.css-cited-thin { border: solid thin gray ; padding: 5pt }
        div.css-cited-medium { border: solid medium black ; padding: 5pt }
        div.figure { page-break-inside: avoid }
        div.note { margin-left: 2em }

        </style>
<link rel="stylesheet" type="text/css" href=
"http://www.w3.org/StyleSheets/TR/W3C-REC">
</head>
<body>
<div class="head">
<a href="http://www.w3.org/"><img src="http://www.w3.org/Icons/w3c_home"
alt="W3C" height="48" width="72"></a>
<h1>Extensible Stylesheet Language (XSL)<br>Version 1.0</h1>
<h2>W3C Recommendation 15 October 2001</h2>
<dl>
<dt>This version:</dt>
<dd>
<a href="http://www.w3.org/TR/2001/REC-xsl-20011015/">
http://www.w3.org/TR/2001/REC-xsl-20011015/</a>
<br>
(
<a href="http://www.w3.org/TR/2001/REC-xsl-20011015/xslspecRX.pdf">PDF by
RenderX</a>,
<a href="http://www.w3.org/TR/2001/REC-xsl-20011015/xslspec.xml">XML file
</a>,
<a href="http://www.w3.org/TR/2001/REC-xsl-20011015/xslspec.html">HTML
(one large file)</a>,
<a href="http://www.w3.org/TR/2001/REC-xsl-20011015/xs011015.zip">ZIP file
</a>
)

</dd>
<dt>Latest version:</dt>
<dd>
```
```
For Help, press F1                    9      44    Read Ovr Block Sync Rec Caps
```

Figure 18.3 Start of Web-delivered XSL specification: underlying HTML

More complicated than our example code, yes. But the process for generating an HTML file from XML is the same as for our data islands example, as shown in Figure 18.4.

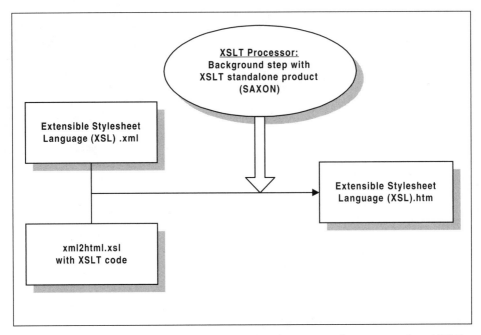

Figure 18.4 Another look at the data islands process for generating HTML

The stylesheet (.xsl file) is a style sheet in name only and in its definition under the XSL specification. In practice it embeds an XSLT program that accomplishes exactly what XSLT code is meant to accomplish: transform data from one XML definition to another. The XSL stylesheet in Figure 18.4 is designed solely to create HTML.

XML TO BEYOND...

The requirement for the printers in this minicase is that the deliverable be a faithful representation of the Web page version and that it be in PDF. Figure 18.5 is the XML content pictured in Figure 18.4, this time rendered as PDF.

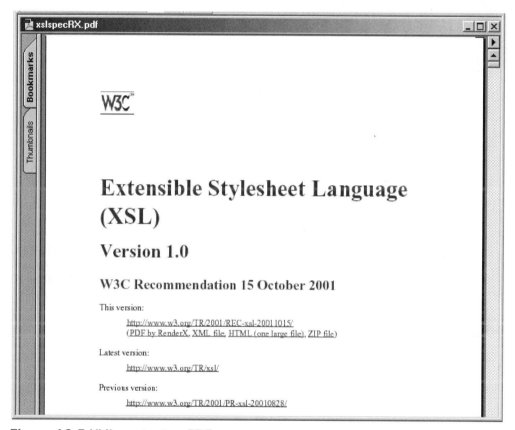

Figure 18.5 XML content as PDF

This rendition is clearly beyond the scope of mere HTML tags. The process for generating this PDF file relies totally on XSL-FO. Figure 18.6 is a summary of that process.

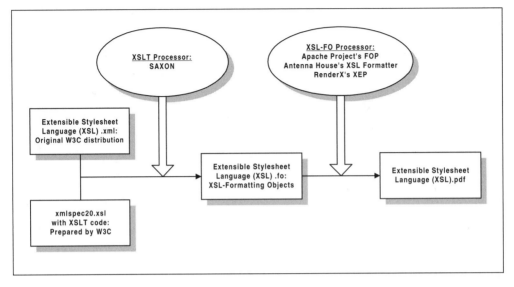

Figure 18.6 Using XSL-FO

  This time in the XSLT step we apply a different conversion style sheet to the XML file: **xmlspec20.xsl**. Unlike the XSL stylesheet in Figure 18.4, this stylesheet is designed strictly to produce XSL formatting objects. A dutiful W3C custodian wrote and continues to maintain their style sheets, and they work for an entire collection of their specifications.

  For our internal experiment, we applied the freely available SAXON XSLT processor and a demonstration version of XEP from RenderX. We used the W3C's own candidate recommendation for XSL-FO as the specimen XML file. After applying the XSL stylesheet **xmlspec20.xsl**, we received the output shown in Figure 18.7.

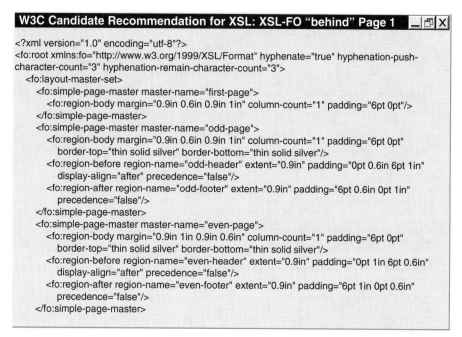

W3C Candidate Recommendation for XSL: XSL-FO "behind" Page 1

```xml
<?xml version="1.0" encoding="utf-8"?>
<fo:root xmlns:fo="http://www.w3.org/1999/XSL/Format" hyphenate="true" hyphenation-push-
character-count="3" hyphenation-remain-character-count="3">
  <fo:layout-master-set>
    <fo:simple-page-master master-name="first-page">
      <fo:region-body margin="0.9in 0.6in 0.9in 1in" column-count="1" padding="6pt 0pt"/>
    </fo:simple-page-master>
    <fo:simple-page-master master-name="odd-page">
      <fo:region-body margin="0.9in 0.6in 0.9in 1in" column-count="1" padding="6pt 0pt"
        border-top="thin solid silver" border-bottom="thin solid silver"/>
      <fo:region-before region-name="odd-header" extent="0.9in" padding="0pt 0.6in 6pt 1in"
        display-align="after" precedence="false"/>
      <fo:region-after region-name="odd-footer" extent="0.9in" padding="6pt 0.6in 0pt 1in"
        precedence="false"/>
    </fo:simple-page-master>
    <fo:simple-page-master master-name="even-page">
      <fo:region-body margin="0.9in 1in 0.9in 0.6in" column-count="1" padding="6pt 0pt"
        border-top="thin solid silver" border-bottom="thin solid silver"/>
      <fo:region-before region-name="even-header" extent="0.9in" padding="0pt 1in 6pt 0.6in"
        display-align="after" precedence="false"/>
      <fo:region-after region-name="even-footer" extent="0.9in" padding="6pt 1in 0pt 0.6in"
        precedence="false"/>
    </fo:simple-page-master>
```

Figure 18.7 *Partial XSL-FO "behind" page 1*

This should look familiar because it is an XML file. Moreover it tested as a well-formed XML file. But this representation of the XSL specification is different because all of the element names (inside the tags) bear the prefix **fo:**. This is a formatting objects (.fo) file. That file was generated by a machine to be consumed by another machine. We added line breaks and spacing to make this sample more readable. But just as a reminder that *structure* alone and not *appearance* is what matters to XML parsers, Figure 18.8 is a larger sample of the same file in the actual unretouched, unformatted and ugly output.

```
┌────────────────────────────────────────────────────────┬──────────┐
│ W3C Candidate Recommendation: Unretouched XSL-FO for Page 1 │ _ 回 X │
├────────────────────────────────────────────────────────┴──────────┤
<?xml version="1.0" encoding="utf-8"?><fo:root xmlns:fo="http://www.w3.org/1999/XSL/Format"
hyphenate="true" hyphenation-push-character-count="3" hyphenation-remain-character-
count="3"><fo:layout-master-set><fo:simple-page-master master-name="first-page"><fo:region-body
margin="0.9in 0.6in 0.9in 1in" column-count="1" padding="6pt 0pt"/></fo:simple-page-
master><fo:simple-page-master master-name="odd-page"><fo:region-body margin="0.9in 0.6in 0.9in
1in" column-count="1" padding="6pt 0pt" border-top="thin solid silver" border-bottom="thin solid silver"/
><fo:region-before region-name="odd-header" extent="0.9in" padding="0pt 0.6in 6pt 1in" display-
align="after" precedence="false"/><fo:region-after region-name="odd-footer" extent="0.9in"
padding="6pt 0.6in 0pt 1in" precedence="false"/></fo:simple-page-master><fo:simple-page-master
master-name="even-page"><fo:region-body margin="0.9in 1in 0.9in 0.6in" column-count="1"
padding="6pt 0pt" border-top="thin solid silver" border-bottom="thin solid silver"/><fo:region-before
region-name="even-header" extent="0.9in" padding="0pt 1in 6pt 0.6in" display-align="after"
precedence="false"/><fo:region-after region-name="even-footer" extent="0.9in" padding="6pt 1in 0pt
0.6in" precedence="false"/></fo:simple-page-master><fo:simple-page-master master-name="blank-
page"><fo:region-body region-name="blank-body" margin="0.9in 1in 0.9in 0.6in" display-align="center"
padding="6pt 0pt" border-top="thin solid silver" border-bottom="thin solid silver"/><fo:region-before
region-name="even-header" extent="0.9in" padding="0pt 1in 6pt 0.6in" display-align="after"
precedence="false"/><fo:region-after region-name="even-footer" extent="0.9in" padding="6pt 1in 0pt
0.6in" precedence="false"/></fo:simple-page-master><fo:simple-page-master master-name="last-
blank-page"><fo:region-body region-name="blank-body" margin="0.9in 1in 0.9in 0.6in" display-
align="center" padding="6pt 0pt" border-top="thin solid silver" border-bottom="thin solid silver"/
><fo:region-before region-name="last-blank-header" extent="0.9in" padding="0pt 1in 6pt 0.6in"
display-align="after" precedence="false"/><fo:region-after region-name="even-footer" extent="0.9in"
padding="6pt 1in 0pt 0.6in" precedence="false"/></fo:simple-page-master><fo:page-sequence-master
master-name="header"><fo:single-page-master-reference master-name="first-page"/><fo:repeatable-
page-master-alternatives><fo:conditional-page-master-reference odd-or-even="odd" master-
name="odd-page"/><fo:conditional-page-master-reference odd-or-even="even" master-name="even-
page"/></fo:repeatable-page-master-alternatives></fo:page-sequence-master><fo:page-sequence-
master master-name="TOC"><fo:repeatable-page-master-alternatives><fo:conditional-page-master-
reference blank-or-not-blank="blank" master-name="blank-page"/><fo:conditional-page-master-
reference odd-or-even="odd" master-name="odd-page"/><fo:conditional-page-master-reference odd-
or-even="even" master-name="even-page"/></fo:repeatable-page-master-alternatives></fo:page-
sequence-master><fo:page-sequence-master master-name="body"><fo:repeatable-page-master-
alternatives><fo:conditional-page-master-reference blank-or-not-blank="blank" master-name="last-
blank-page"/><fo:conditional-page-master-reference odd-or-even="odd" master-name="odd-page"/
><fo:conditional-page-master-reference odd-or-even="even" master-name="even-page"/></
fo:repeatable-page-master-alternatives></fo:page-sequence-master></fo:layout-master-set>
└────────────────────────────────────────────────────────────────────┘
```

Figure 18.8 W3C candidate recommendation: unretouched XSL-FO for page
1

The most notable feature about XSL formatting objects is that this is the part of the XML standard that *really* cares about appearance. In this fragment from the opening print page of the W3C specification, every detail that a professional printer would need for rendering a page is included in the .fo file. This level of detail means that the ratio of formatting information to actual content in an XSL-FO file is often very lopsided. Consider the fourteenth page of the .pdf file (shown in Figure 18.9) that we generated with this .fo file.

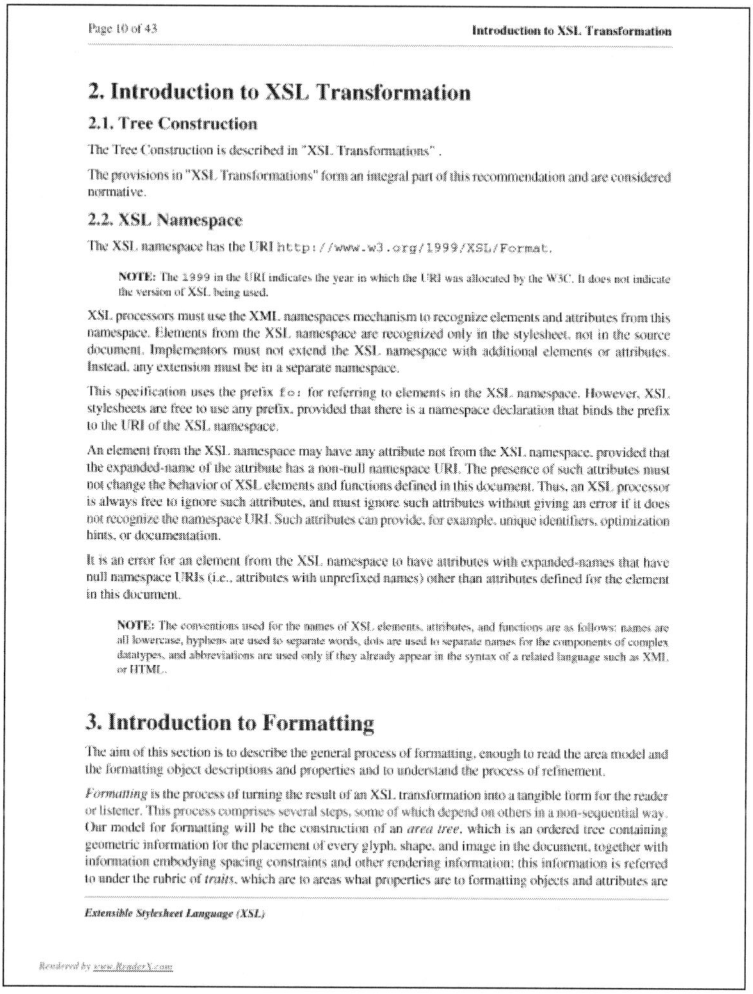

Page 10 of 43 **Introduction to XSL Transformation**

2. Introduction to XSL Transformation

2.1. Tree Construction

The Tree Construction is described in "XSL Transformations" .

The provisions in "XSL Transformations" form an integral part of this recommendation and are considered normative.

2.2. XSL Namespace

The XSL namespace has the URI `http://www.w3.org/1999/XSL/Format`.

NOTE: The `1999` in the URI indicates the year in which the URI was allocated by the W3C. It does not indicate the version of XSL being used.

XSL processors must use the XML namespaces mechanism to recognize elements and attributes from this namespace. Elements from the XSL namespace are recognized only in the stylesheet, not in the source document. Implementors must not extend the XSL namespace with additional elements or attributes. Instead, any extension must be in a separate namespace.

This specification uses the prefix `fo:` for referring to elements in the XSL namespace. However, XSL stylesheets are free to use any prefix, provided that there is a namespace declaration that binds the prefix to the URI of the XSL namespace.

An element from the XSL namespace may have any attribute not from the XSL namespace, provided that the expanded-name of the attribute has a non-null namespace URI. The presence of such attributes must not change the behavior of XSL elements and functions defined in this document. Thus, an XSL processor is always free to ignore such attributes, and must ignore such attributes without giving an error if it does not recognize the namespace URI. Such attributes can provide, for example, unique identifiers, optimization hints, or documentation.

It is an error for an element from the XSL namespace to have attributes with expanded-names that have null namespace URIs (i.e., attributes with unprefixed names) other than attributes defined for the element in this document.

NOTE: The conventions used for the names of XSL elements, attributes, and functions are as follows: names are all lowercase, hyphens are used to separate words, dots are used to separate names for the components of complex datatypes, and abbreviations are used only if they already appear in the syntax of a related language such as XML or HTML.

3. Introduction to Formatting

The aim of this section is to describe the general process of formatting, enough to read the area model and the formatting object descriptions and properties and to understand the process of refinement.

Formatting is the process of turning the result of an XSL transformation into a tangible form for the reader or listener. This process comprises several steps, some of which depend on others in a non-sequential way. Our model for formatting will be the construction of an *area tree*, which is an ordered tree containing geometric information for the placement of every glyph, shape, and image in the document, together with information embodying spacing constraints and other rendering information; this information is referred to under the rubric of *traits*, which are to areas what properties are to formatting objects and attributes are

Extensible Stylesheet Language (XSL)

Rendered by www.RenderX.com

Figure 18.9 Level of detail in .pdf file generated with .fo

(Note: While the header in this sample reads Page 10 of 43, there are four pages of separately numbered front matter. Also the actual document is much larger than 43 pages. We deleted much of the original .xml file to make the demo less unwieldy.)

At the start of Section 2, beginning with the large numeral 2 and counting to the end of subsection 2.1, there are 32 words in all. That includes the numerals and headings. As we might expect, that represents a very modest fragment in the original XML (see Figure 18.10).

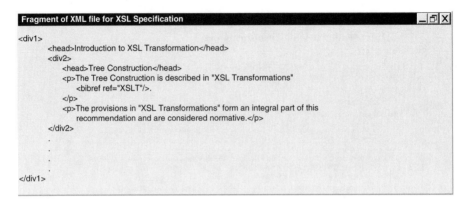

Figure 18.10 Fragment of XML file for XSL specification

Figure 18.11 shows the formatting information required by XSL-FO just for this short passage.

From this pictorial walkthrough we now have a general sense of how each piece of the process—input documents and processing tools—contributes to producing an entirely new product. In this case it is a collection of print-ready pages. But the output could also be HTML, audio, video, or content prepared for delivery on wireless mobile devices.

HOW FORMATTING OBJECTS VIEW A PAGE ....

In Chapter 4 we emphasized that the computer is forever captive to a one-dimensional world. That is still true, even though XSL-FO appears to conduct itself well with pages. The magic that seems to transport the computer to the two-dimensional world of pages is the language underlying XSL-FO. That language is based on a paradigm that treats the page not as strings of characters but as regions of the page's real estate. The following diagram of our Page 10 (see Figure 18.12) illustrates the **regions** of that page.

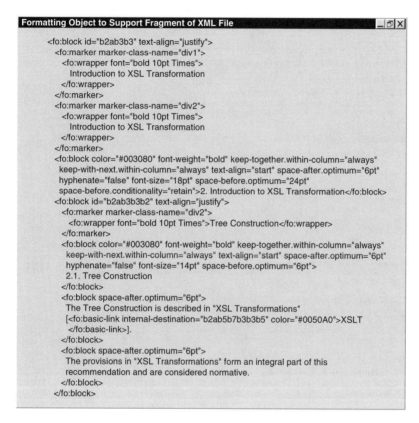

```
Formatting Object to Support Fragment of XML File                    _ 🗗 ✕
        <fo:block id="b2ab3b3" text-align="justify">
          <fo:marker marker-class-name="div1">
            <fo:wrapper font="bold 10pt Times">
            Introduction to XSL Transformation
            </fo:wrapper>
          </fo:marker>
          <fo:marker marker-class-name="div2">
            <fo:wrapper font="bold 10pt Times">
            Introduction to XSL Transformation
            </fo:wrapper>
          </fo:marker>
          <fo:block color="#003080" font-weight="bold" keep-together.within-column="always"
            keep-with-next.within-column="always" text-align="start" space-after.optimum="6pt"
            hyphenate="false" font-size="18pt" space-before.optimum="24pt"
            space-before.conditionality="retain">2. Introduction to XSL Transformation</fo:block>
          <fo:block id="b2ab3b3b2" text-align="justify">
            <fo:marker marker-class-name="div2">
              <fo:wrapper font="bold 10pt Times">Tree Construction</fo:wrapper>
            </fo:marker>
            <fo:block color="#003080" font-weight="bold" keep-together.within-column="always"
              keep-with-next.within-column="always" text-align="start" space-after.optimum="6pt"
              hyphenate="false" font-size="14pt" space-before.optimum="6pt">
              2.1. Tree Construction
            </fo:block>
            <fo:block space-after.optimum="6pt">
            The Tree Construction is described in "XSL Transformations"
            [<fo:basic-link internal-destination="b2ab5b7b3b3b5" color="#0050A0">XSLT
              </fo:basic-link>].
            </fo:block>
            <fo:block space-after.optimum="6pt">
            The provisions in "XSL Transformations" form an integral part of this
            recommendation and are considered normative.
            </fo:block>
          </fo:block>
        </fo:block>
```

Figure 18.11 Formatting Object to Support Fragment of XML File

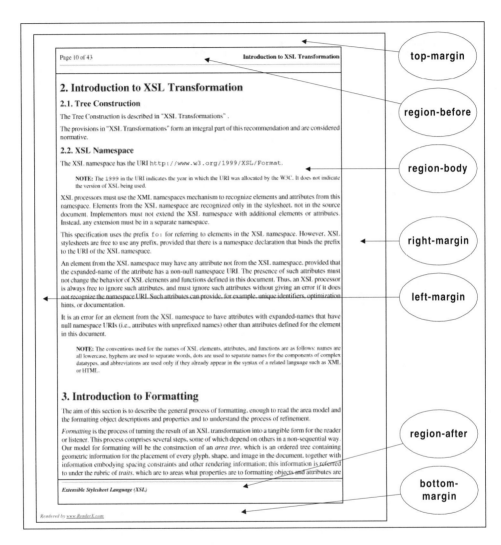

Figure 18.12 An XSL-FO page divided into regions

These names are built into the formatting objects' own language. (Strictly speaking only **region-before**, **body**, and **region-after** are actually used in the XSL-FO style sheet for this document family.)

Using regions, an XSL-FO style sheet defines a master page for each type of page to appear in the final output: how the **body** is to appear, and what goes into the **region-before** and **region-after**.

HOW TO BUILD FORMATTING OBJECTS THAT REALLY FORMAT ....

Figures 18.13 – 18.16 show the actual XSLT code that builds the XSL-FO file. The XSL-FO code that it generates will direct the PDF processor to build the final document. As we observed before, an XSLT program is a curious mix of both its own elements and those of the XML file that it is creating. The way we can tell whose elements are whose is by observing the **prefix** for the various elements: **xsl:** for XSLT's own elements and **fo:** for the XSL-FO file that is in the making. We paraphrase each segment using plain English. The XSLT program itself is the speaker, explaining to us what it wants to see in the final page.

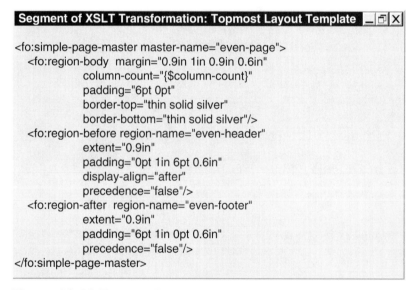

Figure 18.13 Topmost layout template

Figure 18.13: I am naming one of the types of master pages in this document **even-page**. That's for the even numbered pages, whose footers, header, and body information should appear more toward the left side of the page. The page numbers will likewise be on the left. I'm also placing a thin silver rule at both the top and bottom of the body.

```
Segment of XSLT Transformation: Header for Even-Numbered Page ⊟ ⊡ ☒

<fo:static-content flow-name="even-header">
  <fo:list-block font="10pt Times"
            provisional-distance-between-starts="1.5in"
            provisional-label-separation="0in">
    <fo:list-item>
      <fo:list-item-label end-indent="label-end()">
        <fo:block text-align="start">
          <xsl:copy-of select="$page-number"/>
        </fo:block>
      </fo:list-item-label>
      <fo:list-item-body start-indent="body-start()">
        <fo:block text-align="end" font-weight="bold">
          <fo:retrieve-marker retrieve-class-name="div1"
                    retrieve-boundary="page"/>
        </fo:block>
      </fo:list-item-body>
    </fo:list-item>
  </fo:list-block>
</fo:static-content>
```

Figure 18.14 Header for even-numbered page

Figure 18.14: And speaking of headers, here exactly is how I want the headers on even-numbered pages to appear. I'm putting the page number first on the header's line, followed by the caption taken from the new section title on the page (**"div1"**).

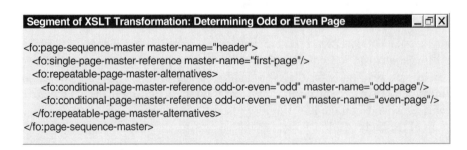

```
Segment of XSLT Transformation: Determining Odd or Even Page          ⊟ ⊡ ☒

<fo:page-sequence-master master-name="header">
  <fo:single-page-master-reference master-name="first-page"/>
  <fo:repeatable-page-master-alternatives>
    <fo:conditional-page-master-reference odd-or-even="odd" master-name="odd-page"/>
    <fo:conditional-page-master-reference odd-or-even="even" master-name="even-page"/>
  </fo:repeatable-page-master-alternatives>
</fo:page-sequence-master>
```

Figure 18.15 Determining Odd or Even Page

Figure 18.15: And how, you may ask, do I know whether I'm even *on* an even-numbered page? Thanks to the built-in smarts of the XML-FO processor who'll be executing the code I'm writing, it will be keeping track of that as it moves through the document. Granted, the XSL-FO program has to be awfully verbose in asking. But in the long conditional element here, I'm having the program ask the processor odd-or-even? If he tells me even, then I'm all set to lay out my stuff using the master page that I named even-page. That's the master page I just showed you above in Figure 18.5.

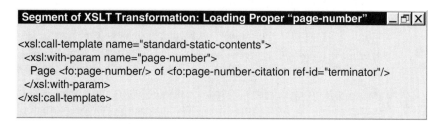

Figure 18.16 Loading proper "page-number"

Figure 18.16: "I thought you might like to see just one small example of where I, the XSLT program, actually tell the XSL-FO processor exactly what to print on the page. You remember the Page (current page number) of 148 that you see in every page header. Well, here is the code that makes that happen (my moment of glory, as it were.) I (**xsl:**) stuff out the string Page, then the XSL-FO processor (**fo:**) brings in the current page number, then I write out of, then he writes the total page count. This is a pretty nice example of how XSLT and XSL-FO work together."

AS THE SPECIFICATION SAYS ....

Extensible Stylesheet Language (XSL)

Version 1.0

W3C Recommendation 15 October 2001

Abstract:

This specification defines the features and syntax for the Extensible Stylesheet Language (XSL), a language for expressing stylesheets. It consists of two parts:

1. a language for transforming XML documents, and

2. an XML vocabulary for specifying formatting semantics.

An XSL stylesheet specifies the presentation of a class of XML documents by describing how an instance of the class is transformed into an XML document that uses the formatting vocabulary.

FIVE REASONS WHY XSL-FO MAKES GOOD BUSINESS SENSE ···

1. *Preservation of investment in structured content.* Once your information is structured and stored as XML, then you can apply as many XSL stylesheets as you wish to that content in order to produce a variety of published products that "play" on a variety of devices.

2. *Minimization of page layout expense.* A single XSL stylesheet can work with an infinite number of XML documents that share the same schema.

3. *Assurance of wide support.* XSL is rapidly becoming a mainstream technology. Over a dozen providers currently support XSL with tools, engines, and add-on products.

4. *Minimal initial outlay.* Many of the same editing and validation tools for creating XML documents also support XSL-FO. This is because an XSL file itself is also XML.

5. *Modest training and run-up costs.* Much of the notation of XSL is taken from cascading stylesheets (CSS), a formatting mechanism that is very familiar to Web page designers.

SUMMARY ··

The XSL Recommendation demonstrates that XML really does concern itself with the appearance and presentation of the final product. And it does so in a very rigorous manner. Translating XML content first to formatting objects—a machine-neutral, non-proprietary intermediate XML renditon—gives us a workflow that is totally portable. The same XSL stylesheet will work with an infinite number of files, if the files comply with the same schema. And with multiple stylesheets, an organization can re-purpose the same content in virtually infinite forms. XSL is not the only way to style XML content. But because it is a native member of the XML family, it makes good sense to consider it seriously.

19 XLink and XPointer

In this chapter...

They Said It...

The links that united her to the rest of humankind—links of flowers, or silk, or gold, or whatever the material—had all been broken. Here was the iron link of mutual crime, which neither he nor she could break.

Nathaniel Hawthorne: The Scarlet Letter

XML content is about more than pages on the screen or in print. It is about creating and tracking fragments of every variety. But part of the larger mission of XML is the dream of hyperlinking, the ability to incorporate related information without physically moving it onto our workbench beforehand. We have grown familiar to the look and feel of HTML hypertext links for Web browsers. But the relationship expressed by an HTML link expresses only a trivial first step in hyperlinking: I am *here* in this document, and I want that information out *there*. XML Linking Language (XLink) departs dramatically from the here-to-there relationship, allowing us to describe every permutation of relationship possible among XML content of any variety. Whereas XML has all along insisted on the separation of structure and appearance, XLink and XML Pointer Language (XPointer) seek the separation of linking apparatus from the actual linked content. The result is a drastic reduction in maintenance effort. A simple but realistic workplace example demonstrates the ability of XLink and XPointer to manage interactive multimedia.

MANAGING LINKS: A BATTLE WE CAN NEVER WIN

Because of the Web's popularity, we are familiar with hyperlinking and the HTML anchor element type for expressing links. But HTML for link management is not only limiting. It can be practically prohibitive.

The following HTML markup (from the news story example in Chapter 2) provides a familiar linking mechanism for Web browsing:

```
<p><font size="+1">This article originates from the KOROLYOV,
 Russia office of the Associated Press. For in-depth coverage,
 log into the <a href="http://www.ap.org">Associated Press</a>
 web site.
   </font>
</p>
```

HTML's **<a>** element is a convenient method for linking the current document with some remote content. But with the convenience comes a risk of high maintenance. If the Associated Press should someday change its URL, without allowing for **www.ap.org** to continue working, then our own Web page would immediately break. Our users would then see the familiar "broken link" error page illustrated in Figure 19.1.

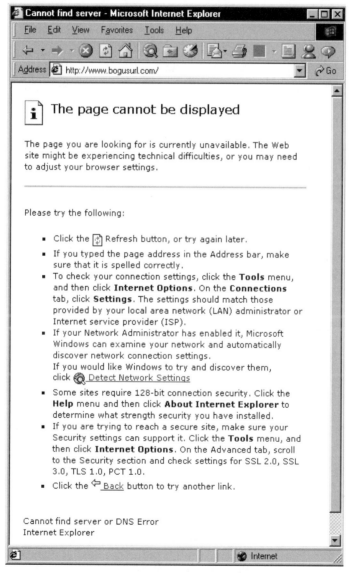

Figure 19.1 A "broken link" error page

The problem is compounded if several thousands of other HTML-encoded pages also were hard-coded with the **www.ap.org** address. The management implication of this is obvious. A change in the address of the **target** content can require hand editing for thousands of pages that reference the address. The Associated Press is not likely to make this happen, but within a large intranet, it would be much more likely and possibly just as detrimental.

HTML-style linking is convenient because we are freed from concern about the color and face of the screen text supporting the link: probably blue and underlined. Also we can assume a certain behavior on the browser's part: Clicking causes another screen to appear. And it will appear only *after* the user's mouse clicks. But these default behaviors of hyperlinking may not be acceptable. We may wish to manage such details directly. That is not possible with HTML alone.

Another severe limitation of HTML links is that they can only point to a single target. We can design around that by making that single target itself to be a list of further links. But each link takes us only to a single target resource. Clearly that is not the nature of fully linked content. We frequently wish for a single item in a document or page to point to many resources simultaneously. This one-to-many model is not possible with HTML.

Another limitation is more subtle but just as critical. When we view a link item on a Web page, we know only that that means "This remote resource is somehow related; click on me and find out how." The author(s) may have supplied explanation on the page, but the link itself explains nothing about its meaning. In other words, HTML by itself has no way to build in the semantics of its links. An HTML link only says this item is linked to that one. Meaningful content demands more. A link should convey the precise basis of a relationship. Is that linked resource the site of a company subsidiary? The names of the king's first-generation offspring? The locations of franchises within this region?

HOW DOES IT WORK?.....................................

At first glance:

XLink Version 1.0 is a full W3C Recommendation as of June 27, 2001, while XML Pointer Language (XPointer) Version 1.0 still is only a working draft as of January 8, 2001. If these specifications are to work in tandem, then why is it worth any of my effort to evaluate a specification that is only half-completed?

No browser comes close to supporting XLink/XPointer as yet. Browser support has been the clincher for most W3C spec activity. That makes me very apprehensive about XLink/XPointer.

Once again, the learning curve implications are not encouraging. XLink requires XPointer, which in turn relies on XPath. And of course XML namespaces are everywhere. True, an XLink file is XML, but the action seems to be in the predefined *attributes* of XLink rather than in elements. All of this tells me that one cannot be a productive XLink developer without mastering a considerable body of XLink internals.

BEYOND THE WEB ....

It is true that the majority of XML technologies are Web-related or Web-intensive. It is also true that the progress of XLink and XPointer toward Web support has been less than encouraging. But this pair of specifications, more than for the rest of the XML family, applies to XML content in any setting. XLink is about content linking, not simply about Web navigation. Linking in this expanded sense is in fact essential for creating a just-in-time media management system, as we shall demonstrate in our case study.

Simple Linking

XLink, as we might expect, can link to remote content (a **remote resource**) in the same way that HTML does with its **<a>** anchor element. In Chapter 2 our HTML demo included a link to the Associated Press. Here is the HTML code behind that demo:

```
<p><font size="+1">
    This article originates from the KOROLYOV, Russia office of the
    Associated Press. For in-depth coverage, log into the
    <a href="http://www.ap.org">Associated Press</a> web site.
        </font>
</p>
```

XLink is able to replicate HTML's link behavior. Here again is the Web coding for the link to the Associated Press, this time rendered as XLink:

```
<p><font size="+1">This article originates from the KOROLYOV,
 Russia office of the Associated Press. For in-depth coverage,
 log into the

<HTMLStyleLink
   xlink:type="simple"
   xlink:href="http://www.ap.org"
   xlink:title="Associated Press"
```

In order to use the XLink attributes in our document (**ourDoc**), we must of course include an XLink namespace declaration in our prolog:

```
<ourDoc xmlns:xlink="http://www.w3.org/1999/xlink">
```

That namespace declaration allows us to prefix each of the XLink attributes with **xlink:** in our own document. This little segment of XLink code says specifically what we can only imply with an ordinary HTML link. Here is what XLink expresses with its rendition of that link:

type-"simple" says that this link originates in our own document, in this **local resource**. It also says that this links to a single **remote resource.**

XLink's attribute **xlink:href** is the same as for HTML.

XLink's attribute **xlink:title** defines the hot text precisely (the passage activated to receive user input).

The advantage in using XLink over HTML linking may appear to be minimal. And since browsers do not as yet generally support XLink, there may not seem to be any advantage. In the big picture, however, there is much to be gained with XLink. The main advantage is that even for a simple link we have control over every aspect of this link's semantics and behavior: exactly when it gets activated and whether it should create a new window, for example. XLink includes an ample suite of attributes that we can apply, even to a simple link.

But let us narrow our focus from Web pages to *linking* alone. We included an XLink apparatus in the above block of XML content to accomplish the same thing as an HTML **<a>** link element. That is precisely the nature of an XLink **simple link**, the kind of embedded link that originates locally (in a **local resource**) and points to a single object (**remote resource**) beyond the current content. This is the only flavor of linking that is available to HTML. Since we are so familiar with HTML's Web page look and feel, it is difficult to imagine links apart from Web pages.

The deliverable for Web pages is content-plus-links. But XLink offers us a totally different sort of deliverable. With XLink and XML files, we can deal separately with all linking matters, allowing us to separate linking from the content it supports. With that separation comes the opportunity to concentrate on *managing* the linking relationships among fragments of content. In our case study, we shall find that XLink separates links from content. That means that some XML supporting files may consist of nothing but links, totally detached from their supported content. Those files—consisting of nothing but linking apparatus—will naturally have the highest incidence of XLink expressions. XLink offers us this breakthrough linking technology through *extended links*.

Extended Links

A major publisher of CD-ROM-based multimedia seeks to provide the highest degree of interactivity possible. The limitations of read-only CD-ROM are well known, including a lock-step, take-it-or-leave-it menu-based approach to sequencing the materials. Even more seriously, the HTML down-cooked content for each CD-ROM product typically includes hundreds of explicit Web addresses, all of them hard-coded, and many of them certain to change even before the CD-ROM product is released. The production department seeks to exploit XML linking technologies to alleviate this chronic two-part downside of CD-ROM-based publishing.

Current practice dictates that HTML is a given because the CD-based material can only be viewed with current Web browsers. As eager as we might be to see broad XML support on browsers, the browsers on most desktops can support only HTML. Furthermore there is no way to halt the migration of live Web-based content so as to preserve the integrity of hard-coded HTTP addresses. And to access that content, the product must continue to use HTTP-style addressing. There would appear to be no straightforward solution to making CD-ROM products any less brittle in its presentation to the user and any more responsive to real-world data migration. So how does the publisher produce linked content that is more easily personalized on the fly and whose links will not break?

PROPOSED XML SOLUTION ....

The solution we offer in this demonstration is an additional *connectivity layer*, consisting of two parts:

1. *A small XML-based digital asset manager* (DIGAM) to broker all Web requests by the user. This is an XML file consisting of XLink and

XPointer expressions, automatically fetched from the publisher when the content is viewed, and stored temporarily on the user's hard disk.

2. *An on-the-fly digital playlist for each of the user's sessions* created by the CD-based display engine. It consists of data captured and transformed from the DIGAM. This also is stored on the user's hard disk only for the duration of the user's session.

The obvious question at the outset is whether any solution that proposes an XLink/XPointer approach is even relevant. If we must deliver to browsers, and if there are only scant product offerings of any kind to support these specifications, then is this demo only a blue-sky exercise?

True, the state of the art is such that wide XLink/XPointer support, including Web browsers, is months or even years away. However there is nothing to hinder the development of special-purpose XLink/XPointer engines, whether or not the specifications are implemented on browsers.

DIGAM: EXECUTIVE TALKTHROUGH......................

We restrict our specimen product to a package that presents a news piece from the archives of each of three news services. The text and image segments of each piece reside as XML on the CD-ROM. All of the direct (i.e., HTML-style) simple links are rendered as XLink. The DIGAM itself, downloaded at the start of the live session, is an XML file. It consists almost totally of links expressed as XLink. Here is the full listing of the DIGAM for this collection:

```
<?xml version="1.0"? standalone="yes">
<!-- A Digital Asset Management system using XLink -->
<!DOCTYPE DAMFile [
        <!ELEMENT DIGAMFile
        (Asset | IPOwner | reposLoc | ownedBy | inReposAt)+>
        <!ATTLIST DIGAMFile
                xlink:type CDATA #REQUIRED>

        <!ELEMENT Asset (mediaTitle)>
        <!ATTLIST Asset
                xlink:type CDATA #REQUIRED
                xlink:href CDATA #REQUIRED
                xlink:title CDATA #REQUIRED
                xlink:label CDATA #REQUIRED>
```

```
        <!ELEMENT IPOwner EMPTY>
        <!ATTLIST IPOwner
                xlink:type CDATA #REQUIRED
                xlink:href CDATA #REQUIRED
                xlink:title CDATA #REQUIRED
                xlink:label CDATA #REQUIRED>

        <!ELEMENT reposLoc EMPTY>
        <!ATTLIST reposLoc
                xlink:type CDATA #REQUIRED
                xlink:href CDATA #REQUIRED
                xlink:title CDATA #REQUIRED
                xlink:label CDATA #REQUIRED>

        <!ELEMENT ownedBy EMPTY>
        <!ATTLIST ownedBy
                xlink:type CDATA #REQUIRED
                xlink:from CDATA #REQUIRED
                xlink:to CDATA #REQUIRED>

        <!ELEMENT inReposAt EMPTY>
        <!ATTLIST inReposAt
                xlink:type CDATA #REQUIRED
                xlink:from CDATA #REQUIRED
                xlink:to CDATA #REQUIRED>

        <!ELEMENT mediaTitle (#PCDATA)>
]>

<DIGAMFile xlink:type="extended"
        xmlns:xlink="http://www.w3.org/1999/xlink">

<!-- Description of each property
        Note: the href address is for the original source.
        The local repository address is stored in the separate section
        of reposLoc locators defined below. -->
        <Asset
                xlink:type="locator"
                xlink:href="http://www.up.org"
                xlink:title="United Press Story"
                xlink:label="UPArch-006">

                <mediaTitle>US Goes to War</mediaTitle>
        </Asset>

        <Asset
                xlink:type="locator"
                xlink:href="http://www.ap.org"
                xlink:title="Associated Press Story"
                xlink:label="APArch-002">
```

```
            <mediaTitle>Normandy Invasion</mediaTitle>
      </Asset>

      <Asset
            xlink:type="locator"
            xlink:href="http://www.Gannett.org"
            xlink:title="USA Today Story"
            xlink:label="GNArch-068">

            <mediaTitle>Germany Surrenders</mediaTitle>
      </Asset>

<!-- Owners of the various properties -->
      <IPOwner
            xlink:type="locator"
            xlink:href="www.Gannett.com/permissions"
            xlink:title="Gannett IP POC"
            xlink:label="GannettPOC"/>
      <IPOwner
            xlink:type="locator"
            xlink:href="www.up.com/permissions"
            xlink:title="UP IP POC"
            xlink:label="UP-POC"/>
      <IPOwner
            xlink:type="locator"
            xlink:href="www.ap.org/permissions"
            xlink:title="AP IP POC"
            xlink:label="AP-POC"/>

<!-- Location of common directory area for made-for-CD versions -->
      <reposLoc
            xlink:type="locator"
            xlink:href="/news/archive/CDVersions"
            xlink:title="CD Versions"
            xlink:label="CD-Directory"/>

<!-- Define the arcs, linking each property with the POC of its owner -->
      <ownedBy
            xlink:type="arc"
            xlink:from="APArch-002"
            xlink:to="AP-POC"/>
      <ownedBy
            xlink:type="arc"
            xlink:from="GNArch-068"
            xlink:to="Gannett-POC"/>
      <ownedBy
            xlink:type="arc"
            xlink:from="UPArch-006"
            xlink:to="UP-POC"/>
```

```
<!-- Define arcs linking each news piece with its local
     repository location -->
     <inReposAt
          xlink:type="arc"
          xlink:from="UPArch-006"
          xlink:to="CD-Directory"/>
     <inReposAt
          xlink:type="arc"
          xlink:from="UPArch-006"
          xlink:to="CD-Directory"/>
     <inReposAt
          xlink:type="arc"
          xlink:from="GNArch-068"
          xlink:to="CD-Directory"/>
</DIGAMFile>
```

The essential observation for this XLink-based manager is that it defines and applies links between its resources. Figure 19.2 is a schematic description of a single asset (a multimedia image, audio file, or video file), showing those resources and the links that express relationships between them.

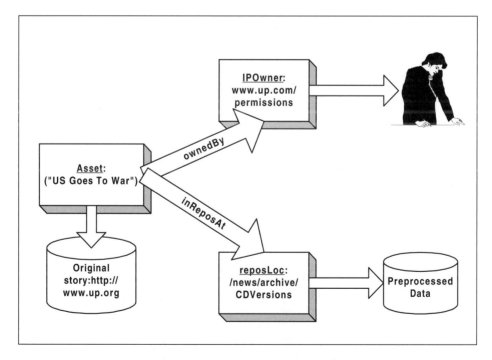

Figure 19.2 *A schematic of a single asset*

Note first that the resources (boxes, original piece, data in repository, person at news editorial) and the arrows connecting them indicate relationships only and not actual data flow. Second, bear in mind that the two links from the asset do not mean go here when I click. They only mean exactly what the picture says. They express relationships: ownership of the asset and physical location information for the asset. It is up to an XLink-aware processor to do with that information whatever it wishes. (One such processor will use these data to create the digital playlist which follows.)

The XML file for the DIGAM is **standalone**, as the prolog says. That means that the file itself contains the XML declaration, including the DTD. In this little discussion, we will match the XML representation of each resource with its portion of the DTD.

While this XLink-heavy file appears a bit unusual, it really is only just another XML file with elements, attributes, and tagged data. Besides the frequency of the prefix **xlink:**, the aspect that is most unfamiliar to us is the density of attributes. Most lines of this file are attributes. That is the most important observation about XLink to keep in mind as we move along.

The XML representation of each asset looks like this:

```
<Asset
       xlink:type="locator"
       xlink:href="http://www.up.org"
       xlink:title="United Press Story"
       xlink:label="UPArch-006">

       <mediaTitle>US Goes to War</mediaTitle>
</Asset>
```

This element and its markup actually contain only a descriptive mediaTitle (US Goes to War). The rest of **Asset** is the suite of Xlink attributes that describe **Asset**. Each of those attributes (**type**, **href**, **title**, and **label**) are part of the XLink specification. We incorporate those attributes into our declaration for Asset so that we may exploit XLink features:

```
<!ELEMENT Asset (mediaTitle)>
<!ATTLIST Asset
       xlink:type CDATA #REQUIRED
       xlink:href CDATA #REQUIRED
       xlink:title CDATA #REQUIRED
xlink:label CDATA #REQUIRED>
```

Commingling our own definition of an element type with XLink's repertoire of attributes is the way XLink/XPointer expressions are to be written.

We examined simple links in the previous section. In fact, there is a simple link (using **href**) for each of the **Asset**s as well. This is the link to the original news piece, as posted on the Internet. We only mention this because it is part of the total DIGAM. We happen not to use this link in our particular application.

Just as each of the three assets has its own XML markup, so does each of the IP owners:

```
<IPOwner
      xlink:type="locator"
      xlink:href="www.up.com/permissions"
      xlink:title="UP IP POC"
      xlink:label="UP-POC"/>
```

But this time the element (**IPOwner**) has no content of its own, as the DTD's definition makes clear:

```
<!ELEMENT IPOwner EMPTY>
<!ATTLIST IPOwner
      xlink:type CDATA #REQUIRED
      xlink:href CDATA #REQUIRED
      xlink:title CDATA #REQUIRED
      xlink:label CDATA #REQUIRED>
```

An **IPOwner** element's sole purpose is to serve as a locator, part of the XLink apparatus for the DIGAM. Exactly the same is true for **reposLoc**. Both of these element types are **EMPTY**, having only attributes and no content of their own.

The final task of this file is to define the two extended links. First we associate each asset with its legal owner. For asset management purposes, we decided to define the publisher's permissions office (point of contact) as the **link end**. With all of the resources having been previously defined, the definition of the **ownedBy** link is straightforward and very readable:

```
<ownedBy
      xlink:type="arc"
      xlink:from="UPArch-006"
      xlink:to="UP-POC"/>
```

Unlike the HTML-style link in our first example, this **xlink:type** is an **arc**. This is the link type that allows us to define link starts and link ends as we please, with no need for physical access to the linked-to content. **xlink:from** identifies the start of the link, and **xlink:to**. identifies the link's end. In our example the from link end is local and the to end is remote. But with the arc mechanism, they could both be remote.

The values assigned to **from** and **to** are the values for **xlink:label** of the **Asset** and of the **IPOwner**.

That completes our tour of the linked resources that support DIGAM. If this were a browser-centric activity, we would probably down translate all of the XLink expressions to HTML. That would provide something that the browser could readily display and that would demonstrate our system. The fact is that for us this linking apparatus is an invisible, embedded XML layer in the total workflow of acquiring, managing, and delivering multimedia. There is nothing remarkable to display because there is nothing to look at! The linked content is a hidden back-room commodity. But while it is hidden, it enables on-the-fly content management in ways never before possible. One of the consumers of DIGAM-linked content is the CD-ROM-based engine that creates the digital playlist. We turn next to this playlist.

DIGITAL PLAYLIST: EXECUTIVE TALKTHROUGH ......

The **playlist** is a mechanism for personalized sequencing. Using live data from the publisher's DIGAM for this electronic product, the presentation engine on the CD-ROM creates the playlist. The playlist, like the DIGAM, consists almost totally of XLink expressions. After it constructs the playlist the engine uses the playlist to fetch the material for each scene and to sequence those scenes for the current session. Here is the full listing for the digital playlist:

```
<?xml version="1.0"? standalone="yes">
<!-- A Digital Asset Management system using XLink -->
<!DOCTYPE DIGAMFile [
      <!ELEMENT DIGAMFile (Asset | IPOwner | reposLoc |
       ownedBy | inReposAt)+>
      <!ATTLIST DIGAMFile
             xlink:type CDATA #REQUIRED>

      <!ELEMENT Asset (mediaTitle)>
      <!ATTLIST Asset
             xlink:type CDATA #REQUIRED
             xlink:href CDATA #REQUIRED
             xlink:title CDATA #REQUIRED
             xlink:label CDATA #REQUIRED>

      <!ELEMENT IPOwner EMPTY>
      <!ATTLIST IPOwner
             xlink:type CDATA #REQUIRED
             xlink:href CDATA #REQUIRED
             xlink:title CDATA #REQUIRED
             xlink:label CDATA #REQUIRED>

      <!ELEMENT reposLoc EMPTY>
      <!ATTLIST reposLoc
             xlink:type CDATA #REQUIRED
             xlink:href CDATA #REQUIRED
             xlink:title CDATA #REQUIRED
```

```
                xlink:label CDATA #REQUIRED>

        <!ELEMENT ownedBy EMPTY>
        <!ATTLIST ownedBy
                xlink:type CDATA #REQUIRED
                xlink:from CDATA #REQUIRED
                xlink:to CDATA #REQUIRED>

        <!ELEMENT inReposAt EMPTY>
        <!ATTLIST inReposAt
                xlink:type CDATA #REQUIRED
                xlink:from CDATA #REQUIRED
                xlink:to CDATA #REQUIRED>

        <!ELEMENT mediaTitle (#PCDATA)>
]>


<DIGAMFile xlink:type="extended"
        xmlns:xlink="http://www.w3.org/1999/xlink">

<!-- Description of each property
        Note: the href address is for the original
        source. The local repository address is stored
        in the separate section of reposLoc locators
        defined below. -->
        <Asset
                xlink:type="locator"
                xlink:href="http://www.up.org"
                xlink:title="United Press Story"
                xlink:label="UPArch-006">

                <mediaTitle>US Goes to War</mediaTitle>
        </Asset>

        <Asset
                xlink:type="locator"
                xlink:href="http://www.ap.org"
                xlink:title="Associated Press Story"
                xlink:label="APArch-002">

                <mediaTitle>Normandy Invasion</mediaTitle>
        </Asset>

        <Asset
                xlink:type="locator"
                xlink:href="http://www.Gannett.org"
                xlink:title="USA Today Story"
                xlink:label="GNArch-068">

                <mediaTitle>Germany Surrenders</mediaTitle>
        </Asset>
```

```
<!-- Owners of the various properties -->
     <IPOwner
           xlink:type="locator"
           xlink:href="www.Gannett.com/permissions"
           xlink:title="Gannett IP POC"
           xlink:label="GannettPOC"/>
     <IPOwner
           xlink:type="locator"
           xlink:href="www.up.com/permissions"
           xlink:title="UP IP POC"
           xlink:label="UP-POC"/>
     <IPOwner
           xlink:type="locator"
           xlink:href="www.ap.org/permissions"
           xlink:title="AP IP POC"
           xlink:label="AP-POC"/>

<!-- Location of common directory area for made-for-CD
     versions -->
     <reposLoc
           xlink:type="locator"
           xlink:href="/news/archive/CDVersions"
           xlink:title="CD Versions"
           xlink:label="CD-Directory"/>

<!-- Define the arcs, linking each property with the
     POC of its owner -->
     <ownedBy
           xlink:type="arc"
           xlink:from="APArch-002"
           xlink:to="AP-POC"/>
     <ownedBy
           xlink:type="arc"
           xlink:from="GNArch-068"
           xlink:to="Gannett-POC"/>
     <ownedBy
           xlink:type="arc"
           xlink:from="UPArch-006"
           xlink:to="UP-POC"/>

<!-- Define arcs linking each news piece with its
     local repository location -->
     <inReposAt
           xlink:type="arc"
           xlink:from="UPArch-006"
           xlink:to="CD-Directory"/>
```

```
        <inReposAt
            xlink:type="arc"
            xlink:from="UPArch-006"
            xlink:to="CD-Directory"/>
        <inReposAt
            xlink:type="arc"
            xlink:from="GNArch-068"
            xlink:to="CD-Directory"/>
</DIGAMFile>
```

The CD-ROM-based product is able to receive (optimally download) an accurate DIGAM for the publisher's product. It converts that XML content to another XML product: the digital playlist. Once created, the digital playlist XLink file is available for any purpose whatever. From the digital playlist, the CD-ROM-based display engine extracts information for two purposes:

1. *To sequence the multimedia scenes properly.* What is proper may have been determined on the basis of the user's stored usage logs, the reader's preferences, the trainee's past performance, or the user's own explicit list. Whatever the basis for the sequence, the engine builds the playlist to sequence the material.

2. *To determine precisely where to access each multimedia item.* Within an HTML-only environment, it was extremely important to enforce the proper path structure for content: which directory would contain images, which directory would contain text, where the icons would be found. With the dynamic environment made possible by XLink, the presentation engine itself can be smarter about where things are stored.

The digital playlist embodies these two essential items of knowledge that the presentation engine requires for each scene: (1) where to find its content and (2) where to go next. It has that information thanks to links. Figure 19.3 is a diagram of that linking relationship.

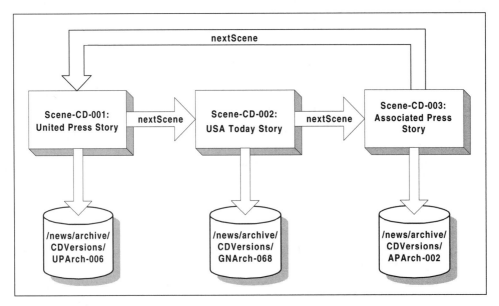

Figure 19.3 Digital playlist linking relationship

Note that in the diagram each scene (here, a story coming originally from a news service's archive) has two links:

A **simple link** to the proper location on the CD-ROM where the content for the scene is stored

An **arc** (extended link) that describes the relationship **nextScene**.

Just as we saw for the DIGAM, the digital playlist first defines its **resources**, the items which play various roles in the linking process. There are only two such items in the playlist: the scene itself and the sequencing link. Here is the definition of **Scene**:

```
<Scene
     xlink:type="locator"
     xlink:href="/news/archive/CDVersions/UPArch-006"
     xlink:title="United Press Story"
     xlink:label="Scene-CD-001" >

  <caption>Normandy Invasion</caption>

</Scene>
```

Like **Asset**, Scene is a **locator**. Its primary payload is linking information. The only content that the element has is the **caption**. Presumably the presentation engine will use that information in some way, but that is of no concern to the linking apparatus.

The other resource is the element defining the link used for the engine's navigation:

```
<nextScene
      xlink:type="arc"
      xlink:from="Scene-CD-001"
      xlink:to="Scene-CD-002"></nextScene>
```

In this **nextScene** element we define a link from the first scene to the second. Note that this link and this link alone will determine the order of presentation. The actual stored order of the scenes on the CD-ROM may be different from that. And the order of presentation for the current user session may be different during the next session.

As we said for the DIGAM, we say again that the digital playlist is not browser-ready. That is not the fault of browser technologies' failure to keep up. Nor is it because the digital playlist is deficient. The Playlist is a supporting mechanism for the presentation engine. The engine is as XLink-aware as it must be to do its job. It will use this linkage information and process the CD-ROM content in the way that it is designed to do. The result may appear as trivial as a repeating slide show. It is not trivial that both the sequence of scenes and the selection material can now be personalized and produced on the fly.

XPOINTER: TWIN OF HYPERLINKING ....

Thus far we have only mentioned XPointer as part of the XLink/XPointer pair of XML specifications. But we have offered no explanation, no demonstration, and no business role for this other hyperlinking technology. Part of the reason we have dedicated only a small part of this chapter to XPointer is that the essentials of XPointer are so straightforward to master and apply to ordinary cases. (The full specification is of course much more complex.)

The motivation for XPointer is the need for greater granularity in addressing content. In practically every example in this book we use generic mechanisms to *point at* files, pages, images, and entire directories. Addressing with HTML's HTTP mechanism does offer a means of breaking through the monolithic addressing brick wall. The original HTML content author may have been foresightful enough to insert an HTML **<a NAME>** or **<a ID>** (**named anchors**) to serve as possible end points of **<a href:>** links. That means that, in a limited sense, HTML already allows us to *point into* a remote document. XPointer carries that much further.

The mission of XPointer is threefold:

1. To allow us to point into XML content rather than simply to point at it.

2. To allow us to point without requiring any preinserted labels in the targeted content.

3. To provide a language with which we can readily navigate to any point in an any instance of XML content of any variety.

How XPointer Points Into

The most helpful way to achieve a strategic grasp of XPointer is to examine common methods that its language uses for identifying very granular objects within some XML content.

Bare-name—Your link to some object requires only that the target element within the location bears an attribute of type **ID**. An XPointer-aware parser will interpret such a name as an XPointer link if it is prefixed with a cross-hatch. Thus **#Case-01** points into the current document at the element whose identification attribute has the value Case-01.

XPath identifiers—An XPath expression can serve as an XPointer if it is prefixed by **#xpointer**. Thus the expression

#xpointer(//example[@application==LegalXML=])

tells the XPointer-aware processor to locate the example element whose attribute application has the value **LegalXML**.

Child Sequences—With only a crosshatch as a prefix, an XPointer-enabled parser will use the following XML tree notation (with slashes) to locate an element: **#/1/5/3/20**. That child sequence expression means "The 20th child of the third child of the fifth child of the topmost element in the tree."

String ranges ()function—This example, adapted from one in the XPointer specification, suggests the extreme level of granularity possible with XPointer:

#xpointer(string-range(//Author,"Henry James",7,0)[2]).

That expression first locates the second **<Author>** element in the current document. Within that element it identifies the string up to but not including the seventh character: **"Henry"** is the result.

The pointing mechanisms of XPointer are more than just reminiscent of XPath. XPointer has in fact co-opted a good share of the XPath methodology for its own purposes.

XLink and XPointer to Achieve the Hyperlink Dream

With XPointer likely to join XLink as a full W3C Recommendation, we are closer to the long-sought goal of hypertext: to allow totally interactive navigation and linking between items of content without labor-intensive markup of all of the actual documents involved. Whereas XLink enables an arm's-distance strategy for managing links, XPointer allows us to penetrate deeply and with great focus into the details of structured information.

AS THE SPECIFICATION SAYS... ....

Abstract of the XML Linking Language (XLink) Version 1.0 W3C Recommendation 27 June 2001:

This specification defines the XML Linking Language (XLink), which allows elements to be inserted into XML documents in order to create and describe links between resources. It uses XML syntax to create structures that can describe links similar to the simple unidirectional hyperlinks of today's HTML, as well as more sophisticated links.

Abstract of the XML Pointer Language (XPointer) Version 1.0 W3C Last Call Working Draft 8 January 2001:

This specification defines the XML Pointer Language (XPointer), the language to be used as the basis for a fragment identifier for any URI reference that locates a resource whose Internet media type is one of text/xml, application/xml, text/xml-external-parsed-entity, or application/xml-external-parsed-entity. XPointer, which is based on the XML Path Language (XPath), supports addressing into the internal structures of XML documents. It allows for examination of a hierarchical document structure and choice of its internal parts based on various properties, such as element types, attribute values, character content, and relative position.

FOUR REASONS WHY XLINK/XPOINTER MAKES GOOD BUSINESS SENSE ....

It is little exaggeration to note that the majority of existing XML systems are really proofs of concept. Some are large-scale and extensive initiatives, to be sure. But the IT community at large has felt that XML is unable to reach out and pull together information in the way that today's workplace demands. XLink and XPointer promise to change that. The benefits to IT will impact where benefits are most needed: in the costly maintenance and life cycle of information. Following are benefits that we have hinted at through this chapter's discussion:

1. *Zero impact on existing content (where linking is required).* Our experience with Web-based HTML has taught us to fear the costs of constant hands-on maintenance of Web page linking. Our brief case study has demonstrated that the cost of maintaining and upgrading links can be drastically reduced. This is because with XLink/XPointer, we need not even touch the actual content. We only need to do minor text editing within the small link products.

2. *Near-zero programming costs for managing links' behavior.* With traditional programming languages alone, the cost for accomplishing what XLink/XPointer expressions can exert over linking would be prohibitive. The days-long learning curve for XLink/XPointer competency is only a tiny fraction of the skill level that would be required for programming and maintenance without these specifications.

3. *Cost-cutting reuse of multimedia.* Because XPointer allows us to link into content, we are able to select content fragments in a more granular fashion without having to rely on the content's internal structure. Internal fragments (video clips, audio passages) that would have been invaluable to us were locked inside whole, unexposed media files. With XPointer we can return to these existing media files and mine them for reusable fragments.

4. *Zero-cost co-option of third-party content.* Prior to XLink/XPointer the only method for external-to-external linking or for linking into remote content was for us to have write-access permission to that content. We would then have to insert link points inside that content. With XLink/XPointer we can easily author linking products that incorporate third-party content, even without the parties' knowledge and without any access to their content.

SUMMARY ....

XLink and XPointer may suffer somewhat from their immaturity. XLink achieved recommendation status only a few months before the time of this writing. And XPointer is still only a working draft. Consequently there is scant support among vendors' products for either. Nevertheless the beneficial impact of these linking specifications is inevitable. We will feel that impact beyond the world of the Web, because linking in this new key is fundamental to enterprise IT for any medium of delivery.

Part 3

XML At Work

20 XML At Work: Manufacturing

In this chapter...

They Said It...

Yer job ain't finished 'til the paper work is done.
anonymous

For some XML evangelists, XML is an exciting hammer in search of nails to pound. But for certain applications, XML is a solution to an already deeply felt need. Electronics products typically are tree-structured in their design. And the manufacturing process typically views them in the same way. Production engineers refer to the description of an electronic product as a structured bill of materials (BOM). A well-tended BOM for an electronics product—with all of its components, subcomponents, connectors, and subassemblies—not only resembles XML. It practically *is* an XML document in the making.

XML belongs in electronics manufacturing because it solves problems and reduces costs. In this chapter we examine an actual BOM, noting how it can support not just production but every aspect of the supplier's activity: manufacturing, purchasing, accounting, engineering, technical writing, and marketing.

USING XML TO ENHANCE MATURE MANUFACTURING TECHNOLOGY ....

The BOM is not a product of XML technology. And unlike other documents, the BOM for a manufactured product is not simply a supporting record. It is virtually an indispensable reflection of the product itself. As we shall see shortly, the BOM encapsulates knowledge and history of the product. Portions of it are typically shared by departments across the entire enterprise. It is also a primary tool for supply chain management—guaranteeing a predictable inventory of components from every vendor and a reliable flow of product to every distributor. If you are seriously involved in any way with designing, creating, producing, and delivering products, the BOM is already an important management tool.

Part of the problem with the BOM is its inherent usefulness. Different pieces of its content are critical to different departments in quite different ways. So the problem is how to expose, extract, and present those various items of BOM knowledge in highly specialized ways. The traditional approach has been to design specialized BOM databases and report generators. The problem with managing that solution is familiar. The databases, computer programs, and report generation products only serve to lock up the BOM within proprietary formats and products and within one-off solutions.

If you work anywhere in a manufacturing supply chain—engineering, software development, or marketing—you probably already access or manage a BOM. Your biggest need is for the ability to translate the BOM to the requirements of your particular department. XML is the ideal solution because it does not require radical data conversion, only a straightforward change in representation of the already structured data.

BOM Basics

Every electronic device, your desktop computer included, consists of a box, inside of which are components like a power supply, printed circuit boards, and hundreds of connectors and pieces of hardware to make it all work. Inside many of the components there are subcomponents (or subassemblies) that also may contain yet more deeply embedded circuit boards, connectors, and yet more hardware. Each circuit board consists of its own etching, its precisely drilled holes, chips and discrete components, and so on.

The traditional way to depict this kind of embedding is with "parts explosions," each an inset that contains a subassembly. The inset then uses an arrow to show where the subassembly is located within the larger product.

The traditional way to describe the structure of an electronics product is with a decimal numbered outline. For each level there is a sequential list of components. Each level of indentation receives another decimal point, as in the following: **1.27.2.82**. That code might designate an item #82 (mounting screw) for the second circuit board in subassembly #27 of the main (level #1) product.

With only those bare essentials—a list of items and the level number of each in a decimal notation—the reader is able to infer which items are components and which are subcomponents.

WHAT DOES A BOM CONTAIN?............................

A bill of materials describes more than just the parts for bins on the assembly bench. It describes everything that comprises the finished product, including the barcode identification labels, instruction labels, and the compliance labels required by law. For each circuit board it lists the art that is printed as an electronic circuit on the board. Even the Ziplock™ bag for the various loose nuts and bolts is identified by item number and level of indentation.

A BOM also contains items that we might say are technically not even there. Every programmable read-only memory (PROM) chip that contains programming code written by the manufacturer has at least two entries on the BOM:

1. The raw (i.e., unprogrammed) PROM as it was received and inventoried from the chip supplier.

2. The program code (as well as its version) written by the software group.

What a BOM Knows

The following BOM report is adapted from that of a real manufacturer of telecommunications equipment. The report's header items are the items of information describing each of the more than 1000 parts in this particular piece of equipment, a telecommunications switching device. These header items are described here.

1. *Level*. The decimal-marked number that identifies the level of embedding or "indentation" of the item.

2. *Item sequence*. The sequence for this item within its own level. For example, there are 13 items within the printed circuit board assembly (level 2) identified as 301643. Those items on the PCB assembly reside at level 3 on the BOM and numbered consecutively as 1–13.

3. *Item number*. This uniquely identifies the item.

4. *Description*. The plain-English description of the item. It typically is full of abbreviations and acronyms, and the full form does not fit on the printed BOM report. But the full form exists in the materials database.

5. *Revision code*. Every item for which some engineering group is responsible for design and upgrades bears a revision code. It is possible that only the engineers will know what the code means for that item. If there is no revision code, then the BOM shows simply that the code is not designated (ND).

6. *Unit of measurement (UOM)*. In this particular BOM, the only two units are "each" and "feet."

7. *Effective date*. The release date of the most recent revision.

8. *Hazard*. If there are any particular warnings for the manufacturing group, they should appear here. In this case, electrostatic discharge, caused by an assembly worker not wearing the proper grounding equipment, may damage the item.

9. *Quantity*. The quantity of this item at this point (sequence and indentation level) of the BOM.

10. *Extended quantity*. The total number of this item, useful only if the UOM (unit of measurement) is other than each.

11. *Engineering change order (ECO) reference designator*. Throughout the life cycle of this product, customers will request and the company will

implement certain fixes and enhancements. It typically requires a long but orderly process before an ECO appears and the revision is released. The ECO reference designator is a pointer to the record that tracks the history behind the revision of the item.

WHO USES THE BOM?......................................

It probably is unfair to say that the BOM is the product's central document for the entire company. But it is safe to assume that the 11 items of information about each part are critical to various functions within the company:

- *Inventory control*. The quantity of each of the thousand of items required to build each product is critical. An unexpected shortage of components could shut down an entire assembly process.

- *Accounting and financial management*. For determining and tracking the cost to build this product, it is necessary to mine periodically the entire list of items in the BOM. Using the suppliers database, it is possible to match BOM parts information with suppliers' costs to determine the cost to build.

- *Purchasing*. With so many components to be ordered from multiple suppliers, it is virtually impossible for a manufacturer to monitor the reorder points for each component by hand. For each component, Purchasing's automated ordering system uses the BOM product number, together with item number, quantity required, and number on-hand (in the inventory database) to trigger a requisition and purchase order.

- *Application engineering*. The engineers who actually design and implement fixes and upgrades to the product rely on the revision identification, release date, and ECO reference as a living history of the product. Whenever a particular fix produces some unforeseen side-effect (usually bad!), the history allows everyone to backtrack to the last known working version. Without this rigorous record, that could be impossible.

- *Production/Manufacturing*. The BOM naturally supplies Manufacturing with a virtual blueprint and requirements definition for the assembly floor: arrangement of bins and assembly benches, bin capacities, wire lengths, connectors, for example.

- *Technical Documentation*. It is virtually impossible for a writer simply to look at a finished product and deduce what is inside. And it is next to impossible to rely solely on engineers' documents (if they even exist). Writers must often become trainees for the products they must document, relying on verbal instructions from engineers. The BOM is among the most reliable sources for their understanding the product. From that the writers can produce the core of installation guides, operations manuals, maintenance manuals, troubleshooting guides, and other supporting documentation.

BOM Workflow

The BOM is clearly a living document. It undergoes constant change because every ECO for the product directly affects the bill of materials: revised part numbers, new or deleted parts, component upgrades, and, of course changed revision levels and dates. It is important therefore that the process of updating the BOM be as straightforward and automated as possible.

For this particular engineering BOM, the only labor-intensive task is to edit the master file (EngBOM.xml) directly with an off-the-shelf XML editing tool (Figure 20.1).

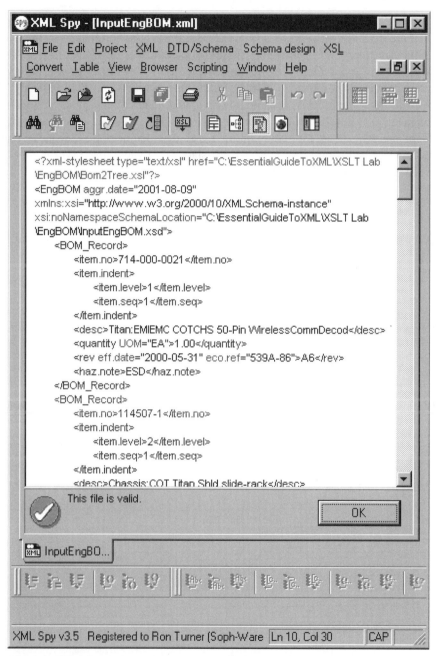

Figure 20.1 Entering the original BOM

Zero-programming "derivatives"

The XML developers in this project are justifiably proud of the clever transformations that are possible with scripts and XSLT. But the production managers are even more appreciative of XML because of the immediate access they have to live XML data without any programming at all. In Chapter 16 we downplayed the ability of Microsoft Internet Explorer to display totally unprocessed (but well-formed) XML. It was not formatted nicely. It came nowhere near matching the most rudimentary Web page layouts. But the various users of the EngBOM.xml content, including even shop floor supervisors, are intimately familiar with the document. So they have virtually no need for styled pages. For them it is satisfactory to view the BOM directly from the browser, as seen in Figure 20.2.

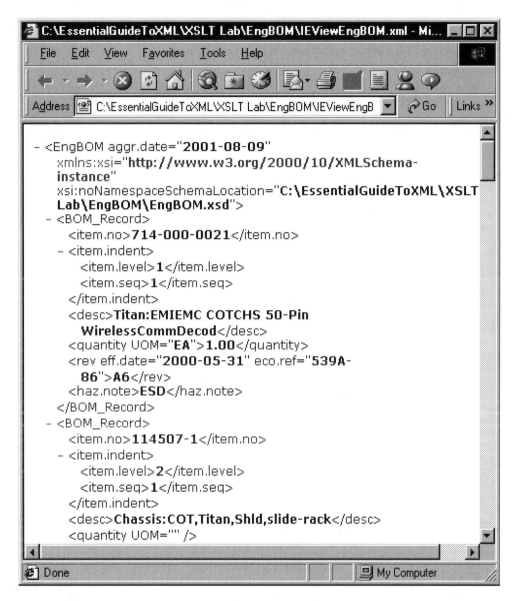

Figure 20.2 Viewing the BOM directly under Microsoft Internet Explorer

This is truly programmerless. The user only must use the browser's **FILE->OPEN** option to display the XML BOM.

Both the Payables and Receivables groups must also have access to certain data within the BOM, but they typically only need to see components' item numbers and descriptions. For them the following Web page rendition in Figure 20.3 is a trusted and valuable tool.

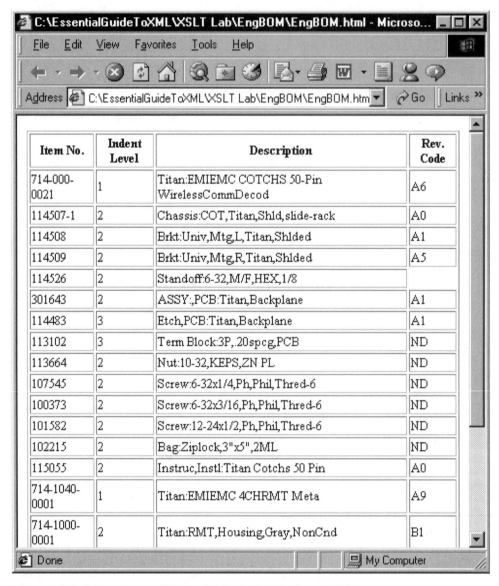

Figure 20.3 Simple rendition of selected data from BOM

This Web page report is generated on the fly, accessing the most current version of the BOM. It uses the simple XML data island approach, also described in Chapter 16. The only programming effort was a one-time 20-minute session to write and test the following .html file:

```
<!DOCTYPE HTML PUBLIC "-//W3C//DTD HTML 4.0 Transitional//EN">
<HTML>

<BODY>

<XML ID="xmlDoc"src = "ViewBOM.xml">

</XML>

<TABLE BORDER = "1" DATASRC = "#xmlDoc">
   <THEAD>
   <TR>
      <TH>Item No.</TH>
      <TH>Indent Level</TH>
      <TH>Description</TH>
      <TH>Rev. Code</TH>
   </TR>
   </THEAD>

   <TR>
      <TD><SPAN DATAFLD = "itemno"></SPAN></TD>
      <TD><SPAN DATAFLD = "itemlevel"></SPAN></TD>
      <TD><SPAN DATAFLD = "desc"></SPAN></TD>
      <TD><SPAN DATAFLD = "rev"></SPAN></TD>
   </TR>
</TABLE>

</BODY>
</HTML>
```

The file referenced above by the highlighted name is a slightly cooked-down version of the BOM XML (only a fragment shown here):

```
<EngBOM>
    <BOM_Record>
        <itemno>714-000-0021</itemno>

            <itemlevel>1</itemlevel>
            <itemseq>1</itemseq>

        <desc>Titan:EMIEMC COTCHS 50-Pin WirelessCommDecod</desc>
        <quantity UOM="EA">1.00</quantity>
        <rev >A6</rev>
        <haz.note>ESD</haz.note>
    </BOM_Record>
    <BOM_Record>
        <itemno>114507-1</itemno>
```

```
        <desc>Titan:EMIEMC COTCHS 50-Pin WirelessCommDecod</desc>
        <quantity UOM="EA">1.00</quantity>
        <rev >A6</rev>
        <haz.note>ESD</haz.note>
    </BOM_Record>
    <BOM_Record>
        <itemno>114507-1</itemno>

            <itemlevel>2</itemlevel>
            <itemseq>1</itemseq>

        <desc>Chassis:COT,Titan,Shld,slide-rack</desc>
        <quantity UOM=""/>
        <rev >A0</rev>
    </BOM_Record>
    <BOM_Record>
        <itemno>114508</itemno>

            <itemlevel>2</itemlevel>
            <itemseq>2</itemseq>

        <desc>Brkt:Univ,Mtg,L,Titan,Shlded</desc>
        <quantity UOM="">1.0</quantity>
        <rev>A1</rev>
    </BOM_Record>
    <BOM_Record>
        <itemno>114509</itemno>

            <itemlevel>2</itemlevel>
            <itemseq>3</itemseq>

        <desc>Brkt:Univ,Mtg,R,Titan,Shlded</desc>
        <quantity UOM="EA">1.0</quantity>
        <rev>A5</rev>
    </BOM_Record>
    <BOM_Record>
        <itemno>114526</itemno>

            <itemlevel>2</itemlevel>
            <itemseq>5</itemseq>

        <desc>Standoff:6-32,M/F,HEX,1/8</desc>
        <quantity UOM="">6.0</quantity>
        <rev></rev>
    </BOM_Record>
```

In order to accommodate the restrictions of our low-grade .html interface to the browser, the original BOM file needed minor adjustments (including some deletions), all very easily accomplished by a nontechnical clerk using a prewritten script. That script likewise requires only a few minutes' one-time effort by a developer.

Repurposing the BOM

We said at the start of this chapter that a bill of materials is tree-structured. When a human engineer or technician reads the BOM, its indentation (tree) structure is obvious. But the original XML file representing the BOM of the product does not express that tree structure in a way that computer can understand. So if we really wanted to create that rendition, it would be necessary to convert the file, adding the intelligence that a human reader uses natively. The first step might be to add a pointer element to each item in the BOM to identify the parent of that item. After running the original XML file through a conversion script (Python), the now-smarter document appears as follows (fragment only):

```
<BOM_Record>
    <item.no>714-0000-0021</item.no>
    <item.indent>
        <item.level>1</item.level>
        <item.seq>1</item.seq>
    </item.indent>
    <desc>Titan:EMIEMC COTCHS 50-Pin WirelessCommDecod</desc>
    <quantity UOM="EA">1.00</quantity>
    <rev eff.date="2000-05-31" eco.ref="539A-86">A6</rev>
    <haz.note>ESD</haz.note>
    <parent>00</parent>
</BOM_Record>
<BOM_Record>
    <item.no>114507-1</item.no>
    <item.indent>
        <item.level>2</item.level>
        <item.seq>1</item.seq>
    </item.indent>
    <desc>Chassis:COT,Titan,Shld,slide-rack</desc>
    <quantity UOM=""/>
    <rev eff.date="2000-10-30" eco.ref="">A0</rev>
    <parent>0101714-000-0021</parent>
</BOM_Record>
<BOM_Record>
    <item.no>114508</item.no>
    <item.indent>
        <item.level>2</item.level>
        <item.seq>2</item.seq>
    </item.indent>
    <desc>Brkt:Univ,Mtg,L,Titan,Shlded</desc>
    <quantity UOM="">1.0</quantity>
    <rev eff.date="2000-10-30">A1</rev>
    <parent>0101714-000-0021</parent>
</BOM_Record>
```

Each of the new parent elements now contains both the identification of its parent (the component within which it is embedded) plus information about its nesting level. This is only one small example of how the BOM record, as exposed *data*, can be easily modified for any purpose whatsoever.

SUMMARY OF XML BOM ....

Because of its inherent structure, a bill of materials is an XML application waiting to happen. Applying XML technologies to this part of manufacturing represents a minimal outlay for development. For some of the derivative products from an XML BOM, there are only minimal one-time costs. With the power of XSLT, other conversion tools, and programming languages, the dynamic BOM can easily be adapted and converted for a wide variety of applications within the organization.

21 XML At Work: Extensible Business Reporting Language

In this chapter...

They Said It...

*You must report to the Volscian lords, how
plainly I have borne this business*

William Shakespeare: Coriolanus

Accounting of any variety invariably entails reporting. Every commercially available accounting product includes reporting utilities for each segment: general ledger, receivables, payables, payroll, inventory, cost accounting, project costing,...whatever packages the accounting system includes. But there is a much wider dimension to financial reporting than simply creating ad hoc reports. All publicly held corporations have an ongoing obligation to issue a wide range of statements and reports. The same is true for business entities within every branch of government. These are meant for wide distribution—to shareholders, auditors, regulators, brokerage firms, news media, creditors, and anyone else who might become a stakeholder. The page format of this information has been highly standardized for decades.

With the escalating demands by regulators, the traffic in business reports has outstripped the ability of many businesses to generate, transmit, and process them manually. The need to automate business reporting has motivated the professional accounting community, led by the American Institute of Certified Public Accountants (AICPA), to host a major XML-based initiative called Extensible Business Reporting Language (XBRL). XBRL is an example of an XML application that is already doing useful work, that has buy-in from a wide spectrum of organizations, and that is spreading globally. This chapter is a brief exhibit of that activity.

ABSTRACT OF THE XBRL SPECIFICATION...............

It is interesting to note in this statement that the XBRL information architects view XBLR not only as a language for creating document instances but as a mechanism for creating wholly new document structures.

> XBRL is the specification for the eXtensible Business Reporting Language. XBRL allows software vendors, programmers and end users who adopt it as a specification to enhance the creation, exchange, and comparison of business reporting information. Business reporting includes, but is not limited to, financial statements, financial information, non-financial information, and regulatory filings such as annual and quarterly financial statements.

> This document defines XML elements and attributes that can be used to express information used in the creation, exchange and comparison tasks of financial reporting. XBRL consists of a core language of XML elements and attributes used

in document instances as well as a language used to define new elements and taxonomies of elements referred to in document instances.[1]

PURPOSE OF XBRL ....

The following extract (also from the Specification) paraphrases the three aspects of information movement that we highlighted in Chapter 5: preparation (encoding), exchange (transfer), and extraction (decoding):

> The XBRL specification is meant to maximize benefits to all stakeholders that use it. The specification is intended to benefit three categories of users: financial information preparers, intermediaries in the preparation and distribution process, and users of financial information. There is also a fourth category of beneficiary, the vendors who supply software and services to one or more of these three types of user. The overall intention is to balance the needs of these groups creating a product that provides benefits to all groups.
>
> The needs of end users of financial information will generally have precedence over other needs when it is necessary to make specification design decisions that may be perceived as benefiting one community at the possible expense of another. XBRL is intended to improve the financial statement product. It facilitates current practice, not change or set new, accounting standards. However, XBRL should facilitate possible changes in financial reporting over the long term.
>
> XBRL will provide users with a standard format in which to *prepare* financial reports that can be subsequently presented in a variety of ways. XBRL will provide users with a standard format in which financial information can be *exchanged* between different software applications. XBRL will permit the automated, efficient, and reliable *extraction* of financial information by software applications. XBRL will facilitate the automated comparison of financial information, accounting policies, notes to financial statements between companies, and other items which users may wish make comparisons that today are performed manually.

TAXONOMIES AND XML SCHEMA ....

The term "taxonomy" is somewhat peculiar to the accounting community. The formal definition within the XBRL specification is as follows:

---

[1] *Luther Hampton, e-Numerate and David Vun Kannon, KPMG LLP, "Extensible Business Reporting Language (XBRL) Specification 2001-6-21." Copyright (c) 2001 XBRL.ORG (AICPA). All Rights Reserved. http://www.XBRL.org/legal/*

Taxonomy. An XML Schema that defines new elements each corresponding to a concept that can be referenced in XBRL documents. XBRL taxonomies can be regarded as extensions of XML Schema, including XML Link based information.

For practical purposes, the AICPA taxonomies are XML Schema definitions. A further discussion in the specification clarifies how "taxonomy" is a natural fit to accounting frameworks.

> An important taxonomy for the purposes of the current specification is the particular taxonomy consisting of elements that correspond to well defined concepts within in the US Generally Accepted Accounting Principles (GAAP) when those principles are applied to Commercial and Industrial (C&I) companies. For example, concepts of 'Accounts Receivable Trade, Gross', 'Allowance for Doubtful Accounts', and 'Accounts Receivable Trade, Net' are different parts of that particular taxonomy. This taxonomy will be used for many examples in this document.

Although any given item can only refer to one taxonomy (is a name in a particular namespace), within any given XML document any number of XBRL items can refer to any number of taxonomies, and taxonomies can be composed together to extend other taxonomies.

The centerpiece of XBRL is the specification "XBRL Taxonomy: Financial Reporting for Commercial and Industrial Companies, US GAAP" (July 31, 2000). That **.xsd** file is located at www.xbrl.org/us/gaap/ci/2000-07-31. In that document, the steering committee (51 participating organizations) is unambiguous about the central role of XML Schema:

> **XML Schema Source File (XSD file)**: This is the official taxonomy. The XSD file is a valid XML file. Other documentation is provided to make using the XSD file information easier.

This is a strong reinforcement of our statement in Chapter 12 that XML Schema is the preferred medium of collaboration. As we noted there, XML Schema alone is able to provide the granular degree of specification that most industries will require.

SAMPLE REPORT...

Figure 21.1 is a sample report, posted at the XBRL Web site (www.xbrl.org):

CONSOLIDATED BALANCE SHEET

Great Plains Software, Inc.

(Dollars in thousands)	MAY 31,	
	1999	1998
ASSETS		
Current assets:		
Cash and cash equivalents	$ 26,983	$ 18,197
Investments	96,700	48,721
Accounts receivable, net	12,593	8,790
Inventories	746	542
Prepaid expenses and other assets	6,340	2,914
Deferred income tax assets	5,542	4,630
Total current assets	148,904	83,794
Property and equipment, net	19,126	8,501
Goodwill and other intangibles, net	3,838	4,946
Deferred income tax assets	3,091	3,318
Other assets	5,293	2,286
Total assets	$ 180,252	$ 102,845
LIABILITIES AND STOCKHOLDERS' EQUITY		
Current liabilities:		
Accounts payable	$ 8,392	$ 4,135
Accrued expenses	11,590	6,941
Income tax payable	--	3,257
Salaries and wages payable	1,031	836
Commissions payable	2,053	2,668
Deferred revenues	23,884	15,133
Total current liabilities	46,950	32,970
Deferred income tax liabilities	109	204
Total liabilities	47,059	33,174
Commitments and contingencies (Note 9)		
Stockholders' equity:		
Common stock, par value $.01 per share: 100,000,000 shares authorized, 15,362,820 shares and 13,720,920 shares issued and outstanding, respectively	154	137
Additional paid-in capital	118,683	67,801
Accumulated other comprehensive loss	(162)	--
Retained earnings	14,518	1,733
Total stockholders' equity	133,193	69,671
Total liabilities and stockholders' equity	$ 180,252	$ 102,845

See accompanying notes to the consolidated financial statements.

Figure 21.1 Sample XBRL report

Under the Hood

The particular workflow for creating, transmitting, capturing, and processing XBRL data will vary from company to company. The taxonomy specifies only the markup of content, not the process for handling it. The following XML data underlies the Current Assets section of the sample report shown in Figure 21.1. We highlight the printed labels text for easy reference. Also we note the match between the labels and the schema's element names (also highlighted). But again, the method for processing the file to produce and format the published report is at the discretion of the local organization.

```
<group type="ci:assets.currentAssets">
   <csh:label>Current assets:</csh:label>
   <group type=
      "ci:cashCashEquivalentsAndShortTermInvestments.cashAndCashEquivalents"
      <label href="xpointer(..)" xml:lang="en">Cash and cash
      equivalents</label>
      <item id="BS-01" period="1999-05-31">26983</item>
      <item id="BS-02" period="1998-05-31">18197</item>
   </group>
   <group type=
      "ci:cashCashEquivalentsAndShortTermInvestments.shortTermInvestments">
      <label href="xpointer(..)" xml:lang="en">Investments</label>
      <item id="BS-03" period="1999-05-31">96700</item>
      <item id="BS-04" period="1998-05-31">48721</item>
   </group>
   <group type="ci:currentAssets.receivablesNet">
      <label href="xpointer(..)" xml:lang="en">Accounts receivable,
      net</label>
      <item id="BS-05" period="1999-05-31">12593</item>
      <item id="BS-06" period="1998-05-31">8790</item>
   </group>
   <group type="ci:currentAssets.inventoriesNet">
      <label href="xpointer(..)" xml:lang="en">Inventories</label>
      <item id="BS-07" period="1999-05-31">746</item>
      <item id="BS-08" period="1998-05-31">542</item>
   </group>
   <group type="ci:currentAssets.prepaidExpenses">
      <label href=
      "xpointer(..)" xml:lang="en">Prepaid expenses and other
      assets</label>
      <item id="BS-09" period="1999-05-31">6340</item>
      <item id="BS-11" period="1998-05-31">2914</item>
   </group>
   <group type="ci:currentAssets.deferredIncomeTaxesCurrentPortion">
      <label href="xpointer(..)"
      xml:lang="en">Deferred income tax assets</label>
      <item id="BS-12" period="1999-05-31">5542</item>
      <item id="BS-13" period="1998-05-31">4630</item>
   </group>
   <label href="xpointer(..)" xml:lang="en">Total current assets</label>
   <item id="BS-14" period="1999-05-31">148904</item>
   <item id="BS-15" period="1998-05-31">83794</item>
</group>
```

And here is the XBRL taxonomy (XML Schema) definition of the element used to generate the first financial entry of the report:

```
<element name=
   "cashCashEquivalentsAndShortTermInvestments.cashAndCashEquivalents"
type="xbrl:monetary">
   <annotation>
      <appinfo>
         <xbrl:rollup to=
         "currentAssets.cashCashEquivalentsAndShortTermInvestments"
         weight="1" order="1"/>
         <xbrl:label xml:lang="en">Cash and Cash Equivalents</xbrl:label>
      </appinfo>
   </annotation>
</element>
```

ADOPTION CURVE ....

Clearly the initial task of launching a successful XBRL initiative is to establish a taxonomy (schema) that precisely describes an accounting standard. The Commercial and Industrial (CI) taxonomy that we just saw is now a maturing and widely adopted specification. But there are many other taxonomy development initiatives underway. Here is the list, based on a recent XBRL progress report:

Other existing taxonomy:

- Draft International Accounting Standards (IAS) Specification is now available at www.iasc.org.uk

U.S. Taxonomies Under Development

- Financial reporting for federal departments and agencies

- Financial reporting for mutual funds

- Financial reporting for financial institutions

- General ledger transactions

- Financial reporting for not-for-profit entities

International Taxonomies Under Development

- Financial reporting for CI Companies, **German GAAP**

- Financial reporting for CI Companies, **Canadian GAAP**

- Financial reporting for CI Companies, **Australian GAAP**

- Financial reporting for **Financial Institutions, Australian GAAP**

- Financial reporting for the **public sector, Australian GAAP**

- Financial reporting for CI, **New Zealand GAAP**

- Financial reporting for CI, **Singapore GAAP**

It is helpful to monitor the rate of XBRL adoption by reading the most recently posted "XBRL Progress Report" at www.xbrl.org. That document features adoptions, professional conferences, points of contact, major projects under way, an XBRL vendor list, and a bibliography.

Adopters

While membership lists may not be totally convincing, the membership of XBRL is an impressive array of organizations (printed here just as it appeared in the progress report):

ACCPAC International, Inc.: ACL Services Ltd.; Advisor Technology Services, LLC; American Institute of CPAs; Arthur Andersen LLP; Asia Securities Printing; Audicon; Bankenverlag K^ln; BDO Seidman, LLP; Beacon IT; Best Software; Bowne & Co., Inc.; Bridge Information Systems; Bryant College; Business Wire; Canadian Institute of Chartered Accountants; CaseWare International Inc.; Certified General Accountants of Canada Association of Canada; Cogniant, Inc.; Council of Koninklijk Nederlands Instituut van Registeraccountants (NIVRA); Countnet.com SA; CPA Australia; CPA2Biz; Crowe, Chizek and Company, LLP; Creative Solutions, Inc.; DATEV e.G.; Defense Finance and Accounting Service (DFAS); Deloitte Touche Tohmatsu; Deutsche Bank; Dresdner Bank; Deutsche B^rse AG; Deutsche Bundesbank; Diva Software; Dow Jones & Company, Inc.; Dresdner Kleinwort Wasserstein; DRSC; DVFA; EDGAR Online, Inc.; eKeeper.com; eLedger.com, Inc.; Elemental Interactive; e-Numerate Solutions Incorporated; ePace! Software; ePartners, Inc.; Epicor Software Corporation; Ernst & Young; Federal Deposit Insurance Corporation; Fidelity Investments; Financial Reporting Solutions (Pty) Ltd.; Financial Software Group; FinArch; First Light Communications, Inc.; FRx Software Corporation; Fujitsu; Gcom2 Solutions; General Electric Company; Global Filings, Inc.; Grant Thornton LLP; Haarmann, Hemmelrath & Partner; Hitachi; Hitachi System and Services; HOLT Value Associates; Hong Kong Society of Accountants; Hyperion Solutions Corp.; IBM; IBMatrix; IDW; I-Lumen, Inc.; Infoteria Corporation; Innovision Corporation; Institute of Chartered Accountants in Australia; Institute of Chartered Accountants in England & Wales; Institute of Chartered Accountants in Ireland; Institute of Management Accountants; International Accounting Standards Committee; International Federation of Accountants; J.P. Morgan Chase; Japan Digital Disclosure Inc.; Japan Notary

Organization; JISA (Japan Information Service Industry Assn); KPMG LLP; KPMG Consulting; Lawson Software; Microsoft Corporation; Microsoft Great Plains Software, Inc.; Ministry of Finance, Singapore; MIP, Inc.; Moody's Risk Management Services, Inc.; Morgan Stanley; Multex.com, Inc.; National Center of Charitable Statistics (NCCS) National Information Infrastructure Enterprise Promotion Association (Taiwan); Navision; NEC Planning Research, Inc. (Japan); NetLedger, Inc.; New River, Inc.; Newtec; Nihon Keizai Shimbun, Inc.; PCA Software; PeopleSoft, Inc.; PPA GmbH; Practitioners Publishing Company; PricewaterhouseCoopers; R.R. Donnelly Financial; Reuters Group LP; RIA; Sage Software; SAP AG; Seattle Pacific University Center for Professional Development; Software AG; Standard and Poor's; Syspro; Takara Printing; Teikoku Data Bank; The Woodburn Group; Thomson Financial; Tokyo Shoho Research; U.S. Census Bureau; XBRL Solutions, Inc.

SUMMARY ....

An industry whose data is consistently structured—either by convention or by federal mandate—is an industry in which XML is likely to thrive and persist. The adoption of XML languages by a large family of collaborators can be difficult without a firm political base. But for accounting practices, that base is well established. The AICPA, with its many GAAPs, provides a highly nutritious setting for XBRL. The momentum that is already in place—among large businesses, regulators, financial institutions, government, and vendors—offers a positive and substantial indicator for the success of XML. That momentum among large-scale early adopters should encourage mainstream business to view XBRL not as a risk but as an issue of best practices.

22 XML At Work: Security

In this chapter...

They Said It...

The merchant, to secure his treasure,
Conveys it in a borrow'd name
Matthew Prior: Song 424

An open standard...*secure*? Self-exposing content...*secure*? Plain text that is humanly readable . . . *secure*? It would seem that a specification whose content is readily transportable, self-exposing, and readable would be anything but secure! XML however is playing a major role in secure systems. XML has established itself as a star player in intelligent access control—specifying exactly *who* gets to see exactly *what*. This data-driven approach to security entails more than physical firewall products. Security of this variety is more sophisticated because an individual can assume different roles within an organization. It is also more complicated because a single item of content will likely contain data elements of varying levels of sensitivity and permissions.

There is more to XML's role in security than defining a markup language. Information architects speak of a "security model," a multilayered system that includes data enrichment, user-to-content policy definitions, role-based access control, confidentiality, enforcement, and markup technology. Live XML-based initiatives and products offer a clear roadmap to an organization seeking a nonproprietary approach to security. The Organization for the Advancement of Structured Information Standards (OASIS), a non-profit, international consortium, hosts a widely representative working group on access control. The Worldwide Web Consortium (W3C) and the Internet Engineering Task Force (IETF) has developed an XML-based specification for digital signatures. IBM offers XML Security Suite for Web-based e-business.

XML is important to security because an organization's security policy must extend across entire networks or clusters of networks. With the advent of B2B exchanges and extranets, an organization's data extends far beyond its physical control; the organization's security must reach out as far as its data. Only an open systems approach will allow for an enterprisewide security implementation that is manageable.

SECURITY IN A NUTSHELL...................................

Authentication and authorization. Conceptually, a security policy is simple and straightforward: "Keep all the bad guys out and let only the good guys in." This is the task of authentication and authorization. Authentication deals with determining whether the visitor is who he says he is. Authorization decides whether that individual may access a particular piece of data or perform a particular function. There is an abundance of off-the-shelf hardware and software products for authentication and authorization.

Role-based access. Authentication and authorization constitute only the "outward-looking" face of security. The problem for the custodian of content is to determine a policy of allowing the proper individuals to access, retrieve, and modify only the proper *data*, or perform a particular function. One major task is to define an access control policy that takes into account not only the *identity* of the user but the *role* of the user as well. For example, Jones as line manager can alter (to predetermined maximum amounts) the pay rate of her immediate staff members, but she cannot modify the terms of their employee contracts unless she has the authority (to act in the role) of a human resources manager. Role-based access control can support that kind of policy.

Granularity. The other major requirement of effective access control is that it must be highly *granular*. For example, certain passages of documents released to plaintiff's and defendant's counsel in the discovery phase of a trial must be "whited out." Some of those passages may only consist of a single sentence or even a single surname or identification number. XML markup, because it is based on elements, allows for element-level access control. As we have seen, an element can be as granular as the schema and markup will allow—in database terms, this is down to the record and field level. So XML provides the mechanism for any level of granularity required.

Data confidentiality and integrity. A third aspect of security focuses on the confidentiality and integrity of content in transit. The provider and the recipient of Web-based information—which may be financial data or private information—must have total confidence that the information will remain hidden and totally intact throughout an exchange. Designers typically implement this protection using data encryption. There are mature and commonly used encryption methods already in use. But XML offers a methodology for easing the exchange of encrypted content.

Digital signatures. For all web-based e-business, it is imperative to verify to the recipient that the sender of some file or transaction is really who he claims to be. A digital signature provides a means for associating a transaction with a particular individual; further, the digital signature is used to verify that the contents of the transaction have not been altered since creation by the sender. Digital signatures, another well-established area of security, are likewise much more straightforward to manage with XML.

USE CASE STUDIES ....

One good indicator of whether an initiative is ready for the workplace is the problem set that it proposes to solve. The OASIS Access Control Technical Committee receives and publishes "Use Case Studies" in the document repository section of its site (http://www.oasis-open.org/committees/xacml/docs/docs.shtml). Each one describes a real-life scenario, including description, actors, triggers, and event flow.[1] The first set deals with financial information. The second is a cluster of use cases for medical records. The third is about XML data of any variety (we selected medical records, as reported by HL7 (XML medical informatics standard) participants. Each excerpt appears with its original language, including the specialized terminology of each area. It is important to note that in every case the human workflow of the data is as significant as the various technologies supporting its security.

Use Case: Cross-Marketing of Financial Information

Brief Description

A telemarketing employee in the insurance affiliate of a consumer bank receives a request to cross-market an insurance product to a consumer banking customer based on the age of the customer and household information derived from other accounts held by parties at the same address.

Scope: Customer Data Use

Participants

1. Employee
2. Customer

Triggers

1. Receipt of cross-marketing request

---

[1]*All of the Use Case Studies in this section Copyright ©The Organization for the Advancement of Structured Information Standards [OASIS] (2001). All Rights Reserved.*

This document and translations of it may be copied and furnished to others, and derivative works that comment on or otherwise explain it or assist in its implementation may be prepared, copied, published and distributed, in whole or in part, without restriction of any kind, provided that the above copyright notice and this paragraph are included on all such copies and derivative works. However, this document itself may not be modified in any way, such as by removing the copyright notice or references to OASIS, except as needed for the purpose of developing OASIS specifications, in which case the procedures for copyrights defined in the OASIS Intellectual Property Rights document must be followed, or as required to translate it into languages other than English.

The limited permissions granted above are perpetual and will not be revoked by OASIS or its successors or assigns.

This document and the information contained herein is provided on an "AS IS" basis and OASIS DISCLAIMS ALL WARRANTIES, EXPRESS OR IMPLIED, INCLUDING BUT NOT LIMITED TO ANY WARRANTY THAT THE USE OF THE INFORMATION HEREIN WILL NOT INFRINGE ANY RIGHTS OR ANY IMPLIED WARRANTIES OF MERCHANTABILITY OR FITNESS FOR A PARTICULAR PURPOSE.

2. Flow of events

Basic Flow

1. Receipt of telemarketing request
2. Employee attempts to access customer data
3. System ensures current time is not during "no-call" dinner hours
4. System ensures request is compliant with provisions of Graham-Leach-Bliley
5. Determine intended use of data, i.e., marketing
6. Determine if insurance affiliate is permitted to access consumer banking data for marketing purposes
7. Determine if customer has given permission for contact related to cross-marketing
8. Determine if parties at same address have given permission for cross-correlation
9. Determine if parties at same address have given permission for exposure of data to other parties at same address
10. Determine if bank use of age is permitted
11. Expose all data
12. Log exposure
13. Employee places call
14. Log results

Use Case Group: Medical Records

This document "Confidentiality Standards, Version 1.2" was written by Meg Kistin Anzalone and Fred Moses of EntitleNet, Inc.

Use Cases

The requirements below were crafted to address the following use cases:

1. Patient (Ms AXS) with abusive ex-spouse who is also insurance subscriber requests restricted access to address and phone portion of record header.
   a. Ms AXS' record document is transmitted to physical therapy facility following diagnosis of acute tendonitis; restriction to address and phone information accompanies transmitted document.

    b. Information regarding services and associated charges are transmitted to outside claims payor. Address and phone restriction follows the information being transmitted, and address and phone of patient are withheld from the EOB.

2. Patient grants entitlement access to psychiatric notes only to primary care doctor. Primary care doctor grants access to patient record to a covering doctor or practice, with entitlement restriction following the transmitted documents so that covering doctor/practice have no access to psych notes.

3. Patient restricts entitlement to HIV screen results, and at a later date presents in the ER with severe trauma; entitlement restrictions are overridden.

4. Patient is him- or herself a caregiver in the medical system in which he or she is being treated. Patient requests entitlement restriction of entire record, granting access solely to primary care doctor. Access to record of services and associated charges are granted to billing staff if billing is done in house.

Confidentiality requirements

- Combinations of individuals or groups may have access to parts or all of a document body.
- Combinations of individuals or groups may have access to parts or all of a document header.
- Entitlement access restrictions to part of a document may be overridden for emergent or critical care situations, or with patient authorization documented.
- Access entitlement can change over time and context.
- Access entitlement restrictions can be added by healthcare givers or by patients.
- Entitlement restriction removal and entitlement granting can only be by documented patient authorization.
- Access entitlement and entitlement restrictions must travel with the document transmission.

In one of the responses, Fred M. Behlen, Ph.D., Assistant Professor of Radiology, The University of Chicago offered the following:

> Many people assume that a patient 'owns' his/her patient records, whereas 'ownership' is actually a bundle of rights that does not perfectly apply to pa-

tient records. It's worthwhile to remind standards developers and implementers to remember that access controls may also apply to the patient.

Here's what I would propose:

5. Patient's psychiatrist receives information from patient's family member which psychiatrist believes could be harmful to the patient or others if disclosed to the patient. In accordance with law in patient's state, psychiatrist marks this information as not to be disclosed to patient. Patient requests release of psychiatric records to himself. Access to the restricted documents is denied.

6. Patient in previous example follows legally mandated procedures (e.g., appeals to the state Health Department) and obtains an order for release of records. Entitlement restrictions are overridden.

Use Case: XML Resources (Medical Record)

This excerpt is from a document written by Michiharu Kudo. In this excerpt there is an ample description of the advantages of XML. There is also a set of separate XML data views, one for the patient and one for the patient's family. The level of granularity for these specialized views is the entire **record** element, the element containing all of the actual medical chart information. These views are driven by the data contained in the **informed   consent** section of the complete XML **medical_record**.

This application illustrates how the XML access control can be applied to the domains that require more complicated access control specifications such as a context dependent access control. This application is taken from the medical domain. A medical record stores medical history such as diagnosis results and the chemotherapy history for a patient. The advantages of representing medical records in XML format would be a platform-independent plain-text format and the features of the digital signature. It is often said that patients want to be properly informed by the doctor in charge so they can give their informed consent to treatment. One way to achieve this goal is for the doctor and the patient to sign a document which confirms that the patient was well informed and consented to the procedure. Since XML provides a mechanism to store the digital signature inside the document, XML is an appropriate format to represent medical records.

The medical record we use in this example consists of three sections: a general information section, a medical record section, and an informed consent section. The general information section is used for storing the patient's name and the date she/he checked in, which can be read by many people. The record section is used for storing diagnosis results and the therapeutic history, which is basically read only by the medical staff. The informed consent section is used for recording the grant of informed consent, which should not be modified once it has been written.

```xml
<?xml version="1.0"?>
<!DOCTYPE medical_record SYSTEM "medical_record.dtd">
<medical_record>
  <general_info>
    <hospital_info>
      <name>ABC Hospital</name>
      <department>Surgery</department>
    </hospital_info>
    <patient_info>
      <name>Patricia</name>
      <age>60</age>
      <sex>female</sex>
      <health_insurance>123456</health_insurance>
      <family>Frank</family>
    </patient_info>
    <hospitalization_info>
      <registration>2000-09-01</registration>
      <in>2000-09-14</in>
      <out></out>
    </hospitalization_info>
  </general_info>
  <!-- ========================================= -->
  <record>
    <diagnosis_info>
      <diagnosis>
        <item type="primary">Gastric Cancer</item>
        <item type="secondary">Hyper tension</item>
      </diagnosis>
      <pathological_diagnosis>
        <diagnosis>
          <item type="primary">Well differentiated adeno carcinoma</item>
        </diagnosis>
        <date>2000-10-05</date>
        <malignancy type="yes"/>
      </pathological_diagnosis>
    </diagnosis_info>
    <therapy_info>
      <operation>
        <method_of_surgery>total gastrectomy</method_of_surgery>
        <date>2000-09-20</date>
      </operation>
      <chemotherapy>
        <div>
          <prescription>5-FU 500mg and CDDP 10mg /day x10days</prescription>
          <start_date>2000-10-10</start_date>
          <end_date>2000-10-21</end_date>
        </div>
```

```
        <po>
          <prescription>5-FU 200mg/day</prescription>
          <start_date>2000-12-01</start_date>
          <end_date/>
        </po>
      </chemotherapy>
    </therapy_info>
  </record>
  <!-- ========================================== -->
  <informed_consent>
    <family_consent>
      <date>2000-09-13</date>
      <disclosure_to_patient>no</disclosure_to_patient>
    </family_consent>
    <patient_consent>
      <date>2000-09-19</date>
    </patient_consent>
  </informed_consent>
</medical_record>
```

A set of access control policies is described as follows:

1. Doctor and nurse can read the entire medical records.

2. The doctor in charge can write every element of the medical record (unless the policy explicitly specify the denial of access).

3. The hospital staff can read general information.

4. Patients can read their own general information.

5. A patient's family can read his/her family's general information.

6. A hospital receptionist can write a patient's name in a blank medical record.

7. Patients can read their own medical records only after informed consent has been given and the family has agreed to the disclosure of the results of the diagnosis.

8. A patient's family can read their family's medical records if informed consent have been given.

9. Even the doctor in charge cannot modify the informed consent section once it has been granted.

The following XML is Patricia's view (patient). Since her psychiatrist believes that this diagnosis information could be harmful to the patient, she is allowed to read only general information.

```
<?xml version="1.0"?>
<!DOCTYPE medical_record SYSTEM "medical_record.dtd">
<medical_record>
  <general_info>
    <hospital_info>
      <name>ABC Hospital</name>
      <department>Surgery</department>
    </hospital_info>
    <patient_info>
      <name>Patricia</name>
      <age>60</age>
      <sex>female</sex>
      <health_insurance>123456</health_insurance>
      <family>Frank</family>
    </patient_info>
    <hospitalization_info>
      <registration>2000-09-01</registration>
      <in>2000-09-14</in>
      <out/>
    </hospitalization_info>
  </general_info>
</medical_record>
```

The following XML is Patricia's family's view. They are allowed to read Patricia's diagnosis information.

```
<?xml version="1.0"?>
<!DOCTYPE medical_record SYSTEM "medical_record.dtd">
<medical_record>
  <general_info>
    <hospital_info>
      <name>ABC Hospital</name>
      <department>Surgery</department>
    </hospital_info>
    <patient_info>
      <name>Patricia</name>
      <age>60</age>
      <sex>female</sex>
      <health_insurance>123456</health_insurance>
      <family>Frank</family>
    </patient_info>
    <hospitalization_info>
      <registration>2000-09-01</registration>
      <in>2000-09-14</in>
      <out/>
    </hospitalization_info>
  </general_info>
  <record>
    <diagnosis_info>
      <diagnosis>
        <item type="primary">Gastric Cancer</item>
        <item type="secondary">Hyper tension</item>
```

```
        <pathological_diagnosis>
          <diagnosis>
            <item type="primary">Well differentiated adeno carcinoma</item>
          </diagnosis>
          <date>2000-10-05</date>
          <malignancy type="yes"/>
        </pathological_diagnosis>
      </diagnosis_info>
      <therapy_info>
        <operation>
          <method_of_surgery>total gastrectomy</method_of_surgery>
          <date>2000-09-20</date>
        </operation>
        <chemotherapy>
          <div>
            <prescription>5-FU 500mg and CDDP 10mg /day x10days</prescription>
            <start_date>2000-10-10</start_date>
            <end_date>2000-10-21</end_date>
          </div>
          <po>
            <prescription>5-FU 200mg/day</prescription>
            <start_date>2000-12-01</start_date>
            <end_date/>
          </po>
        </chemotherapy>
      </therapy_info>
    </record>
</medical_record>
```

ENCRYPTION ....

IBM's XML Security Suite[2] includes an encryption tool. The element
credit_payment in the following XML record contains sensitive information.

```
<?xml version="1.0"?>
<!DOCTYPE customer_order SYSTEM "custord.dtd">
<customer_order>
    <items>
      <item>
        <name>Turnip Twaddler</name>
        <qty>3</qty>
        <price>9.95</price>
      </item>
```

---

[2]The code excerpts in this section are from "The XML Security Suite: Increasing the security of e-business," by Doug Tidwell, Cyber Evangelist, developerWorks XML Team. http://www-4.ibm.com/software/developer/ library/xmlsecuritysuite/index.html

```
      <item>
         <name>Snipe Curdler</name>
         <qty>1</qty>
         <price>19.95</price>
      </item>
   </items>
   <customer>
      <name>Doug Tidwell</name>
      <street>1234 Main Street</street>
      <city state="NC">Raleigh</city>
      <zip>11111</zip>
   </customer>
   <credit_payment>
      <card_issuer>American Express</card_issuer>
      <card_number>1234 567890 12345</card_number>
      <expiration_date month="10" year="2004"/>
   </credit_payment>
</customer_order>
```

The documentation with Security Suite shows how to modify the product's Java programming code with a minimum of effort to perform element-level encryption. In this case we wish to encrypt only the **credit_payment** element. The result is as follows (unreadable encryption code is truncated in this sample):

```
<customer_order>
   <items>
      <item>
         <name>Turnip Twaddler</name>
         <qty>3</qty>
         <price>9.95</price>
      </item>
      <item>
         <name>Snipe Curdler</name>
         <qty>1</qty>
         <price>19.95</price>
      </item>
   </items>
   <customer>
      <name>Doug Tidwell</name>
      <street>1234 Main Street</street>
      <city state="NC">Raleigh</city>
      <zip>11111</zip>
   </customer>
   <EncryptedElement algorithm="DES/CBC/PKCS5Padding" contentType="text/xml"
encoding="base64" iv="S5Rirg//pNQ=">vJqNpDrQT1vmCVbyGJfIwdIDBYoGXGmutgz6TVGoF
xNEN5OiKw8pmtxFixz5hOChOXgTtPqktQhEHO5+vLOLAFgIioDIRQGHHmHng3CLd+8tvrT8wxPBCF
d2TGXW2tqSepam0ZxdmwUXwNSAgaR8hmiromD+bh+tDomPv7eFZ4no5ft3JG3t0trLlwVupF/5vaI
uUkkgyG8x9AcS/kXJxHpmM=peqGzIMf+8A=</EncryptedElement>
</customer_order>
```

The sensitive data is now encrypted. Although the encryption itself is plain text and humanly readable, the only way that the receiver can de-encrypt the data is by receiving the proper encryption key from the sender.

DIGITAL SIGNATURES ....

The concept behind digital signatures is similar to authentication. Authentication is a step in the process of allowing or disallowing a user onto a network or into a database. It seeks to verify that a user is who she/he says she/he is. A digital signature, on the other hand, is part of a transmitted record. It verifies that the author of the record really is the same person claimed within the record itself. The digital signature is as good as a handwritten one in the eyes of the law. (The W3C Proposed Recommendation for XML-Signature Syntax and Processing refers to digital signature as digital authentication.) Another feature of digital signatures is that a sender of a document that includes a digital signature cannot repudiate that it was sent. Both of these features of digital signatures are essential for safe and successful e-commerce.

Digital signature relies on public-key infrastructure (PKI), a pervasive security standard for all of industry. With PKI it possible to encrypt and transfer money and sensitive data securely.

There are two steps to creating a digital signature as part of a transmitted record:

1. The user applies a transformation procedure to the record, the result being a "hash" of the record. There are several such transformations available.

2. The user then applies a private key to encrypt the hash. That key is issued to the user directly by a public-private key authority.

The now-encrypted hash, plus the sender's public key, constitute the digital signature of the file. Note that the sender's digital signature is unique for every record.

Here is an example of a digital signature, represented as XML. The element **SignatureValue** contains the value of the digital signature, the result of the two-step "cook-down" above. That element and the element containing the public key are highlighted.

```
<?xml version='1.0'?>
<!DOCTYPE Signature SYSTEM "xmldsig-core-schema.dtd" [
<!ENTITY dsig "http://www.w3.org/2000/09/xmldsig#">
   <!ENTITY % SignatureProperty.ANY '| ts:timestamp'>
   <!ELEMENT ts:timestamp (#PCDATA)>
   <!ATTLIST ts:timestamp
```

```
<Object>
  <SignatureProperties>
    <SignatureProperty Target="#MyFirstSignature">
      <ts:timestamp xmlns:ts=
          "http://www.example.org/rfc/rfcxxxx.txt">
        this is a test of the mixed content model</ts:timestamp>
    </SignatureProperty>
  </SignatureProperties>
</Object>
</Signature>
```

The title of Section 8.1.1 in the W3C proposed recommendation reads "Only What is Signed is Secure." The gist of this section is that sometimes we must allow certain parts of transmitted content to remain "uncovered" by digital signature. But it is little exaggeration to apply that statement to all of electronic exchange. Now that digital signature syntax and procedures have been totally formalized by the W3C as an XML technology, we can honestly say that XML is not simply a participant but an active player in Internet security.

SUMMARY ....

XML, as a markup mechanism, does not in itself make anything secure. But where access to actual content is an issue, XML fills crucial security roles for e-business. XML is the backbone for open-systems access control. It has facilitated straightforward solutions to complex and dynamic role-based access problems. The same XML that conveys recognizable text content can just as readily incorporate elements of encrypted data, still as plain text. XML's agility with encrypted data allows it also to be the purveyor of digital signatures, the essential requirement for safe Internet business. The wider the domain of an organization's connectivity, the greater the need for XML-based security solutions.

23 XML At Work: Law and the Courts

In this chapter...

They Said It...

The law is a very imperfect mechanism. If you press exactly the right buttons and are also lucky, justice may show up in the answer. A mechanism is all the law was ever intended to be.

Raymond Chandler

In this workplace visit, we examine two significant aspects of XML and the law: (1) XML markup and multiple use (reuse) of statutes from the Michigan Compiled Law initiative and (2) XML-based infrastructure for court records, developed by LegalXML. The second group of exhibits is of particular technological interest because they demonstrate a workable strategy for publishing native XML on a Web browser. In addition, it is useful to see how LegalXML's XML methodology incorporates and displays non-XML graphic images.

MICHIGAN STATE LAW ....

It is no longer acceptable for an ordinary citizen to have to go to a law library to find a particular statute. As with archived information of every type, we now expect (or hope) to access laws online. While most states make their legal codes available in electronic form, we feature the Lemon Law from the Michigan Compiled Laws collection.[1] (This is a consumer protection law providing legal remedies to purchasers of new automobiles which prove to be beyond repair.) In Chapter 9 we also referenced this project, noting how a consumer advocacy group might use (and repurpose) the full XML text of a state law, if the XML form were available.

There is a substantial "back room" effort to prepare the statutes first as XML. Once they are in XML, the site specialists apply automated procedures to generate

---

[1]*Content of the Lemon Law excerpt used in this discussion Copyright © 2001 Legislative Council, State of Michigan. Screens, formatted text, and .pdf files courtesy of www.MichiganLegislature.org. Michigan Compiled Laws: Complete Through PA 117 of 2001. A free service provided by The Michigan Legislative Council, House of Representatives and Senate. DISCLAIMER: The Michigan Compiled Laws is the compilation of Michigan laws in force (including the Constitution of the State of Michigan of 1963, as amended), arranged without alteration, under appropriate heads and titles. The laws presented on this site are not intended to replace official versions of such laws on file with the Secretary of State. Further, the Legislature presents this information, without warranties, express or implied, regarding the information's accuracy, timeliness, or completeness. If you believe the information presented on this site is inaccurate, out-of-date, or incomplete, or if you have any technical problems accessing or reading the information, please address any concerns to the Library of Michigan via an email message, or by calling (517)373-3842.*

Web-displayable .html, downloadable formatted pages for printing, and PDF files.
Figure 23.1 is the start and end of the Web browser's rendition of the Lemon Law.

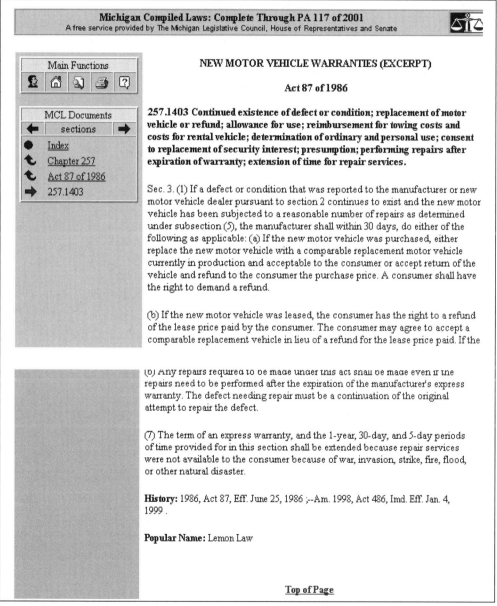

Figure 23.1 Michigan Lemon Law (web page rendition)

And here is a sample of the underlying XML for Section 1407.253:

```
<section.mcl docID="mcl-257-1403">
    <excerptinfo>
      <statuteeditorshead>NEW MOTOR VEHICLE WARRANTIES
       (EXCERPT)</statuteeditorshead>
      <statuteorigin>Act 87 of 1986</statuteorigin>
    </excerptinfo>
    <sectref mclnum="257.1403" sectionlabel="3" mclchap="257"
     mclsect="1403"> 257.1403</sectref>
    <catchline>Continued existence of defect or condition;
     replacement of motor vehicle or refund; allowance for use;
     reimbursement for towing costs and costs for rental vehicle;
     determination of ordinary and personal use; consent to
     replacement of security interest; presumption; performing
     repairs after expiration of warranty; extension of time for
     repair services.</catchline>
    <section-body>
      <section-number>Sec. 3.</section-number>
      <paragraph>
        <paragraph-number>(1)</paragraph-number>
        <p>If a defect or condition that was reported to the
          manufacturer or new motor vehicle dealer pursuant to
          section 2 continues to exist and the new motor vehicle
          has been subjected to a reasonable number of repairs as
          determined under subsection (5), the manufacturer shall
          within 30 days, do either of the following as
          applicable:</p>
        <paragraph>
            <paragraph-number>(a)</paragraph-number>
            <p>If the new motor vehicle was purchased, either
            replace the new motor vehicle with a comparable
            replacement motor vehicle currently in production
            and acceptable to the consumer or accept return of
            the vehicle and refund to the consumer the purchase
            price. A consumer shall have the right to demand a
            refund.</p>
        </paragraph>
        <paragraph>
            <paragraph-number>(b)</paragraph-number>
            <p>If the new motor vehicle was leased, the consumer
            has the right to a refund of the lease price paid by
            the consumer. The consumer may agree to accept a
            comparable replacement vehicle in lieu of a refund
            for the lease price paid. If the consumer agrees to
            accept a replacement vehicle, the lease agreement
            shall not be altered except with respect to the
            identification of the vehicle.</p>
        </paragraph>
      </paragraph>
```

```
<paragraph>
    <paragraph-number>(2)</paragraph-number>
    <p>The purchase price or lease price includes the cost of any
       options or other modifications installed or made by or for the
       manufacturer, and the amount of all other charges made by or for
       the manufacturer, less a reasonable allowance for the consumer's
       use of the vehicle, and less an amount equal to any appraised
       damage that is not attributable to normal use or to the defect or
       condition.  A reasonable allowance for use is the purchase or
       lease price of the new motor vehicle multiplied by a fraction
       having as the denominator 100,000 miles and having as the
       numerator the miles directly attributable to use by the consumer
       and any previous consumer prior to his or her first report of a
       defect or condition that impairs the use or value of the new
       motor vehicle plus all mileage directly attributable to use by a
       consumer beyond 25,000 miles. If a vehicle is replaced or
       refunded under the provisions of this section, if towing services
       and rental vehicles were not made available without cost to the
       consumer, the manufacturer shall also reimburse the consumer for
       those towing costs and reasonable costs for a comparable rental
       vehicle that were incurred as a direct result of the defect or
       condition.</p>
</paragraph>
<paragraph>
    <paragraph-number>(3)</paragraph-number>
    <p>If a court or an alternative dispute settlement procedure
       described in section 5 determines that a consumer has provided
       sufficient evidence that the vehicle did not provide reliable
       transportation for ordinary personal or household use for any
       period beyond the first 25,000 mileage usage period of the
       vehicle, the court or the alternative dispute settlement
       procedure may reduce the vehicle usage deduction for mileage
       beyond the first 25,000 mileage usage period only for the period
       beyond the 25,000 mileage usage period that the court or
       alternative dispute settlement procedure determines that the
       vehicle did not provide useful transportation for ordinary
       personal or household use. To determine if the vehicle did or did
       not provide useful transportation for ordinary personal and
       household use, the court or the alternative dispute settlement
       procedure shall consider all of the following:</p>
    <paragraph>
        <paragraph-number>(a)</paragraph-number>
        <p>The number of repairs.  </p>
    </paragraph>
    <paragraph>
        <paragraph-number>(b)</paragraph-number>
        <p>The cost of the repairs.</p>
    </paragraph>
```

The underlying XML form of the law is not available to the public. But because that text is XML, the office is able to render the statute in two other options, each downloadable. Figure 23.2 shows formatted text (partially shown here), suitable for immediate printing.

257.1403 Continued existence of defect or condition; replacement of motor vehicle or refund; allowance for use; reimbursement for towing costs and costs for rental vehicle; determination of ordinary and personal use; consent to replacement of security interest; presumption; performing repairs after expiration of warranty; extension of time for repair services.

Sec. 3. (1) If a defect or condition that was reported to the manufacturer or new motor vehicle dealer pursuant to section 2 continues to exist and the new motor vehicle has been subjected to a reasonable number of repairs as determined under subsection (5), the manufacturer shall within 30 days, do either of the following as applicable: (a) If the new motor vehicle was purchased, either replace the new motor vehicle with a comparable replacement motor vehicle currently in production and acceptable to the consumer or accept return of the vehicle and refund to the consumer the purchase price. A consumer shall have the right to demand a refund.

(b) If the new motor vehicle was leased, the consumer has the right to a refund of the lease price paid by the consumer. The consumer may agree to accept a comparable replacement vehicle in lieu of a refund for the lease price paid. If the consumer agrees to accept a replacement vehicle, the lease agreement shall not be altered except with respect to the identification of the vehicle.

(2) The purchase price or lease price includes the cost of any options or other modifications installed or made by or for the manufacturer, and the amount of all other charges made by or for the manufacturer, less a reasonable allowance for the consumer's use of the vehicle, and less an amount equal to any appraised damage that is not attributable to normal use or to the defect or condition. A reasonable allowance for use is the purchase or lease price of the new motor vehicle multiplied by a fraction having as the denominator 100,000 miles and having as the numerator the miles directly attributable to use by the consumer and any previous consumer prior to his or her first report of a defect or condition that impairs the use or value of the new motor vehicle plus all mileage directly attributable to use by a consumer beyond 25,000 miles. If a vehicle is replaced or refunded under the provisions of this section, if towing services and rental vehicles were not made available without cost to the consumer, the manufacturer shall also reimburse the consumer for those towing costs and reasonable costs for a comparable rental vehicle that were incurred as a direct result of the defect or condition.

(3) If a court or an alternative dispute settlement procedure described in section 5 determines that a consumer has provided sufficient evidence that the vehicle did not provide reliable transportation for ordinary personal or household use for any period beyond the first 25,000 mileage usage period of the vehicle, the court or the alternative dispute settlement procedure may reduce the vehicle usage deduction for mileage beyond the first 25,000 mileage usage period only for the period beyond the 25,000 mileage usage period that the court or alternative dispute settlement procedure determines that the vehicle did not provide useful transportation for ordinary personal or household use. To determine if the vehicle did or did not provide useful transportation for ordinary personal and household use, the court or the alternative dispute settlement procedure shall consider all of the following: (a) The number of repairs.

(b) The cost of the repairs.

Figure 23.2 Michigan Lemon Law (preformatted text rendition)

Figure 23.3 shows a fragment of the .pdf version.

257.1403 Continued existence of defect or condition; replacement of motor vehicle or refund; allowance for use; reimbursement for towing costs and costs for rental vehicle; determination of ordinary and personal use; consent to replacement of security interest; presumption; performing repairs after expiration of warranty; extension of time for repair services.

Sec. 3. (1) If a defect or condition that was reported to the manufacturer or new motor vehicle dealer pursuant to section 2 continues to exist and the new motor vehicle has been subjected to a reasonable number of repairs as determined under subsection (5), the manufacturer shall within 30 days, do either of the following as applicable:

(a) If the new motor vehicle was purchased, either replace the new motor vehicle with a comparable replacement motor vehicle currently in production and acceptable to the consumer or accept return of the vehicle and refund to the consumer the purchase price. A consumer shall have the right to demand a refund.

(b) If the new motor vehicle was leased, the consumer has the right to a refund of the lease price paid by the consumer. The consumer may agree to accept a comparable replacement vehicle in lieu of a refund for the lease price paid. If the consumer agrees to accept a replacement vehicle, the lease agreement shall not be altered except with respect to the identification of the vehicle.

(2) The purchase price or lease price includes the cost of any options or other modifications installed or made by or for the manufacturer, and the amount of all other charges made by or for the manufacturer, less a reasonable allowance for the consumer's use of the vehicle, and less an amount equal to any appraised damage that is not attributable to normal use or to the defect or condition. A reasonable allowance for use is the purchase or lease price of the new motor vehicle multiplied by a fraction having as the denominator 100,000 miles and having as the numerator the miles directly attributable to use by the consumer and any previous consumer prior to his or her first report of a defect or condition that impairs the use or value of the new motor vehicle plus all mileage directly attributable to use by a consumer beyond 25,000 miles. If a vehicle is replaced or refunded under the provisions of this section, if towing services and rental vehicles were not made available without cost to the consumer, the manufacturer shall also reimburse the consumer for those towing costs and reasonable costs for a comparable rental vehicle that were incurred as a direct result of the defect or condition.

Rendered 10/17/2001 2:45:34 PM   Page 2   MCL Complete Through PA 117 of 2001

© 2001 Legislative Council, State of Michigan   *Courtesy of www.MichiganLegislature.Org*

Figure 23.3 Michigan Lemon Law (PDF rendition)

Usage History

The Michigan Compiled Laws project most definitely demonstrates XML at work in a socially responsible manner. The following list of commonly requested documents (and the category of each legislative act) reflects a profile of personal needs among a wide population.

- Lemon Law (vehicles)
- Crime Victim's Rights, Ethnic Intimidation, Firearms Law, Sex Offender Regis Act, Stalking (law enforcement)
- Landlord Tenant Act (housing)

- Clean Indoor Air (health)
- Adoption Code, Child Abuse and Neglect Prevention, Child Custody Act (family law)
- Setting Aside Convictions (courts)
- Consumer Protection (commerce)

LEGALXML

The courts are clogged. That is a common complaint heard from judges, politicians, and anyone seeking a legal remedy or relief. A significant factor in case backlog is the movement of information. A coalition of legal professionals has proposed an XML standard for court records that promises to ease the workflow, which an abundance of paper handling has created. This case study is of particular interest to us first because it demonstrates a technology at work—serious work. Moreover it represents the hard work of collaboration necessary to propagate a suite of XML schemas to solve real problems. This workplace did not have the luxury of inventing entirely new information systems. So the XML schemas reflect much of the data structures and information items familiar to court records managers and users.

LegalXML was founded in November 1998. Its members include lawyers, developers, application vendors, judges, and court personnel. Its motto is "Developing XML Standards for the Legal Community." Its vision statement is "to provide core XML Document Standards and Protocol Standards to assist the people and organization who support and administer the legal system in increasing its overall efficiency and effectiveness." It describes itself as follows:

A nonprofit organization comprised of volunteer members from private industry, non-profit organizations, government, and academia. The mission of Legal XML is to develop open, nonproprietary technical standards for legal documents.

The following exhibits demonstrate how LegalXML delivers native XML documents to the user's Web browser for display.[2] The most significant effort on the part of LegalXML, however, is the intensive human dedication and collaboration that the initiative has required. This is consistent with what we have noted throughout this book.

---

[2]*All of the examples of documents, as well as the excerpts from style sheets and schemas, Copyright ©1999–2001 LegalXML, Inc. All Rights Reserved. Special thanks to Rolly Chambers, LegalXML Legal Work Group cochair who assisted with this exhibit.*

How It Works

We noted rather emphatically in Chapter 17 that it is not safe to ship XML content blindly to a user's browser. We learned that Microsoft has extended the capability of its Internet Explorer, so we capitalized on that extension...and were disappointed. From that lesson we learned we must adhere strictly to the HTML standard in order for the content to "play" properly on all popular browsers.

But what if we choose deliberately to exploit a particular vendor's current technology? That is the approach taken by LegalXML. In this case, the publication of its XML documents assumes the user's browser to be Internet Explorer 5.5 or better. It furthermore assumes that the XML processor MSXML3 is installed in the browser and is working properly. Note that, unlike Microsoft's "extension" discussed in Chapter 17, the functionality of XML in Internet Explorer is not a Microsoft proprietary feature. All browser providers are currently providing or will soon provide standard XML support.

The "magic" of native-XML-on-the-browser is the ability of Internet Explorer to apply style sheets to a document. In the traditional HTML-only scenario, the server ships HTML pages and the browser renders them directly as best it can. With style sheets, the protocol between the server and client is somewhat more refined:

1. Server receives a request from the client (user's computer) in the usual fashion.
2. Client's browser receives the file, noting that it is an .xml file.
3. Client browser's XML intelligence (Internet Explorer's MSXML3, in this case) examines the .xml file and discovers callouts (in the header info) to the .xsl (style sheet) and .dtd (schema) files.
4. MSXML3 has the browser request the required .xsl/.dtd files from the server.
5. MSXML3 now does its client-side styling of the .xml file, based on the description of structure in the DTD and of the style in the .xsl file.

This exhibit is notable because it represents true on-the-fly processing by an XML processor. We shall now view screen renditions, as well as the XML, style sheet, and schema notations responsible.

Pirate's Complaint

The whimsical example in Figure 23.4 demonstrates how the browser, powered by an XML processor, is able to apply a DTD and a style sheet in order to produce the following display:

IN THE PIMA COUNTY CONSOLIDATED JUSTICE COURTS	115 N. CHURCH AVE., TUCSON , AZ 85701	
Plaintiff **John Paul Jones** Address Tucson, AZ 857XX (520) XXX-XXXX Ext. XXXX (Name/Address/Phone)	Case No.: CV 01-xxxxx SUMMONS/ COMPLAINT/ ANSWER Small Claims Division	Defendant **Jean Pirate LaFitte** Address Tucson, AZ 85712 (520) XXX-XXXX Ext. XXXX (Name/Address/Phone)

Notice and Summons
TO THE ABOVE-NAMED DEFENDANT: Jean Pirate LaFitte { SEAL} YOU ARE DIRECTED TO ANSWER THE CLAIM OF THE PLAINTIFF WITHIN TWENTY (20) DAYS IN THE SMALL CLAIMS DIVISION OF THE COURT CITED ABOVE. IF YOU DO NOT APPEAR AND DEFEND YOURSELF, A JUDGMENT MAY BE ENTERED AGAINST YOU. If you wish to defend against the Plaintiff claim, you must pay a fee at the time you file your answer. **Requests for reasonable accommodation for persons with disabilities must be made to the court by parties at least three (3) Business days in advance of a scheduled court proceeding.**
Date: 04-Mar-01   Clerk's Signature: *s/ L. M. Jacobs, IV,*   L.M. Jacobs, IV, Clerk, Small Claims Division

PLAINTIFF CLAIM
The defendant owes me $2500 for the following reasons: Goods I bought from the defendant were defective and return was not allowed. Pirates are not good vendors.

Date: 04-Mar-01   Plaintiff's Signature: *s/ John Paul Jones* , John Paul Jones, Plaintiff

NOTICE TO DEFENDANT: If you contest this claim, you must write your Answer in the spaces below and file it in the Small Claims Division of the Court named above within twenty (20) days of the date of service of the Claim. You must also PAY A FEE at the time you file your Answer. Failure to file an Answer within the twenty (20) days may result in a judgment being entered against you.
DEFENDANT ANSWER
I do not owe the Plaintiff because:

Date_____   Defendant's Signature: _____   Jean Pirate LaFitte, Defendant

CERTIFICATE OF SERVICE OF MAILING BY PLAINTIFF

I, John Paul Jones, Plaintiff in this action, certify that I have appointed the Clerk of the Court as my agent to complete service of process on the Defendant.

Date: 04-Mar-01   *s/ John Paul Jones* , John Paul Jones, Plaintiff

CERTIFICATE OF SERVICE BY DEFENDANT

I, Jean Pirate LaFitte, Defendant in this action, certify that I have appointed the Clerk of the Court as my agent to complete service this Answer on the Plaintiff.

Date_____   _____   Jean Pirate LaFitte, Defendant

WARNING: YOU DO NOT HAVE THE RIGHT TO APPEAL THE DECISION OF THE HEARING OFFICER OR THE JUSTICE OF THE PEACE IN A SMALL CLAIMS COURT. IF YOU WISH TO PRESERVE YOUR RIGHT TO APPEAL, YOU MAY HAVE YOUR CASE TRANSFERRED TO THE JUSTICE COURT PURSUANT TO SEC. 22-504, SUBSECTION A, ARIZONA REVISED STATUTES, IF YOU REQUEST SUCH TRANSFER AT LEAST TEN DAYS PRIOR TO THE DAY OF THE SCHEDULED HEARING.

JP 118 4/96 ORIGINAL-COURT; GREEN-RETURN OF SERVICE; CANARY-DEFENDANT; PINK-DEFENDANT; GOLDENROD-PLAINTIFF

Figure 23.4 Complaint (converted from XML to HTML)

The following XML notation is the header information (metadata and case caption) of the actual file that the XML-enabled browser interprets and processes:

```xml
<?xml version="1.0" encoding="UTF-8"?>
<!DOCTYPE Legal SYSTEM "./dtd/courtdocument(10).dtd">
<?xml-stylesheet type="text/xsl" href="./xsl/smcl2html(06032001).xsl"?>
<Legal>
   <CourtDocument FilingType="SmallClaims" SpecialHandling="No"
      ID="d001.xxxxx" Version="1.0">
      <MainDocument>
         <DocumentMetadata>
            <Creator>
               <FullName>Rolly Chambers</FullName>
            </Creator>
            <Filer>
               <BasicActor ActorType="Person" RoleType="Party">
                  <FullName>John Paul Jones</FullName>
                  <RoleName>Plaintiff</RoleName>
               </BasicActor>
            </Filer>
            <Identifier ID="document.1-xxxxx"/>
            <DocumentType>Summons</DocumentType>
            <Format>text/xml</Format>
            <BasicDocumentInformation>
               <DocumentStatus DocumentStatus="Draft"/>
               <Privacy Privacy="Unsealed"/>
            </BasicDocumentInformation>
         </DocumentMetadata>
         <CaseCaption>
            <Court CourtType="State">
               <CourtName>IN THE PIMA COUNTY CONSOLIDATED JUSTICE
                  COURTS</CourtName>
               <CourtDivision>Small Claims Division</CourtDivision>
               <BasicAddress Type="Business">
                  <AddressLine>115 N. CHURCH AVE.,</AddressLine>
                  <City>TUCSON </City>
                  <State>AZ</State>
                  <PostalCode> 85701</PostalCode>
               </BasicAddress>
            </Court>
            <FullCaseNumber>Case No.: CV 01-xxxxx</FullCaseNumber>
            <BasicActor ID="a001" RoleType="Party" ActorType="Person">
               <GivenName>John</GivenName>
               <MiddleName>Paul</MiddleName>
               <FamilyName>Jones</FamilyName>
               <RoleName>Plaintiff</RoleName>
```

```
    <BasicAddress Type="Business">
       <AddressLine>Address</AddressLine>
       <City>Tucson</City>
       <State>AZ</State>
       <PostalCode> 85712</PostalCode>
    </BasicAddress>
    <Phone Type="Business">(520) XXX-XXXX Ext. XXXX </Phone>
 </BasicActor>
 <DocumentTitle>SUMMONS</DocumentTitle>
</CaseCaption>
         :
         :
```

Note that the XML file identifies to the browser the schema (**.dtd**) and style sheet (**.xsl**) files (highlighted) that it needs in order for the browser to render the XML document properly.

Here is a fragment of the DTD that describes the top level of the document:

```
<!ELEMENT MainDocument (DocumentMetadata, CaseCaption, DocumentBody,
          DocumentSigner*, ProofOfService?, Attachment*)>
<!ENTITY % DocumentMetadata.content "Creator , Filer , Identifier ,
          DocumentType ,
          Description? , Subject? , Coverage? , Reference? , Format ,
          BasicDocumentInformation? , FilingInformation?">
          :
          :
<!ELEMENT DocumentMetadata (%DocumentMetadata.content;)>
          :
          :
<!ENTITY % CaseCaption.content "Court , FullCaseNumber? , (CaseTitle? ,
          (BasicActor | Vs)*),
          DocumentTitle , AssociatedCase*">
<!ELEMENT CaseCaption (%CaseCaption.content;)>
```

In this excerpt, the highlighted elements **DocumentMetadata** and **Case-Caption** rely on the entity declarations **DocumentMetadata.content** and **CaseCaption.content** to spell out exactly the subelements of each. The XML processor uses this DTD to find its way around the document as it applies the styling information.

The style sheet for this file processes the XML by creating HTML. It uses XMLT elements to capture XML content and insert HTML tags in the proper places. Here is a fragment that creates the court information at the top of the document, based on information in the **<CaseCaption>** element.

```
<!-- This template displays the contents of the <CaseCaption> element in
the underlying XML document. -->

<xsl:template match="CaseCaption">

<!--
************************************************************************
-->

<!-- This displays the contents of the <CourtInformation> element within
the <CaseCaption> tag. The <CourtInformation> element contains information
about the name, type, address and location of the court in which the case
has been filed. -->

<TD WIDTH='60%'><P ALIGN='LEFT'>
   <FONT SIZE='2' FACE='Times New Roman'>
      <xsl:value-of select="Court/CourtName"/>
   </FONT></P></TD>
   <TD WIDTH="20%"><P ALIGN="CENTER">
   <FONT SIZE='2' FACE='Times New Roman'>
      <xsl:value-of select="Court//AddressLine"/>
   </FONT></P></TD>
   <TD WIDTH="20%"><P ALIGN="RIGHT">
   <FONT SIZE='2' FACE='Times New Roman'>
      <xsl:value-of select="Court//City"/>,
      <xsl:value-of select="Court//State"/> 
      <xsl:value-of select="Court//PostalCode"/>
   </FONT>
   </P>
</TD>
```

As we noted in Chapter 17, XSLT notation is a mixture of XSLT elements (for processing XML) and HTML tags (for inserting HTML markup into the new file).

Federal Court Order

We turn next to a typical legal document, a court order from a federal district court. Again, there is underlying XML, which references a DTD and a style sheet. But the notable feature of this single document is that it manages and displays non-XML content as well as XML text. Figure 23.5 through 23.8 display the entire court order package, converted on the fly from XML.

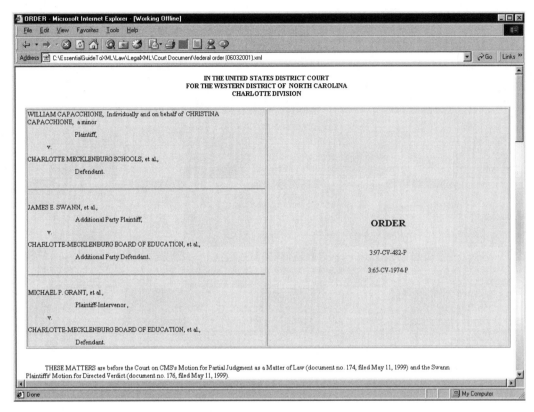

Figure 23.5 Court Order (transformed to HTML)

Once again, the style sheet called out in the XML file uses XSLT to convert the XML to HTML for display of the form portion of the document (Figures 23.5 and 23.6). But the balance of this document (appearing within the same XML record) is quite different (See Figures 23.7 and 23.8).

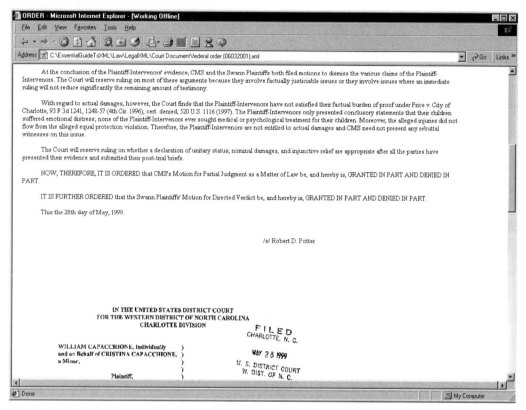

Figure 23.6 Continuation of Court Order Form and Start of Image

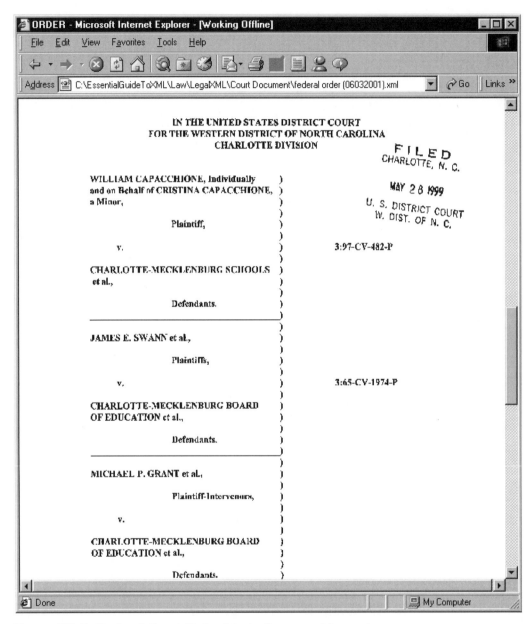

Figure 23.7 Body of Court Order (start of scanned image)

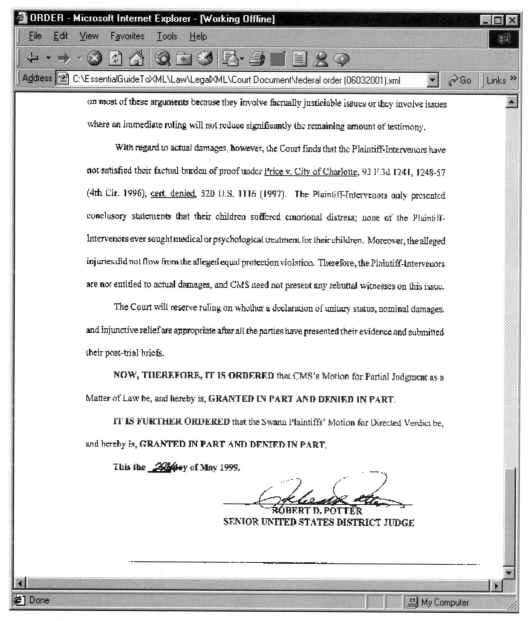

on most of these arguments because they involve factually justiciable issues or they involve issues where an immediate ruling will not reduce significantly the remaining amount of testimony.

With regard to actual damages, however, the Court finds that the Plaintiff-Intervenors have not satisfied their factual burden of proof under Price v. City of Charlotte, 93 F.3d 1241, 1248-57 (4th Cir. 1996), cert. denied, 520 U.S. 1116 (1997). The Plaintiff-Intervenors only presented conclusory statements that their children suffered emotional distress; none of the Plaintiff-Intervenors ever sought medical or psychological treatment for their children. Moreover, the alleged injuries did not flow from the alleged equal protection violation. Therefore, the Plaintiff-Intervenors are not entitled to actual damages, and CMS need not present any rebuttal witnesses on this issue.

The Court will reserve ruling on whether a declaration of unitary status, nominal damages, and injunctive relief are appropriate after all the parties have presented their evidence and submitted their post-trial briefs.

NOW, THEREFORE, IT IS ORDERED that CMS's Motion for Partial Judgment as a Matter of Law be, and hereby is, GRANTED IN PART AND DENIED IN PART.

IT IS FURTHER ORDERED that the Swann Plaintiffs' Motion for Directed Verdict be, and hereby is, GRANTED IN PART AND DENIED IN PART.

This the ___ day of May 1999.

ROBERT D. POTTER
SENIOR UNITED STATES DISTRICT JUDGE

Figure 23.8 Body of Court Order (end of scanned image)

The interesting item in this application is that the XML content encapsulates non-XML notation, two scanned image files in this case. The images are decidedly inferior to directly rendered HTML, as is always the case. But the XML-enabled browser is able to fetch and display these image files along with the HTML on the same page, just as browsers have always been able to do. The encoding within the XML file to accomplish this is straightforward.

```
<Attachment ID = "att001" Number = "page 1">
       <AttachmentContent MimeType = "image/gif"
        href = "./images/order1a.gif">
               <DocumentTitle>.gif image of order</DocumentTitle>
       </AttachmentContent>
</Attachment>
<Attachment ID = "att002" Number = "page 2">
       <AttachmentContent MimeType = "image/gif"
        href = "./images/order2a.gif">
               <DocumentTitle>.gif image of order</DocumentTitle>
       </AttachmentContent>
</Attachment>
```

Using that notation, the XML processor applies the following XSLT style sheet logic to generate an HTML **<IMG>** block for the browser to display..

```
<xsl:template match="Attachment">
       <xsl:for-each select="AttachmentContent">
       <P/>
               <xsl:if test="@MimeType='image/gif'">
                       <IMG>
                               <xsl:attribute name="SRC">
                                       <xsl:value-of select="@href"/>
                               </xsl:attribute>
                       </IMG>
               </xsl:if>
       </xsl:for-each>
</xsl:template>
```

"RAW" XML ON A WEB BROWSER AFTER ALL? ......

In Chapter 16 we viewed how Internet Explorer, without the assistance of XML-enabled processing, can render XML, but to a very limited extent. In this case study we have seen that a browser equipped with an XML processing engine can do far more. But while the server can now send native XML to the browser for desktop (on-the-fly) processing, it must do so by conforming absolutely to the constraints of the browser's XML product. To the extent that XML add-ons like MSXML3 are totally XML-conformant, we can expect to see many more applications like those from LegalXML.

24 XML At Work: WAP & WML

In this chapter...

They Said It...

My business is roaming at large.
William Wordsworth: The Excursion

The Wireless Application Protocol (WAP) Forum is a global consortium of wireless technology providers. The forum's Web site (www.wapforum.org) lists 160 full members and 196 associate members.

The protocol itself is not a single standard or specification but a collection of specifications, 55 in all. These in turn are clustered under 15 functional areas which represent every aspect of wireless technologies: Protocols (nine specifications for the low-level management of messaging), Security (six specifications), Push (eight specifications for delivering server-initiated information), and the Wireless Application Environment (10 specifications). The specification for WML is part of this latter functional area.

While the forum is not related to the Worldwide Web Consortium, it borrows heavily from specifications released by the W3C. As our exhibit will show, WML is an enhanced HTML. For this XML language to function properly for wireless delivery, every WML instance of content must be valid. In that regard it is practically the same as Extensible Hypertext Markup Language (XHTML), which is currently a W3C working draft.

WIRELESS MARKUP LANGUAGE ....

While WML represents only one of over 50 WAP specifications, the markup language is the most visible aspect of WAP among the XML community. A WML file looks very much like HTML but with added features to support wireless technologies. The primary unit of information in WML is the **card**, and a group of cards comprise a **deck**. A WML file must be valid XML content in order for it to "play" on a wireless device. This means that the content must conform strictly to the WAP Forum DTD.

How It Works

Just as a Web browser must be able to process HTML, a WAP device must be able to process WML. This means that it must be able to (1) parse WML on its own, (2) use tags to assign predefined screen font styles, and (3) execute hyperlinking. Those links may join segments within the WML content itself, or they may take the user to the outside world.

The WAP device we use in this exhibit is a freely available emulator product called M3Gate, developed by the Russian firm Numeric Algorithm Laboratories (www.numeric.ru). As a WML development tool on a standard computer, M3Gate interacts with an installed Web browser. M3Gate includes an XML parser from The Apache Software Foundation (an open systems group). Once the emulator has been installed, the user needs only to double-click on a .wml file in order to launch M3Gate.

WIRELESS EXHIBIT: INTERACTIVE PROFESSIONAL TRAINING PLANNER ....

In this demonstration, the user has received an interactive edition of a course catalog for an upcoming XML meeting. Her personalized package is an extract, containing only the management track. She browses the catalog, an abstract-only version that is edited for small-screen viewing. She then returns a live reservation for a selected session by launching an e-mail directly from the session topics page. Figure 24.1 shows the top-level menu of the management training sessions.

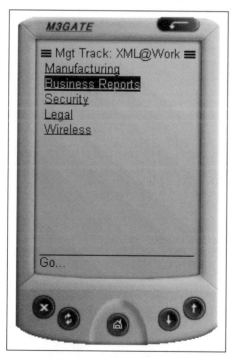

Figure 24.1 Top-level menu of Management Training Planner

When the user selects Go in the lower-left corner of the screen, the page for the Business Reports session appears. It contains the header identifying the session, the topics to be covered, and a link for registering. This is shown in Figure 24.2.

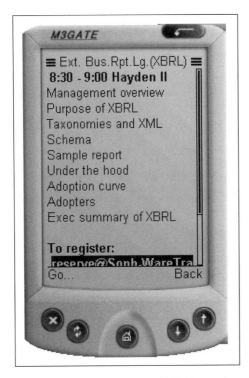

Figure 24.2 Abstract of XBRL session

Next, the user presses the down arrow to scroll to the bottom of the page (Figure 24.3).

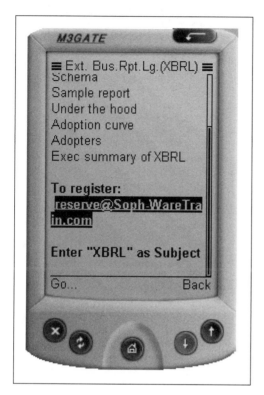

Figure 24.3 Bottom of the screen

The user now can activate the device's mail system by selecting Go. Once the mail is sent, she will then be automatically registered for the XBRL session.

WML Behind the Planning Package

It takes many layers of technology in order to create a total WAP-conforming application. For our discussion, we are inspecting only WML. For this demonstration, only a single file, consisting of a deck of six cards (four are visible here) was required. Here is the initial portion of the file.

```
<?xml version="1.0"?>
<!DOCTYPE wml PUBLIC "-//WAPFORUM//DTD WML 1.1//EN"
"http://www.wapforum.org/DTD/wml_1.1.xml">

<wml>
      <card id="mgtTrack" title="Mgt Track: XML@Work">
             <p>
             <a href="#manufacturing">Manufacturing</a><br/>
             <a href="#reports">Business Reports</a><br/>
             <a href="#security">Security</a><br/>
             <a href="#law">Legal</a><br/>
             <a href="#wireless">Wireless</a>
             </p>
      </card>

      <card id="manufacturing" title="Manufacturing">
              <p>
              <b>8:00 - 8:30: Hayden II</b><br/>
              Management overview<br/>
              Leveraging a mature technology<br/>
              Bill of materials Basics<br/>
              What does a BOM contain?<br/>
              What a BOM "knows"<br/>
              Who uses the BOM?<br/>
              BOM workflow<br/>
              Zero-programming "derivatives"<br/>
              Repurposing the BOM<br/>
              Summary of XML BOM<br/><br/><b>
              To register:<br/>
              <a href="reserve@Soph-WareTrain.com">reserve@Soph-
              WareTrain.com</a><br/><br/>
              Enter "manufact" as Subject</b><br/>
              </p>
      </card>

      <card id="reports" title="Ext. Bus.Rpt.Lg.(XBRL)">
              <p>
              <b>8:30 - 9:00 Hayden II</b><br/>
              Management overview<br/>
              Purpose of XBRL<br/>
              Taxonomies and XML Schema<br/>
              Sample report<br/>
              Under the hood<br/>
              Adoption curve<br/>
              Adopters<br/>
              Exec summary of XBRL<br/><br/><b>
              To register:<br/>
              <a href="reserve@Soph-WareTrain.com">reserve@Soph-
              WareTrain.com</a><br/><br/>
              Enter "XBRL" as Subject</b><br/>
              </p>
      </card>
```

```
        <card id="security" title="Open Standards Security">
                <p>
                <b>9:30-10:00 Kettering I</b><br/>
                How can "open" be secure?<br/>
                Security in a nutshell<br/>
                Use case studies<br/>
                Encryption<br/>
                Digital signature<br/>
                Exec summary of XML-based security<br/>
                To register:<br/>
                <a href="reserve@Soph-WareTrain.com">reserve@Soph-
                WareTrain.com</a><br/><br/>
                Enter "security" as Subject</b><br/>
                </p>

        </card>
        :
        :
</wml>
```

The card whose id is mgtTrack contains only the live links to pages of session topics (Figure 24.1). The card **report** underlies the page depicted in Figures 24.2 and 24.3. The live link to the training provider's e-mail-based reservation system is near the end of each card. Consequently, the user must scroll to the end of the page in order to send that mail (see Figure 24.3).

HAS WAP'S TIME COME?...................................

Unlike every other initiative and specification in this book, WAP and the WAP Forum represent a nonmainstream effort in XML. That has created a predictable amount of unrest within the larger markup community. Nevertheless the participation of over 350 serious information technology providers and the relative maturity of the many WAP specifications should convince us that, regardless of political fluctuations, WAP is an XML technology here to stay.

25 It's Up to You: Ten Questions You Should Ask About XML

In this chapter...

They Said It...

Go, and do likewise.

Luke 10:37 (New King James Version)

OVERVIEW...

XML represents a paradigm, a distinctive way of perceiving and managing content. But there is no single strategy for going with XML. The decision to embark on even a small XML initiative entails evaluation and decision of many varieties. No single set of XML tools will fit all organizations' needs. We have suggested many value propositions in the Benefits sections of the technologies chapters. But only a few of those may actually spell out added value for your organization. We have suggested frequently that certain aspects of XML require new skill sets, a factor that deserves serious thought. And we have emphasized the impact that XML technologies may have on information workflow. This constitutes yet another point of management decision, likely the most far-reaching.

This book is about XML technologies, and we have offered an executive-level survey of issues, core topics, and usage exhibits. But technologies in themselves do not solve problems for an organization. Every XML provider and promoter touts XML as neat stuff, but only you can evaluate whether XML as a standard is sufficiently mature and workplace-proven and whether a judicious application of XML is a sensible approach to solving your organization's IT problems. Get past the hype and decide: Will XML deliver value for your organization?

DECISION MAKER'S LIST ....

This discussion should serve as a starter exercise in XML decision-making. Based on the XML topics and technologies covered, we suggest 10 questions to place before your organization. We invited you in the Introduction to jump to this list before starting through the chapters. Now that you have had an up-close look at pieces of XML technologies, we invite you to apply this brief checklist periodically to your own workplace.

1. Is XML becoming a significant factor in our industry's business?

Your industry, trade group, or business sector interest group may already have formulated its own XML specification. The specification may be for a full-blown markup language, like Business Reporting Markup Language (BRML) for financial reporting. If so, you are already seeing promotions for XML training and tools that will help you get on board.

XML in your industry may be less visible than an actual markup language. It may be an XML method of transferring certain types of information, an XML approach to integrating systems, or a requirement for your particular firm to make its Web browsers more XML-aware.

If XML is becoming not simply a nice-to-do but a need-to-do agenda for your company to do business, then it is safe to assume that XML is making its own business case. If that is true, then you are likely to enjoy the benefits of shared experiences and lessons learned across a wide community of your colleagues. No single IT director need shoulder the costly burden of being the first adopter.

2. Is the Internet becoming more central to information flow for our organization?

Information moves. Your organization likely creates and manages a substantial body of information that has clearly quantifiable value. But no information, regardless of how valuable, is of any real worth until it can be retrieved, transmitted, exchanged, and delivered. The Holy Grail of easy information transfer has been a prime motivator in management information systems (MIS) for decades. The Internet has provided a significant piece of the puzzle for making that dream come true. As planetary plumbing, the Internet provides a totally vendor-independent method of moving information. You do not have to be an open systems bigot to appreciate the enormous benefits that the Internet brings to business information.

The other major piece of the information transfer puzzle is the information itself. In order for Internet-based content to be suitable for transfer, the transfer will be more straightforward if the format and notation of the content is also vendor-free (open). So if your company is already investing in greater Internet activity for its mission-critical content, then XML is a natural next step to consider.

*3. Is it becoming critical for us to have total **control** as well as **ownership** of our content?*

All of the content your organization creates—financial, journalistic, educational, manufacturing, legal, personnel, historical, artistic—is your intellectual property. But legal *ownership* of property is not the same as total *control*. You may own the copyrights to millions of items packaged as multimedia products, but those items may be locked into proprietary formats—databases, page layout products, word processors, and so forth. Yielding some control to IT products has always been part of business practice.

But there are probably certain portions of your organization's content that you must control . . . totally and over a very long life cycle. You cannot continue to expose such mission-critical, long-lived content to the risk of vendors' failing support and obsolete proprietary formats.

XML goes far beyond the markup of text. As this book demonstrates, it also deals with the management of content. To the extent that you can acquire and maintain *control* over your property, you can guarantee your safe *ownership* of the property.

4. Are we finding the current or announced releases of our database, content management, communications, and Internet software and tools to be identified as XML-aware or XML-enabled?

Look closely at the Web pages of your vendors' database, editing, publishing, and content management products. You are likely to spot XML-aware, XML-enabled, or even XML-native among the features in product release announcements. Look for conversion tools that will allow you to convert to and from XML on the fly. Follow the progress of browser software to really see how native the native XML can be in order for the browser to deliver XML on the desktop.

To the extent that your providers are implementing various parts of the XML specification, your company's own investment in XML development is reduced and is more secure. The critical mass of XML-aware products is another huge indicator that XML has indeed crossed the chasm of widespread acceptance.

*5. Does the availability and maturity of XML tools and products appear to be adequate for **our** business?*

Broad acceptance is good. But for XML to make its case in your organization, you must be certain that there are adequate XML tools and products that solve real problems in your company. An XML-pure database that requires you to convert all of your legacy data to XML might not be cost-effective. An XML database that allows your legacy data to coexist with pure XML data would be a prudent choice.

Suppose you need an XML editing tool for entering large volumes of financial data that is peculiar to your industry. If a general-purpose XML editor requires three days' training for a data entry operator, then it might be better to invest in a conversion tool. A right-sized XML conversion tool can take traditional data (records created by semiskilled data entry clerks) and convert them to XML.

Part of the tools question entails the level of XML sophistication among your organization's developers. The simplicity of XML makes it feasible to develop XML tools in-house for performing many of the mundane conversion and management tasks you will likely require. (See question 9.)

6. Can we identify certain XML candidate projects that are limited in scope and that would serve as safe and convincing proofs-of-concept?

If you are contemplating an XML initiative in your organization, you should assume that even if it were straightforward, it would not be easy. It is therefore necessary for you first to ignore all of the evangelistic XML hype that you have heard (even the occasional flowery claims in this book). You must concentrate on actual benefits that you expect to demonstrate for your project. Third, you must scale the first project to a size that guarantees your success. Choose a pilot project that you can easily get your arms around.

An example of a showcase first project would be to transform your company's published reports from XML to Web pages on the fly. That would be a straightforward project, challenging but rewarding in terms of lessons learned and new technologies acquired. (The core technologies presented in this book offer a road map.)

An example of a non-candidate first project would be the wholesale conversion of massive amounts of legacy data to XML. The learning curve for that would be prohibitively costly, and tangible results that can be demonstrated to senior executives (the ones who gave you the money to perform this experiment) would be hard to come by.

The best criterion for a properly scaled first project is that one can be completed with a minimum of outside help and maintained entirely by internal personnel. (See question 9.)

Launching an initiative with new technologies always requires up-selling, before, during, and after the first project. It is much easier to spin to management a report of a success (no matter how small the victory) than a report of a failure (no matter how small).

The long-term destiny of your organization is dependent upon the success or failure of your XML pilot project. Failure will mean that XML may not be considered again for several quarters (and/or not on your watch). Success, on the other hand, will pave the way for forays into deeper XML waters. For the XML pilot, failure is not an option. Choose the pilot project with great care.

7. Are there identifiable portions of our information that could be multipurposed to achieve a business advantage?

The term *repurpose* has been abused by open systems protagonists. But it is a concept that makes convincing business sense. Given some information asset, so the argument goes, it is prudent for you to leverage your investment in that asset by generating new uses, new revenue, and new cost reductions from the asset. If you own the copyright on the text and multimedia of a college science textbook, for example, you might seek to repackage the product as a syndicated training product. It would require additional development to enhance the product, but you would repurpose the original content, modifying that as little as possible.

XML is good at repurposing. The cases of content conversions we demonstrate in this book are only a small example. XML derives its power to repurpose from the ease it offers for developers to manipulate content. This, as we explain in the earlier chapters of the book, is because XML content is highly self-exposing.

If your organization is sensing that certain sectors of your content should be re-used in new ways, then it is highly likely that you should seek for ways that XML can help.

8. Is there a need for more granular (i.e., user-specific and item-specific) control over access to and delivery of our organization's information?

Consumers of your information come to you with different needs. Customers, suppliers, regulatory officials, board members, accountants, auditors, internal manag-ers, employees, and job hunters all have different requirements. Easy, but controlled, dissemination of information has been an on-going goal of MIS for decades. Question 2 describes how the Internet has helped resolve that. But targeting the information has been an MIS headache from the beginning. This is why every database product in-cludes a reporting tool, a means of shaping the delivery of information in a way that suits the user.

With Internet- and browser-based delivery, the customization bar has been raised. The user now expects that a catalog company's online system will learn and re-member his or her precise interests and purchasing history. He or she furthermore can expect to see in the online catalog only those items that are of interest. This drive for highly granular profiling and secure access is behind many XML initiatives. (See Chapter 22.)

The best indicator of whether or not your organization is ready for an XML-based granularity initiative is the amount of frustration expressed by the IT persons re-sponsible for generating reports. If certain programmers' jobs have degenerated into writing customized reporting scripts, it is time to consider how XML can help.

9. Is the climate of our IT workplace such that information workers would wel-come change for the sake of their own career enrichment?

There are typically two major management concerns over the launch of an XML initiative: the human-side impact on *workflow* and the new skills requirements for XML *development*.

There is no doubt that processing content for an XML-based system will entail change: new processes and procedures, new learning requirements, and obsolescence of entire skill sets and positions. Planning for an XML initiative therefore requires as much care in personnel management as it does for the technology itself. We mentioned up-selling to management in question 6. But the task of selling your initiative to rank-and-file information workers is arguably more critical and more difficult.

The sales pitch to the rank-and-file is not the same pitch as for management. The value propositions to management are completely different than those for developers and system/data administrators. If it is done properly, those workers should welcome the new skills they will need to acquire. That means that XML training and support will be crucial. If that planning is in place, then much of the success of XML in your organization is assured.

But high-side XML skills sets are also problematic. What do your developers need to learn or what kind of developers do you need to recruit in order to do XML? The following ten questions are supplied by O'Reilly and Associates, a premier source of XML information. The questions may help you to qualify a good training course (for your internal developers), a good candidate for hire, or a good consultant. The Web-based article by Brian Buehling appeared at O'Reilly and Associates' xml.com site as "Top 10 Interview Questions When Hiring XML Developers." [1] You are already familiar with many of these topics from having read this book.

- Describe the differences between XML and HTML.
- Describe the role that XSL can play when dynamically generating HTML pages from a relational database.
- Give a few examples of types of applications that can benefit from using XML.
- What is DOM and how does it relate to XML?
- What is SOAP and how does it relate to XML?
- Can you walk us through the steps necessary to parse XML documents?
- Give some examples of XML DTDs or schemas that you have worked with.
- Using XSLT, how would you extract a specific attribute from an element in an XML document?
- When constructing an XML DTD, how do you create an external entity reference in an attribute value? [a trick question!]
- How would you build a search engine for large volumes of XML data?

10. Do we now perceive XML as an established way of doing business with information and not just as the Next Big Thing?

---

[1]*Published April 11, 2001 on xml.com at http://www.xml.com/pub/a/2001/04/11/10questions.html. Copyright © 2000 O'Reilly & Associates, Inc. Used with permission.*

By now this should be a rhetorical question. The overall *objective* of this book is to help you see that XML is more than just the Next Big Thing. The specific *goal* of the book is to help you determine whether XML has a legitimate place in your business.

If you are beyond viewing XML as just another buzzword, and if you are now convinced that XML can create real value in your organization, then you are ready for some serious next steps in XML.

Index

 Solutions from experts you know and trust.

| Articles | Free Library | eBooks | Expert Q & A | Training | Career Center | Downloads | MyInformIT |

Login   Register   About InformIT

Topics

Operating Systems
Web Development
Programming
Networking
Certification
and more...

**Expert
Access**

**Free
Content**

www.informit.com

✓ Free, in-depth articles and supplements

✓ Master the skills you need, when you need them

✓ Choose from industry leading books, ebooks, and training products

✓ Get answers when you need them - from live experts or InformIT's comprehensive library

✓ Achieve industry certification and advance your career

Visit *InformIT* today
and get great content
from PH
PTR

Prentice Hall and InformIT are trademarks of Pearson plc /
Copyright © 2000 Pearson

Prentice Hall: Professional Technical Reference

Back | Forward | Reload | Home | Search | Guide | Images | Print | Security | Stop

PH PTR

http://www.phptr.com/

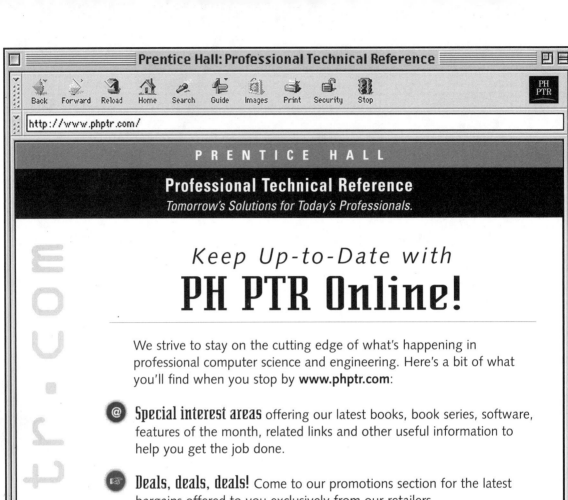

PRENTICE HALL

Professional Technical Reference
Tomorrow's Solutions for Today's Professionals.

Keep Up-to-Date with

PH PTR Online!

We strive to stay on the cutting edge of what's happening in professional computer science and engineering. Here's a bit of what you'll find when you stop by **www.phptr.com**:

@ Special interest areas offering our latest books, book series, software, features of the month, related links and other useful information to help you get the job done.

Deals, deals, deals! Come to our promotions section for the latest bargains offered to you exclusively from our retailers.

$ Need to find a bookstore? Chances are, there's a bookseller near you that carries a broad selection of PTR titles. Locate a Magnet bookstore near you at www.phptr.com.

! What's new at PH PTR? We don't just publish books for the professional community, we're a part of it. Check out our convention schedule, join an author chat, get the latest reviews and press releases on topics of interest to you.

✉ Subscribe today! Join PH PTR's monthly email newsletter!

Want to be kept up-to-date on your area of interest? Choose a targeted category on our website, and we'll keep you informed of the latest PH PTR products, author events, reviews and conferences in your interest area.

Visit our mailroom to subscribe today! **http://www.phptr.com/mail_lists**

www.phptr.com